The
Other Hand
of God

THE
OTHER HAND
OF GOD

The Holy Spirit as the Universal Touch and Goal

Kilian McDonnell, O.S.B.

A Michael Glazier Book

LITURGICAL PRESS COLLEGEVILLE, MINNESOTA

www.litpress.org

A Michael Glazier Book published by the Liturgical Press

Design by Frank Kacmarcik, Obl.S.B.

Library of Congress Cataloging-in-Publication Data

McDonnell, Kilian.
    The other hand of God : the Holy Spirit as the universal touch and
    goal / Kilian McDonnell.
        p.   cm.
    "A Michael Glazier book."
    Includes bibliographical references and index.
    ISBN 0-8146-5171-2
        1. Holy Spirit—History of doctrines.   I. Title.
BT119.M42 2003
231'.3—dc21   2003047622

To

Dr. Cecil M. Robeck, Jr.,

scholar, trail-blazer, friend,

and co-chair with me for many years in the

International Classical

Pentecostal/Roman Catholic Dialogue.

Table of Contents

Foreword

"Had we but world enough and time," as the poet Andrew Marvell, in a quite different context, used to say. I originally planned for this volume to include major sections on the church and on the feminine Spirit in the Syriac tradition. Research for these chapters is complete, but the advance of years—I am eighty-one as I write this foreword—has made it advisable to proceed to publication without them.

Along with trinitarian theologians such as Catherine Mowry LaCugna, I believe that Father, Son, and Spirit language is normative. However, I do not use masculine pronouns for the persons of the Trinity except when quoting others who do.

Though I work with historical persons and periods, I proceed as a systematic theologian. This means that certain works and themes will occur often in these pages, but viewed from a variety of angles.

I wish to thank my editors, Dr. Patrick Henry, Dr. Miranda Henry, and Sr. Dolores Schuh. Rarely does an author have editors with such a range of expertise. They have correctly read my mind.

Abbreviations

CCh	Corpus Christianorum
CCCM	Corpus Christianorum Continuatio Medievalis
CCSL	Corpus Christianorum Series Latina
CSCO	Corpus Scriptorum Christianorum Orientalium
CSEL	Corpus Scriptorum Ecclesiasticorum Latinorum
CSS	*Credo in Spiritum Sanctum*, ed. José Sariva Martins, 2 vols. (Vatican City: Libreria Editrice Vaticana, 1983)
Dörries, *DSS*	Hermann Dörries, *De Spiritu Sancto: Der Beitrag des Basilius zum Abschluss des trinitärischen Dogmas* (Göttingen: Vandenhoeck & Ruprecht, 1956)
Kelly, *Creeds*	J.N.D. Kelly, *Early Christian Creeds*, rev. ed. (New York: Harper & Row, 1978)
Kelly, *Doctrines*	J.N.D. Kelly, *Early Christian Doctrines*, 5th. ed. (New York: Harper & Row, 1976)
MS	*Mysterium Salutis*, Johannes Feiner and Magnus Löhrer, eds., 7 vols. (Einsiedeln: Benziger, 1965–1976)
PG	Migne, Patrologia Graeca
PL	Migne, Patrologia Latina
SC	Sources Chrétiennes

Come Holy Spirit

Come Creating Spirit,
Enter the minds of those who are your own,
Fill with grace from heaven
The hearts you created.

We call you Paraclete,
Gift of God Most High,
Living Spring, Fire, Love,
And Inward Balm.

Touch of the Father's right hand,
You give seven gifts for us.
Truly, you are the Father's promise,
Gifting tongues with speech.

Flame light into our senses,
Flood love into our hearts,
Fix in enduring power
Our frail bodies.

Drive our foes far off,
And give us a long peace;
With you to lead and guide us,
May we avoid all harm.

Grant us through you to know the Father,
And also to understand the Son,
That we may always believe you,
Who are the Spirit of them both.

To God the Father be glory,
And to God the Son, who rose
From the dead, and to God the Paraclete,
World without end, Amen.

Translated by Eleonore Stump and Kilian McDonnell, O.S.B.

Chapter 1

To Do Pneumatology Is to Do Trinity

In a 1989 study entitled *The Forgotten Trinity,* the British Council of Churches noted a revival of interest in the Trinity. It would be difficult to name a major theological movement of the recent past that has not sought to incorporate the Trinity; in turn, these movements have themselves modified the way we view the Trinity. Liberation and feminist movements have reformulated or reinterpreted trinitarian theology. All theological traditions—Protestant, Anglican, Orthodox, Roman Catholic—have seen reactions against a trinitarian tradition that had become alienated from the piety of the faithful; pre-eminent among these reappraisals is Catherine Mowry LaCugna's *God For Us: The Trinity and Christian Life.* In *Trinity and the Kingdom,* Jürgen Moltmann presents the Trinity as a model of "social personalism and personal socialism." In *God the Economist,* M. Douglas Meeks closes the gap between the trinitarian God and political economy, while Michael and Kenneth Himes, in *Fullness of Faith: The Public Significance of Theology,* use Trinity to fashion a public theology for such issues as human rights.[1]

In broad terms this revival has been sparked by the theologies of Karl Barth and Karl Rahner, the two dominant trinitarian theologians of the twentieth century. Barth presents the Trinity as the

[1] *The Forgotten Trinity.* The Report of the B. C. C. Study Commission on Trinitarian Doctrine Today, 3 vols. (London: British Council of Churches, 1989) 1.4. LaCugna (San Francisco: Harper, 1991). Moltmann (New York: Harper & Row, 1981) 157–58. Meeks (Minneapolis: Fortress, 1989). Himes (New York: Paulist, 1993). One could also mention Leonardo Boff, *Trinity and Society* (Maryknoll: Orbis, 1988).

revelation of God as Lord before the "first theological word" is uttered. Trinity is the basic supposition, the horizon, the umbrella under which any theology is made possible. For Barth, Trinity belongs to the prolegomenon of theology. Rahner's dictum—"the 'economic' Trinity is the 'immanent' Trinity, and the 'immanent' Trinity is the 'economic' Trinity"—cited endlessly in twentieth-century trinitarian discussion, itself assures Rahner a place in the history of trinitarian reflection. Rahner's intent, reinforced by Piet Schoonenberg, is to relate Trinity to God's saving acts in time and space, away from a speculative concern for inner-trinitarian life.[2]

Alongside this revival of interest in the Trinity is another retrieval—recovery of the doctrine of the Spirit. As recently as 1985 one could still speak of the Spirit as the forgotten God and of pneumatology as neglected, the "Cinderella" of theology,[3] but today publications abound. However, the revival of trinitarian doctrine and renewed theological interest in the Holy Spirit have not so far converged in any significant way. There have been some attempts to bring christology and pneumatology together in a viable Spirit christology, but with insufficient attention to the determinative dynamic of trinitarian life, though there are some notable exceptions.[4]

[2] Barth, *Church Dogmatics* (Edinburgh: T. & T. Clark, 1936) 1/1:339–560. Rahner, *The Trinity* (New York: Seabury, 1974) 22. Rahner (24) adds a qualification: "No adequate distinction can be made between the doctrine of the Trinity and the doctrine of the economy of salvation." This was not sufficient to save Rahner from widespread criticism for making the two-way road between immanent and economic Trinity into a resolution of the mystery, a kind of mitigated rationalism. The criticism has some justification. Schoonenberg, "Trinity–the Consummated Covenant. Theses on the Doctrine of the Trinitarian God," *Studies in Religion/ Sciences Religieuses* 5 (1975–1976) 111–16. Both Barth and Rahner have been criticized: Jürgen Moltmann, *History and the Triune God* (New York: Seabury, 1992) 125–42; Yves Congar, "The 'Economic' Trinity and the 'Immanent' Trinity," in his *I Believe in the Holy Spirit* (New York: Seabury, 1983) 3:11–18; Hans Urs von Balthasar, *Theo-Drama* (San Francisco: Ignatius, 1992) 508; Paul D. Molnar, "The Function of the Immanent Trinity in the Theology of Karl Barth: Implications for Today," *Scottish Journal of Theology* 42 (1989) 367–99.

[3] Kilian McDonnell, "A Trinitarian Theology of the Holy Spirit?" *Theological Studies* 46 (1985) 191–93.

[4] Among these exceptions: Jürgen Moltmann, "'The Fellowship of the Holy Spirit': On Trinitarian Pneumatology," *History and the Triune God*, 57–69 (originally published in *CSS* 2.921–38); Walter Kasper, *Jesus the Christ* (New York:

It is not enough to have the Spirit related to the divine threeness. The issue is not just Trinity of persons, but the trinitarian dynamic. One model of this dynamic is God reaching through the Son in the Spirit to touch and transform the world and church to lead them in the Spirit through the Son back to God. Within this rhythm—the dynamic of life from the Father to the Father—is to be found the extension of trinitarian life beyond the divine self to cosmos and church in the missions of the Son and the Spirit. The Son and the Spirit function, in Irenaeus's graphic image, as the two hands of the Father at work in history to change, transfigure, and open the way back to the source and goal of all, the Father.[5] Irenaeus, grounding his vision in scripture (Rom 5:8-11; 8:26-30; 2 Cor 5:18-21; Gal 4:4-7), knew that naked threeness is not enough. If pneumatology and christology are not kept within this movement, they lose their primary location (Eph 1:3-14; 2:4-5, especially 18-22; Rom 8:3-17; Gal 4:4-6; 1 Cor 6:12-20).

Without this trinitarian cycle of life, without the Father as source and future end, we lose purpose and objective. "You are like stones for a temple of the Father prepared for the edifice of God the Father, hoisted to the heights by the crane of Jesus Christ, which is the cross, using for a rope the Holy Spirit. Your faith pulls you up, and love is what leads you to God." Here Bishop Ignatius of Antioch (ca. 35–ca. 107) demonstrates how firmly trinitarian language was rooted in the faith of the church at an early date, and how the goal of salvation is the Father. Elsewhere, on his way to martyrdom, he again makes God the goal: "Let me imitate the passion of my God [Christ]. . . . The living water [the Spirit as in John 7:38] murmurs within me and says 'Come to the Father.'"[6] Irenaeus (ca. 130–ca. 200), nearly a century later, shows the pattern in a clearer form: "Such is the order, such is the rhythm, such is the movement through which the human person, created and modeled, becomes the image and the resemblance of the uncreated God.

Paulist, 1976) 240–74, and *The God of Jesus Christ* (New York: Crossroad, 1986) 198–229.

[5] *Against Heresies* 5.6.1; SC 153.72.

[6] *To the Ephesians* 9:1; SC 10.64–66. *To the Romans* 6, 7; SC 10.114–16. W. R. Schoedel, *Ignatius of Antioch* (Philadelphia: Fortress, 1985) 66, n. 6.

To Do Pneumatology Is to Do Trinity

The Father decides and commands, the Son executes and models, the Spirit nourishes and grows . . . thus approaching the uncreated [God]."[7] History, time, and the church have an end in God, into whom they pour themselves.

BACKWARD DEVELOPMENT OF CHRISTOLOGY AND THE QUESTION OF IDENTITY

Trinitarian reflection arose in the post-biblical era in response to the quite unsystematic triadic tradition within the New Testament itself.

When Jesus prays in his native Aramaic, he addresses God as "Abba" (Mark 14:36), which is equivalent to "Papa" in English. Jesus himself spoke little of the Spirit—indeed, extremely little—and it would be a misplaced question to ask if he ever thought of the Spirit as a person.[8]

The relation of the Spirit to the divine sonship of Jesus was expressed first in the pre-Pauline hymn of Romans 1:3-4 ("The gospel concerning his Son, who was descended from David according to the flesh and was declared to be Son of God with power according to the spirit of holiness by resurrection from the dead, Jesus Christ our Lord"). Only after considerable theological reflection did Matthew (3:16-17) relate the Spirit to the ministry of Jesus, beginning with Jesus' baptism by John the Baptist. On the question of the identity of Jesus, Raymond E. Brown sees regressive theologizing of three themes: divine proclamation of identity, the begetting of God's Son, and the agency of the Holy Spirit. The backward development of the christological moment within the New Testament, establishing the identity of Jesus, is from resurrection (Rom 1:3-4), to the baptism of Jesus (Mark 1:9-11; Matt 3:13-17; Luke 3:21-22), to conception (Luke 1:26-38), to pre-existence (John 1:1).[9]

The association of the Spirit with the Father and the Son in the

---

[7] *Against Heresies* 4.38.3; SC 100.955. See also 5.5.1; SC 153.64.

[8] The conservative exegete Franz J. Schierse thinks that Mark 3:28-30 is perhaps the single "Spirit" text which can claim authenticity as a word of Jesus. "Die neutestamentliche Trinitätsoffenbarung," *MS* 2.98.

[9] *The Birth of the Messiah* (Garden City: Doubleday, 1977) 125, 138–43. When speaking of pre-existence, Brown adds Colossians 1:15, and notes that conception christology and pre-existent christology were harmonized in Matthew and Luke. See also Ernst Käsemann, *Romans* (London: SCM, 1980) 10, who refers to Philippians 2:6 and John 1:1.

Great Commission of Matthew 28:19-20 raises the question of the Spirit's personality but does not settle it. Even if John Meier goes too far when he asserts that one can "hardly imagine a more forceful proclamation . . . of the Spirit's distinct personality" than the listing of the Spirit on equal terms with the Father and the Son in the baptismal command, still the formulation must not be disregarded. "One does not baptize people in the name of a divine person, a holy creature, and an impersonal divine force."[10]

There is some development of triadic content in New Testament books written at a later date, especially Ephesians and the Fourth Gospel. The first chapter of Ephesians has a triadic mentality behind it, and 4:1-5 concerning the unity of the church, takes its character from a triadic baptismal catechesis. John, though pre-dogmatic and unsystematic, comes closer to the developed post-biblical trinitarian doctrine than any other New Testament author, not only in the Prologue, but also in the Farewell Discourses of chapters 14–17, reflecting the remembered teachings of Jesus on relations of Father, Son, and Holy Spirit.[11]

IN THE SPIRIT GOD TOUCHES CHURCH AND WORLD: THE TRIADIC TEXTS

Exegetes have reached no consensus on the exact number or content of triadic texts. Whether a text is considered truly triadic depends in each instance on how an exegete interprets *pneuma*. Many scholars agree on 2 Corinthians 1:21-22, Galatians 4:6, and Romans 8:9-11.[12] But if a text is to be considered triadic in a proper sense, there needs to be some equivalence between Father, Son, and Spirit.

In Romans, Paul (unlike John) does not understand *pneuma* as a

---

[10] *Matthew* (Wilmington: Glazier, 1980) 371–72.

[11] *The Forgotten Trinity*, 2.10. Rudolf Schnackenburg, *Brief an die Epheser* (Zürich: Benziger, 1982) 162, 163, 168, 171; there is a double triad present: Spirit, Lord, God (and Father), and also one Lord, one faith, one baptism. Edmund J. Fortman, *The Triune God: A Historical Study of the Doctrine of the Trinity* (Grand Rapids: Baker, 1972) 29.

[12] Francis Martin, "Pauline Trinitarian Formulas and Church Unity," *Catholic Biblical Quarterly* 30 (1968) 200–01. Otto Kuss, *Der Römerbrief* (Regensburg: Pustet, 1963–78) 583–84.

personal being distinct from the Father and the Son, but approaches Spirit as in some Old Testament texts (e.g., Ezek 36:26; Isa 44:3) where *ruach* means God's outgoing activity and presence to the world in a creative, quickening, renewing way. But still, in Romans Spirit is already the vivifying power of the risen Christ. "God's spirit" has become "Christ's Spirit." The Spirit, while not losing autonomous identity, takes on the personality of Christ.[13]

In the triadic formulations the relation of the Spirit to the Father and Son is not always clear, though there are personal relations between the three, even when not in the differentiated sense of later trinitarian development. Romans 8:9-11 seems to be "a clear triadic text" which provides a basis for the post-biblical development.[14]

What in the biblical text led the later church to use this kind of language? The scriptures give more than presuppositions. The placing of the Spirit alongside two undoubted personal beings can throw light on the character of the Spirit—a kind of identifying by proximity. The Spirit belongs in some sense to the nature of God, and comes forth from God, is the "act" of God; only the Spirit searches the depths of God (1 Cor 2:10-12). If God is personal, then the Spirit is personal, in spite of the difficulties of applying

---

[13] Joseph Fitzmyer, *Romans* (New York: Doubleday, 1993) 480. Wilhelm Thüsing, *Per Christum in Deum: Studien zum Verhältnis von Christozentrik und Theozentrik in den paulinischen Hauptbriefen* 2nd ed. (Munster: Aschendorff, 1968) 163, says that while Paul uses "through the Spirit," he probably means "through the pneumatic Christ," and conversely, "through Christ" perhaps means "through the Spirit." Such a line of thought does not imply that Paul made no distinction between Christ and the Spirit. Raymond E. Brown, *The Gospel According to John XIII–XXI* (Garden City: Doubleday, 1970) 1139, says that for John, the Paraclete is "the personal presence of Jesus in the Christian while Jesus is with the Father." See also James D. G. Dunn, *Jesus and the Spirit* (Philadelphia: Westminster, 1975) 318–26.

[14] Kuss, *Römerbrief*, 582. Fitzmyer, *Romans*, 481. Gerhard Delling, *Worship in the New Testament* (Philadelphia: Westminster, 1962) 56, considers 1 Cor 12:4-6, 2 Cor 13:13, and Eph 4:4-6 as constituting the most important evidence for triadic teaching in Paul, all others deriving from these three. Jane Schaberg, *The Father, Son, and the Holy Spirit: The Triadic Phrase in Matt 28:19b* (Chico, Calif.: Scholars, 1982) 7, says that "there may be no evidence of a conscious effort to establish a triadic conception of God, a tri-unity, but there is indication that thoughts were moving in that direction." See also Brendan Byrne, *Romans* (Collegeville: The Liturgical Press, 1996) 238.

"person" to one who does not have a face.[15]

What Paul says about the Spirit in a "partly unsophisticated, partly unfinished, partly imprecise" manner can lead to misinterpretation when the church is forced by historical necessities (e.g., heresy) to make its theological position precise and clear—which sometimes requires new conceptualizations.[16] If the doctrine of the Trinity does not come from the New Testament, it comes from nowhere. This must be recognized even if a triadic tradition in the New Testament is not yet a conscious trinitarianism. The texts are fluid and we cannot sort out with precision what was still in flux. The impulses, the instincts of faith discerned in the biblical texts are part of a developing history which becomes clear in and through a post-biblical struggle.

THE ORDERING OF THE DIVINE NAMES

Is the order of names in a given text really significant? Is it dictated by context? Does rhetoric determine order, or is it arbitrary? Do the texts allow a decision between these three possibilities? Placing too much emphasis on the order is clearly hazardous.

To speak of triadic biblical models is tempting, but appropriate only in a qualified sense. What we find is a triadic mind-set, a habit of thought—less a firm affirmation and more an intimation, like Ben Shahn's portrait of Caligula that is simply a curved line and a dot. Model is shorthand for the triadic mindset within the New Testament.

Five models are proposed here. Texts may well fit in more than one, but the point is the discernment of the role of the Spirit, not fine-tuning of the models.

(1) The Effective Act Model: God–Spirit–Christ/Son (Gal 4:6; [Matt 1:18; Luke 1:26-35; Acts 15:7-11])—the Spirit as the dynamic of God's outreach.

(2) The Kyrios Model: Christ/Jesus–God–Spirit (2 Cor 1:21-22; 2 Cor 13:13; [Acts 2:32-33])—Christ as the Lord of the

---

[15] Schierse, "Die neutestamentliche Trinitätsoffenbarung," *MS* 2.88. F. X. Durwell, "Pour une christologie selon l'Esprit," *Nouvelle Revue Théologique* 114 (1992) 664.

[16] Kuss, *Römerbrief*, 575, 582–83.

Spirit, and the meaning of that lordship for the role of the Spirit in history.

(3) Historical Model: Spirit–Christ–God/Father (1 Cor 12:4-6; Eph 4:4-7)—the order of history and experience.

(4) Access Model: Christ–Spirit–Father (Eph 2:18-22)—the Spirit has exclusive rights of access to the Father.

(5) Sending Model: God/Father–Christ/Son/Jesus–Spirit (Rom 8:3-17; Eph 1:3-14; [Matt 28:19; Acts 5:30-32; John 1:14, 29-34; 14:16; 15:26; possibly 1 John 1:1-4; 3:23-24])—based on the missions of the Son and the Spirit from the Father.[17]

These models demonstrate that the triadic form is well established; how much meaning can be attached to the differing orders of the names is less clear. We must exercise caution in building theological systems on the models when there are exegetical questions for which we have no answers—for instance, how great a role does rhetoric play in the ordering of the names in a given instance?

New Testament experience implies God as a differentiated unity, as unity in plurality.[18] In the biblical period binitarian patterns (mention only of Father and Son) also had a strong hold on religious thought. The post-biblical church, after struggling through biblical obscurities, especially as regards the Spirit, focused on strong indications within the New Testament that plurality in unity was trinitarian rather than merely binitarian. The predominant New Testament view seems to be a combination of the Effective Act (Father–Son–Spirit) and the Historical (Spirit–Son–Father) Models.[19] But whatever the model, there is a habit of mind which sees the Spirit as the place of mediation whereby God touches the church and the world and sets them on the road back to God.

The order of the names is in service of a theological intent—the Spirit stands at the beginning of a new history of the new creation, namely, at the conception of Jesus (Matt 1:20; Luke 1:35), and at

[17] This model has the same pattern as David Coffey's procession model. Coffey's models, however, *Deus Trinitas: The Doctrine of the Triune God* (New York: Oxford University Press, 1999) 46–65, are of the immanent Trinity.

[18] E. C. Colwell, "A Definite Rule for the Use of the Article in the Greek New Testament," *Journal of Biblical Literature* 52 (1933) 12–21.

[19] Geoffrey Wainwright, *Doxology* (London: Epworth, 1980) 99.

the first moment of the church's existence (Acts 1:1-4). The movement—individual, ecclesial, cosmic—makes possible an integral trinitarian view, in which the redemption of the created order and social transformation is caught up in the free movement of creation and the children of God from the Father back to God.

Chapter 2

Struggling with Ambiguity

Though our contemporary use of "person" as a category has little to do with whatever we can extract from the New Testament witness, we cannot do without it. Even Augustine is embarrassed by the term "person" and asks his readers' indulgence for using it. But the twelfth-century Richard of St. Victor thinks that an act of the Spirit led to the recognition of the term "person" in the church, so that everyone, even rustics, could understand the Trinity.[1]

No one has come up with a workable category to replace person, so for now we have to stay with the term. Karl Rahner and Franz J. Schierse suggest that we return to the original experience of salvation, the meeting of the sinful human being with the merciful Father in heaven through Jesus Christ who sends the Spirit.[2] This puts the Spirit at the center of the attempt to come to terms with "person" because it is through the Spirit that one experiences the Son and the Father.

[1] Karl Rahner and Karl Lehmann, "Kerygma und Dogma," *MS* 1.694. Augustine, *On the Trinity* 7.6.11. Michael Schmaus, *Die psychologische Trinitätslehre des heilgen Augustinus* (Münster: Aschendorff, 1927) 148. Leo Scheffczyk, "Uneingelöste Traditionen der Trinitätslehre," *Trinität: Aktuelle Perspektiven der Theologie*, Eugen Drewermann et al., eds. (Freiburg: Herder, 1984) 68, 71. Richard of St. Victor, *On the Trinity* 4.5; 4.4; PL 196.933: *nomen personae in ore omnium, etiam rusticorum, versatur.* Heinz Wipfler, *Die Trinitätsspekulation des Petrus von Poitiers und die Trinitätsspekulation des Richard von St. Viktor. Ein Vergleich* (Münster: Aschendorff, 1965) 53, n. 43.

[2] Rahner, "Der Dreifaltige Gott als Transzendenter Urgrund der Heilsgeschichte," *MS* 2.343–44; *The Trinity* 106. Franz J. Schierse, "Die neutestamentliche Trinitätsoffenbarung," *MS* 2.93.

According to Paul, Christ is the image of God (2 Cor 4:4; see Col 1:15). The Spirit has neither a countenance nor a name. Can one be a person having neither face nor name? Though one can find in both Paul's and John's presentations of the Spirit characteristics of a person, the questions remain: Is a move from personification to personhood justified? Can we find here early traces of later developments as regards person? Both Leo Scheffczyk and Otto Kuss think some concept of person is present in the New Testament texts, while Schierse leaves the question open, fearing that to relate the biblical doctrine to the later understanding of person leads to tritheism.[3]

THE BINARY TENDENCY IN THE NEW TESTAMENT

The trinitarian history of the Spirit is blurred by the New Testament's tendency to engage in trinitarian talk about the Father and the Son without mentioning the Spirit. There are binary doxologies in Paul (1 Cor 8:6; 1 Tim 2:5-6; 6:13-14). Schierse remarks, "There appears to be no 'place' for a third divine person alongside of the Father and the Son." The character of the Spirit is indeterminate in other ways too. The Fourth Gospel attempts to show the similarity between Christ and the Spirit, while the later tradition is at pains to distinguish them. Paul drew on the figure of Wisdom for the pre-existent Christ and the Spirit—some interpreters think this obscures the distinction. David Brown says it was Paul's charismatic experience on the road to Damascus that collapsed the distinction between Christ and the Spirit.[4]

But the principal cause of confusion is "the Lord is the Spirit"

[3] Jacques Guillet, "The Spirit of God," *Dictionary of Biblical Theology*, Xavier Léon-Dufour, ed. (New York: Seabury, 1973) 571. Scheffczyk, "Lehramtliche Formulierungen und Dogmengeschichte der Trinität," *MS* 2.150. Otto Kuss, *Der Römerbrief* (Regensburg: Pustet, 1963–78) 580–83. Schierse, "Trinitätsoffenbarung," *MS* 2.120–21.

[4] Kelly, *Creeds*, 19–20. Schierse, "Trinitätsoffenbarung," *MS* 2.112. Raymond E. Brown, *The Gospel According to John XIII–XXI* (Garden City: Doubleday, 1970) 1141: "The Spirit is the life of Jesus. As in John's eschatology, where the Spirit assumes the features of Christ, so here, Christ is 'spiritualized.' This relation obscures the distinction between Jesus and the Spirit such that pneumatology almost gets lost in christology." Gary M. Burge: *The Anointed Community: The Holy Spirit in the Johannine Tradition* (Grand Rapids: Eerdmans, 1987) 110. David Brown, *The Divine Trinity* (Lasalle, Ill.: Open Court, 1985) 194.

(2 Cor 3:17). The identity between the Lord and the Spirit is not formal, logical; it is dynamic, illuminating, an identity in experience. The verse is not a speculative reflection on the divine nature. For believers, the Lord is experienced as the end-time Spirit, so the assertion about the Spirit is a christological statement. The text is not saying Lord and Spirit are identical in every way.[5]

What, then, does scripture mean in saying that the Spirit comes down on Mary? The angel says, "The Holy Spirit will come upon you . . . therefore the child to be born will be called Son of God" (Luke 1:35). Is what descends impersonal power? "Jesus, full of the Holy Spirit, returned from the Jordan and was led by the Spirit in the wilderness" (Luke 4:1); "Jesus, filled with the power of the Spirit, returned to Galilee" (Luke 4:14). Is this impersonal power? "At that same hour Jesus rejoiced in the Holy Spirit" (Luke 10:21). Is this impersonal inspiration? These passages imply wisdom, something divine in the Son of God. Does a higher being dwell in the man Jesus? Or is Jesus identified with the higher being? At the very least, they mean that Jesus is near to God.[6]

Though the phrase "in the presence of God and of Christ Jesus and of the elect angels" (1 Tim 5:21) is probably to be understood in an eschatological context, the text caused trouble in the post-biblical period because opponents of the Spirit's divinity asked, "Why did the Apostle not make mention of the Holy Spirit after naming Christ, but rather mentions the elect angels?" Athanasius, Basil, and Didymus the Blind all had to deal with this verse in their defense of the divinity of the Spirit.[7] Other texts are unclear whether the Spirit or an angel is acting (Acts 8:26, 39; 23:9). In the final

[5] Felix Porsch, *Pneuma und Wort: Ein exegetischer Beitrag zur Pneumatologie des Johannesevangeliums* (Frankfurt am Main: Knecht, 1974) 202. James D.G. Dunn, *Christology in the Making: A New Testament Inquiry into the Origins of the Doctrine of the Incarnation* (Philadelphia: Westminster, 1980) 146, 147. Ingo Hermann, *Kyrios und Pneuma* (Munich: Kösel, 1961) 51, 52. Neill Quinn Hamilton, *The Holy Spirit and Eschatology in Paul* (Edinburgh: Oliver and Boyd, 1957) 15–16, 83. Schierse, "Trinitätsoffenbarung," *MS* 2.119.

[6] Basil Studer, *Trinity and Incarnation* (Collegeville: The Liturgical Press, 1993) 38.

[7] Athanasius, *Letters to Serapion* 1.10–14, 119; SC 15.99–108, 121. Basil, *On the Holy Spirit* 13.28–30; SC 17bis.348–352. Didymus the Blind, *On the Trinity* 2.19; PG 39.548c.

book of the Bible the whole of revelation is said to be the work of the angel Jesus sends (Rev 1:1; 22:6, 16). In the early post-biblical period—indeed, in the later strata of the New Testament—there is a mixing of angelology and pneumatology.[8]

The ambiguity of the biblical text is at the basis of the post-biblical uncertainty. As Basil Studer notes, the post-biblical authors understood the Spirit *(pneuma)* as the breath of life, the superior part of the soul, the cosmic soul, divine life imparted to humankind, the divine being, the element of divinity in Christ, and the Spirit who is placed alongside the Father and the Son in the baptismal formula.[9]

THE IDENTITY CRISIS IN THE POST-BIBLICAL PERIOD

This imprecision in the biblical text did not hinder Clement of Rome at the end of the first century from recognizing the "independent" character of the Spirit: "We have one sole God, one sole Christ, and one sole Spirit of grace who has been poured out on us, and one sole call in Christ."[10] But for many, the scriptural unclarity, together with the tendency to speak of the Spirit in "power" categories (Luke 1:17; 24:49; 1 Cor 2:4; 1 Thess 1:5; Eph 3:16; Acts 6:5, 6; 10:38), and the lack of firm teaching on the Spirit as person, led in the post-apostolic period to difficulties in distinguishing Christ and the Spirit.

The Apostolic Fathers tend to identify the Logos with the Spirit. Justin Martyr (ca. 100–ca. 165), who proposes a distinct trinitarian faith against the charge of atheism, mentions the baptismal formula four times but is hazy about the distinction between Christ and the Spirit. The apologists—ca.120–220: Aristides, Justin, Tatian, Athenagoras, Theophilus, Minucius Felix, Tertullian—trying both to establish the Christians' right to exist and to convert the educated classes, repeat the clear trinitarian baptismal formula without giving

[8] Jean Gribomont, "Esprit, pères grecs," *Dictionnaire de Spiritualité* 4.1258. George Montague, *The Holy Spirit: Growth of a Biblical Tradition* (New York: Paulist, 1976) 329.

[9] *Trinity and Incarnation*, 38. On the ambiguity of the Spirit in the *regulae fidei*, see Joseph Moingt, *Théologie trinitaire de Tertullien: Histoire, doctrine, méthodes*, 4 vols. (Paris: Aubier, 1966–1969) 1.79.

[10] *To the Corinthians* 46.6; SC 167.176. See also the formula of an oath in 58.2; SC 167.192.

much theological attention to the Spirit. Their whole concern is for Logos christology.[11]

GROPING THE WAY

Early pneumatology is still groping its way. In *On First Principles*, Origen, though a committed trinitarian, has difficulty fitting the Spirit into his systematics.[12] But there simply was not much debate about the Spirit in the days of emerging trinitarian doctrine. In fact, it was only in the quarter-century immediately preceding the Council of Constantinople in 381 that the Spirit became a matter of serious discussion.

Augustine, writing as a fairly young presbyter, reflects on the paucity of theological reflection on the Spirit, though he would certainly have known of Ambrose's and Basil's books, both entitled *On the Holy Spirit*. About two years before he became bishop in 395, Augustine was still saying "as yet, the subject of the Holy Spirit has not been so extensively and thoroughly covered by the learned and outstanding commentators on the sacred scriptures as to enable us to see readily what is also proper to him whereby we call him neither the Father nor the Son, but the Holy Spirit. They simply proclaim him to be the gift of God, so that we may believe that God does not communicate a gift less perfect than himself." Augustine would say that the Father generates and the Son is generated, but the only distinctive character of the Spirit is "gift of God." Augustine would have been especially careful about his formulation, as the text of *On the Faith and the Creed* was prepared for a synod of African bishops in October 393.[13]

Both at the beginning and the end of the fourth century there

---

[11] Harry A. Wolfson, "The Identification of the Logos and the Holy Spirit," *The Philosophy of the Church Fathers*, 2nd ed. (Cambridge: Harvard, 1964) 183–91. Kelly, *Doctrines*, 102. Justin, *First Apology* 6; 61.3, 10–13; 65.3; 67.2, in *Saint Justin: Apologies*, André Wartelle, ed. (Paris: Études Augustiniennes, 1987) 104, 182, 188, 190.

[12] Kilian McDonnell, "Does Origen Have a Trinitarian Doctrine of the Holy Spirit?" *Gregorianum* 75, 1 (1994) 5–35.

[13] *On Faith and the Creed* 9.19; 8, in *Augustine: De Fide et Symbolo*, E. P. Meijering, ed. (Amsterdam: Gieben, 1987) 118, 161. Johannes Quasten, *Patrology* 4 vols. (Westminster, Md.: Christian Classics, 1986) 4.369.

was little theological reflection on the role of the Spirit, in spite of Origen's major contribution earlier. When the Spirit's status became a matter of dispute, no common grammar was available. At hand were some biblical triadic texts, especially Matthew 28:19, and the *regulae fidei,* too generic to respond to the specific question that eventually arose about the divinity of the Spirit. Theologians had *homoousios* (of one substance) for the Son, but no comparable technical vocabulary for the Spirit. In the past, and into the fourth century, they used binitarian Father and Son language to speak about the Spirit.

FATHER AND SON CARRY THE TRINITARIAN ARGUMENT

When the question of the divinity of the Spirit became pressing, theological reflection was aided by the trinitarian mode in which christological questions were approached. If the full identity of the Son is established by reference to the trinitarian dynamic, then that seemed a safe way to approach the identity of the Spirit.

Prior to the fourth century the discussion about God was so dominated by the Father/Son relationship that some of the early authors were suspected of being binitarians rather than true trinitarians in their doctrine of God. But the suspicion is unfounded. A binitarian mentality (mention of only Father and Son) was precisely that—a mentality, a habit—not a firm theological stance excluding the Spirit. The Trinity is not denied; rather, it is presupposed. Authors who theologize in this binitarian fashion also cite the text of Matthew 28:19, and incorporate liturgical rites of baptism.

Even those who include the Spirit in their theological reflection— e.g. Athenagoras, Irenaeus, Tertullian, Hippolytus in *Against Noetus,* and especially Origen—often argue in a binitarian mode. Tertullian is irrevocably committed to the trinitarian vision; he is the first Latin theologian to use the word *trinitas,* and in a context where he is speaking of the Spirit.[14] But in *Against Praxeas,* where he gives his best teaching on the Trinity, he argues in a binitarian mode for the first twenty-five of the thirty-one chapters.

[14] *On Modesty,* 21,16: SC 394.274. This is not just a problem for antiquity. Because biblically the trinitarian impulse is located in christology, there is a tendency even today to speak of the Trinity in terms of the relation of the Father and the Son. The Spirit is not given equal time and, attitudinally, not always equal stature.

The Other Hand of God

Origen is trinitarian in intent, and he clearly wants to include the Spirit, on which he is expansive. It is not on mere sufferance that he accepts the Spirit, but he is at a loss as to what to do with the Spirit in terms of formal theological organization. It is hardly surprising that the first scholar to produce a theological synthesis did not produce an eternally valid formulation. Origen's piety is trinitarian in grand style, not binitarian. But he struggles. On the question of distinction and unity in the Trinity, he speaks only of the Father and the Son, as did nearly everyone else.[15]

Even those who wanted to vindicate the full rights of the Spirit alongside the Father and the Son guarded their language. Especially after the Council of Nicaea there was much confusion. Many volleys and blasts were launched without a great deal of precise attention to the shadows that were the targets. We must, therefore, be careful about attaching labels to these early authors. People of integrity and orthodox intentions were groping even after Nicaea. Obscurities fueled a "war of suspicion."[16] The application of *homoousios* to the Son in the creed of Nicaea inaugurated a period of great confusion because so many did not accept it. Only when that controversy cooled, and the church moved toward the Council of Constantinople in 381, did the Spirit surface as an issue of debate. Reluctant to introduce new language, the participants sought to redefine the old terms and to build hedges around them.

Nicaea had no need to say more than "and [we believe] in the Holy Spirit," since the Spirit was not at issue, but the credal formula of Nicaea committed the church to the equality and divinity of the Spirit, even if not expressly stated. The celebration of the liturgy, Christian experience, and the logic of the council's creed, together with the necessity of responding to those who openly denied the divinity of the Spirit, would eventually bring the church to a more explicit affirmation of the Spirit's relation to the Father and the Son.

BUT IT IS NOT IN SCRIPTURE!

No one wanted to go beyond scripture. Though the Nicenes accepted

---

[15] Wolf-Dieter Hauschild, *Gottes Geist und der Mensch: Studien zur frühchrist-lichen Pneumatologie* (Munich: Kaiser, 1972) 138, 149. Wolfson, *Philosophy of the Church Fathers*, 317.

[16] Wolfson, 377.

the non-scriptural *homoousios* for the Son in relation to the Father, they were hesitant to use it of the Holy Spirit, though they were convinced the Spirit is equal and divine. Athanasius, Didymus the Blind, and the Cappadocians had to grapple with the objections of some who pointed out, quite rightly, that on the divinity of the Spirit the scriptures are silent, if one requires direct, explicit testimony. Nicaea's "and [we believe] in the Holy Spirit" is an expression, not of doubt as to the divinity of the Spirit, but of the failure of scripture to be explicit, and of the reluctance of the council to say more than scripture says.

No one but Athanasius dared to use the term *homoousios* of the Spirit before 358. It was a risk—bold, audacious, wholly without precedent. Athanasius is fully conscious that he is breaking new ground. Still, he is careful. He never applies *theos* to the Spirit, though he comes close. He says that the Spirit "is no creature, but is one with the Son as the Son is one with the Father, [the Spirit] is glorified with the Father and the Son, and *confessed as God with the Word.*"[17]

Athanasius, who had been the most outspoken defender of the church's faith regarding the Son, is thus also one of the earliest champions of the church's faith concerning the Spirit. He inspired Basil, whose *On the Holy Spirit* has been called "the most brilliant theology of the Holy Spirit in the East." Basil argues in a binitarian mode in sections 6.13 through 8.21, though the purpose of the tract is to establish that "the same honor" *(homotimos)* is due to the Spirit as to the Father and Son—in other words, the Spirit is divine. As we shall see, Basil wants to ascribe equal honor to the Spirit without actually using the technical word for it, namely, *homotimos.* Not only is the tract guarded in its language; Basil is willing to show it only to a select circle of the like-minded. The closest he comes to *homoousios* language in *On the Holy Spirit* is found late in the treatise, after much preparation of the ground: The Spirit "is divine in nature *(theion tē phusei),* infinite in greatness." In a letter, he approves of *homoousios* applied to the Spirit, but even here the term is directly applied to the Son and only indirectly to the Spirit. Basil is shy of

---

[17] *Letters to Serapion* 1.27, 31; SC 15.133, 139, 165. C. R. B. Shapland, *The Letters of Saint Athanasius concerning the Holy Spirit* (New York: Philosophical Library, 1951) 133, n. 7, contends that Athanasius uses *homoousios* of the Spirit in 3.1. Actually he uses it of the Son and then ascribes it "likewise" to the Spirit.

saying more than that "the Son is recognized as being consubstantial *(homoousios)* with the Father, and the Holy Spirit, enjoying the same honors, is numbered and adored with them."[18]

[18] H. B. Swete, *On the Early History of the Doctrine of the Holy Spirit* (Cambridge: Deighton and Bell, 1873) 47. Gribomont, "Esprit, pères grecs," 4.1271. Studer, *Trinity and Incarnation*, 183; Pia Luislampe, *Spiritus vivificans. Grundzüge einer Theologie des Heiligen Geistes nach Basilius von Caesarea* (Münster: Aschendorff, 1981) 162–88. Hermann Dörries, *De Spiritu Sancto: Der Beitrag des Basilius zum Abschluss des trinitärischen Dogmas* (Göttingen: Vandenhoeck & Ruprecht, 1956) 121. Basil, *On the Holy Spirit* 23.54; SC 17bis.444. Basil, *Letter* 90.2, in *Lettres*, Yves Courtonne, ed., 3 vols. (Paris: Société d'Édition "Les Belles Lettres," 1957–1966) 1:196.

Chapter 3

The Way of Doxology

Faith in the Trinity arose not from learned speculation but out of the experience of Christian life, especially worship: "The grace of the Lord Jesus Christ, the love of God, and the communion of the Holy Spirit be with all of you" (2 Cor 13:13) likely comes out of the liturgy. First Corinthians 8:6, "there is one God, the Father, from whom are all things and for whom we exist, and one Lord, Jesus Christ, through whom are all things and through whom we exist," probably comes from a baptismal liturgy. Ivan Havener suggests that New Testament credal statements, including Trinitarian ones, are not declaratory, "baptismal confessions," but "baptismal acclamations." Whatever the factors that contributed to their formation, "the earliest dogmas were largely understood as doxologies, as confessional praises of God. . . . Dogma is thought liturgy; liturgy is prayed dogma"—hence the mutuality and harmony between liturgy and faith expressed in "the law of prayer is the law of faith" (*lex credendi lex statuat supplicandi*) of Prosper of Aquitaine.[1]

[1] Hans Dietrich Wendland, *Die Briefe an die Korinther* (Göttingen: Vandenhoeck & Ruprecht, 1968) 259. Franz J. Schierse, "Die neutestamentliche Trinitätsoffenbarung," *MS* 2.126. Jerome Murphy-O'Connor, "The First Letter to the Corinthians," *The New Jerome Biblical Commentary*, Raymond E. Brown et al., eds. (Englewood Cliffs: Prentice Hall, 1990) 806. Havener: "The Credal Formulae of the New Testament: A History of the Scholarly Research and a Contribution to the On-going Study" (Ph.D. diss., University of Munich, 1976) 542. Walter Kasper, "Geschichtlichkeit der Dogmen?" *Stimmen der Zeit* 179 (1967) 407. Prosper: Denzinger–Schönmetzer, *Enchiridion Symbolorum Definitionum et Declarationum de Rebus Fidei et Morum*, 246.

The Spirit of the Son, whom God has sent into the hearts of the children, cries "Abba! Father!" (Gal 4:6), reflecting not doctrinal decision but Christian experience. This "Abba!" cry of the faithful in Romans 8:15 probably comes out of the liturgical experience of baptism—the cry of the baptized is also the cry of the Spirit. Trinitarian definition and description are in another dimension; here we have joyous encounter with the transcendent mystery within the celebration of the *koinonia*. The trinitarian awareness of Justin Martyr, the earliest witness to an expansion of the third credal article on the Spirit, was shaped by "the fervent common prayers" of the liturgy of baptism and Eucharist.[2]

The trinitarian dynamic Father–Son–Spirit–Son–Father provides a key to understanding Irenaeus's view of both the universal history of salvation and the Christian's experience of baptism. Irenaeus traces the rhythms of trinitarian movement from the absolute source, the Father, to the absolute goal of eschatology, the Father. "The Spirit in advance prepares for the Son of God, and the Son leads [the believer] to the Father, and the Father gives [the believer] incorruptibility and eternal life which results in the vision of God for those who see him. Likewise those who see the light are in the light and participate in his splendor. For the glory of God gives life." For Irenaeus, Spirit is the linchpin in this divine progress through our history, locking in the movement so there is no slippage in approaching the Father: "Therefore the baptism of our rebirth comes through these three articles, granting us rebirth unto God the Father, through His Son, by the Holy Spirit. For those who are bearers of the Spirit of God are led to the Word, that is, to the Son; but the Son takes them and presents them to the Father; and the Father confers incorruptibility. So without the Spirit there is no seeing the Word of God, and without the Son there is no approaching

[2] Dieter Lührmann, *Der Brief an die Galater* (Zurich: Theologischer Verlag, 1978) 69. Otto Küss, *Römerbrief* (Regensburg: Pustet, 1963–1978) 2.602–3. Ernst Käsemann, *Commentary on Romans* (Grand Rapids: Eerdmans, 1980) 227–28; Joseph Fitzmyer, *Romans: A New Translation with Introduction and Commentary* (New York: Doubleday, 1993) 498–99. Justin, *Apology* 1.65,67, in *Apologies*, André Watrelle, ed. (Paris: Études augustiniennes, 1987) 188–92. Hans-Jochen Jaschke, *Der Heilige Geist im Bekenntnis der Kirche* (Münster: Aschendorff, 1976) 25.

the Father; for the Son is the knowledge of the Father, and the knowledge of the Son is through the Holy Spirit."[3]

BASIL: DOXOLOGY INSTEAD OF TECHNOLOGY

BASIL: DOXOLOGY INSTEAD OF TECHNOLOGY

Basil's *On the Holy Spirit* arises out of a dispute as to the right way to give glory to God—indeed, doxology is the theme of the whole book. Again and again he returns to doxology in making a trinitarian argument; the logic of his claims for the divinity of the Spirit is baptism, faith, doxology.[4]

All the Cappadocians set themselves against those who do "technology" instead of theology, that is, who use purely rational, logical categories to speak of mystery. Basil and the two Gregories, themselves educated in the school of the sophists, resist the transposition of the experience of faith into excessive dialectics, proofs, syllogisms, abstruse language, artificial analysis, intemperate conceptuality, irrefutable logic devoid of adoration, without respect for the laws arising out of the holy mystery they are contemplating. In a word, they oppose rationalism in trinitarian doctrine while promoting a consistent and rationally defensible doctrine of God.[5]

Those who have departed from the tradition, Basil complains, are "not ashamed to describe the creator of the universe with language fit for a hammer or a saw." Basil is incensed at the use of carpentry language for the divine transcendence. The trinitarian mystery surpasses all intelligence and "defies language." None of the Cappadocians is against philosophical rigor, least of all Gregory of Nyssa, who offers an extensive philosophical refutation of technology in his

[3] Basil Studer, *Trinity and Incarnation* (Collegeville: The Liturgical Press, 1993) 60. Irenaeus, *Against Heresies* 4.20.5; SC 100.638, 640; *Demonstration of the Apostolic Preaching* 7; SC 406.92. Albert Houssiau, "Le baptême selon Irénée de Lyon," *Ephemerides Theologicae Lovaniensis* 60 (1984) 57.

[4] Dörries, *DSS*, 54, 148f., 154.

[5] Basil, *On the Holy Spirit* 3.5; SC 17bis.264; Gregory of Nazianzus, *Discourse* 31.18; SC 250.310; Gregory of Nyssa, *Against Eunomius* 1; PG 45.297, 337; 7; PG 45.741; 12; PG 45.905, 1021. See also Clement of Alexandria, *Miscellaneous Studies (Stromata)* 2, 19, 4; SC 30.58. E. Vandenbussche, "La Part de la dialectique dans la théologie d'Eunomius 'le technologue,'" *Revue d'histoire ecclésiastique* 40 (1944) 47–72, especially 49 n. 1. R.P.C. Hanson, "The Transformation of Images in the Trinitarian Theology of the Fourth Century," *Studia Patristica* 17/1 (Oxford: Pergamon, 1982) 112.

Against Eunomius. Their quarrel is with the assumption that our "mental narrowness" is adequate. Nor does Basil believe that alongside appropriate metaphysical speculation there is a second way, the doxological. Rather, he takes reason up into divine knowing and adoration, into contemplation, the true philosophy. He mines biblical categories and aesthetics for his vocabulary: beauty, light, illumination, joy, grandeur, splendor, radiance, dance—hence the hymnodic quality of much of Basil's writing on the Spirit. "To glorify is nothing else but to enumerate his wondrous properties" by repeating the multiple glories bestowed on us.[6]

The question of right praise, doxology, arose when Basil, presiding at a celebration, finished the liturgy by using two different forms of the doxology. The ancient form was "glory to God, the Father through *(dia)* the Son in *(en)* the Holy Spirit." The second form praised "God the Father with *(meta)* the Son with *(syn)* the Holy Spirit." Some of those celebrating with Basil at the liturgy, offended by this second form, accused him of using "strange and contradictory words." Basil's opponents used the ancient formula "with the same ease with which they breathe air." *On the Holy Spirit* is apparently Basil's vindication of the propriety of also using "with" (*meta* and *syn*) in a doxology, since the scriptures themselves attest no fixed assignment of prepositions to specific divine persons. Basil argues that the use of "with" is, in fact, customary, and he cites precedents. But he is by no means sanguine about the success of his efforts in a tumultuous climate where, he notes with some weariness and sarcasm, "everyone is a theologian," a complaint repeated by Gregory of Nazianzus some six years later. Basil's intent is not to displace the "through" and "in" using only "with," but to use them side by side, in a hermeneutical dialectic, so that the Arian interpretation of "through" and "in" is excluded.[7]

[6] Basil, O*n the Holy Spirit* 3.5; SC 17bis.266; 28.70; SC 17bis.498; 4.6; SC 17bis.268; 8.17; SC 17bis.304. Pia Luislampe, *Spiritus vivificans. Grundzüge einer Theologie des Heiligen Geistes nach Basilius von Caesarea* (Münster: Aschendorff, 1981) 32.

[7] Basil, *On the Holy Spirit* 1.3; SC 17bis.256; 1.3; SC 17bis.258; 25.58; SC 17bis.456; 4.6 and 5.7–12; SC 17bis.268–84; 25.58; SC 17bis.45; 29.74; SC 17bis.510, 512; 30.77; SC 17bis.526. Gregory of Nazianzus, *Discourse* 27.3; SC 250.76. Joseph Jungmann, "Reaction of the Arian Struggles on Liturgical

The question of what is the right way to praise God arises out of liturgical worship and the solution is stated in terms of right liturgy. One gives to the Spirit equal honor *(homotimia)* with the Father and the Son as in the celebration of baptism. "We glorify God both in the Spirit and with the Spirit." Why? Because we believe as we are baptized, and we glorify as we believe. The profession of faith, which arises out of our baptism, is therefore "the origin and mother of doxology." One must jealously guard "the baptismal teaching, the confession of faith and the giving of the doxology"—the three are inextricably bound. Illumination does not come from the outside, but from being inseparably "joined to the Spirit of knowledge. . . . The way to divine knowledge ascends from one Spirit through the one Son to the one Father."[8] Like Irenaeus, Basil has doxology return in the Spirit through Christ, the same route in the reverse "direction" by which God's glory, the divine blessings, descends to us, that is, through Christ in the Spirit. After God has reached us through Christ in the Spirit, the ascending return lays down the doxological highway.

For Basil the communion *(koinonia)* of the Spirit with the Father and the Son means that "only the Spirit can adequately glorify the Lord." Glory given *in* the Holy Spirit through the Son to the Father is not a matter of just ranking the Spirit with the dignity of the Father and the Son, but a recognition of our own radical incapacity. "Of ourselves we are not capable of giving glory, but in the Spirit we have the aptitude." Because objects placed near something brilliant themselves take on its splendor, the "glory of the Spirit is changed into [the believer's] glory, not stingily, or dimly, but with abundance."[9]

Gregory of Nyssa argues in a similar way. "The Spirit is the glory" because the Spirit belongs to that "revolving circle of glory moving from like to like" within the Trinity. The path of glory is first of all marked out in the rhythms of divine life. However, Gregory extends the glory beyond the triune life. He sees the divine glory operative

Prayer. The Dispute over the Doxology," in his *The Place of Christ in Liturgical Prayer* (Staten Island, N.Y.: Alba House, 1965) 172–90.

[8] Basil, *On the Holy Spirit* 27.68; SC 17bis.488, 490; 10.26; SC 17bis.338; 18.47; SC 17bis.412.

[9] Ibid., 18.46; SC 17bis.410; 26.63; SC 17bis.474; 21.52; SC 17bis.436.

at three levels: within the Trinity, between the Trinity and humankind, and in humankind itself. If the Spirit is not glory, then the
Spirit could not unify life within the Trinity, and as a result the
Trinity would cease, humankind would remain a collection of individuals, without the inner unity which glory gives. "We also repeat
[the circle] in prayer, glorifying the Son by means of the Spirit, and
the Father by means of the Son."[10] The Spirit is the entrance into
the circle of glory.

RICHARD OF ST. VICTOR: THE TRINITARIAN TROUBADOUR

Making a leap forward to the Middle Ages, we meet another trinitarian theologian with a doxological passion, Richard of St. Victor,
one of the most influential theologians of the twelfth century. His
writings on the Trinity are probably the most distinguished trinitarian contribution between Augustine and the time of Bonaventure
and Thomas Aquinas, though he is not above criticism.

Richard had "almost a stormy appetite" for defending and docu-
menting theological propositions. He was very learned, well-informed
on the questions and controversies of the day, including the methods
of the schools, though he was primarily an exegete. For a long time
he was known mostly as a writer of mystical treatises. In trinitarian
history he is significant because, though largely indebted to Augustine, he "found a new way into the mystery" of the Trinity. Richard
was the first to leave the path of aprioristic thinking, marked out by
Augustine and Anselm, and stumble toward God on the road of
experience.[11]

Richard approached plurality of persons in one God by using the

[10] *Oration* ("When all things are subjected to him"), in *Opera*, Werner Jaeger,
ed. (Leiden: Brill, 1952–) 3/2.21–22. Martien Parmentier, "The Doctrine of the
Holy Spirit in the Works of Gregory of Nyssa," *Ekklesiastikos Pharos* 58 (1976)
420–21. Gregory of Nyssa, *Against the Macedonians* 22; PG 45.1329.

[11] Hans Urs von Balthasar, *Richard von Sankt-Victor: Die Dreieinigkeit* (Einsiedeln:
Benziger, 1980) 21. Friedrich Überweg and Bernhard Geyer, *Die patristische und
die scholastische Philosophie* 13th ed. (Basel: B. Schwabe, 1956) 267. Jean Chatillon,
"Richard v. St. Viktor," *Lexikon für Theologie und Kirche* 3rd ed. 8.1294. Michael
Schmaus, "Die Trinitätslehre des Simon von Tournai," *Recherches de théologie
ancienne et médiévale* 3 (1931) 373. Franz Courth, *Trinität in der Scholastik*
(*Handbuch der Dogmengeschichte*) (Freiburg: Herder, 1985) II/1b.65, 66.

dynamics and dialectics of love. Augustine had the procession of the Son by intelligence and that of the Spirit by love. Richard had both proceed by love. Basing himself on 1 John 4:8 ("Whoever does not love does not know God, for God is love") and on verse 16 ("God is love, and those who abide in love abide in God, and God abides in them"), he describes divine love in its trinitarian structure. He draws especially on two books: the Bible and nature, noting the harmony between them. To these he adds a third book, the human person. Experience, whether biblical or in his contact with friends, was a treasury on which he drew. He moved away from the abstract categories and attempted a more empirical, experiential approach.[12]

Richard of St. Victor shares with the Cappadocians a trinitarian mysticism, a spiritual dynamism, the personal quest for the mystery of the triune God going beyond academic inquiry. He confesses that "it is not science which stimulates me to this audacious task" of writing on the Trinity. "I am rather impelled by a fire which burns in my soul." Richard's ardor is not sufficient to move God beyond silence. "And if I am not successful in coming to my goal? And if I fail in my task? Then what? I will have had the joy of seeking the face of my Lord, of having employed all of my strength, without truce, to run the course, to vex myself, to exhaust myself. . . . I have done what is possible, I have not found [the mystery of the triune God], but I have searched. I have called and he is the one who has not answered." The blame is God's. It is not surprising that Dante says of Richard: "as a contemplative, he was more than a man."[13] Richard represents all those who have ever taken this distressing path of writing about the Trinity, who have sought to feed at the heart of the most personal of all mysteries, only to find on their plate the dry bones of distinctions.

Richard is important also because he looks upon the Trinity as the supreme object of contemplation. Nonetheless, he grants that be-

---

[12] For a critique of Richard's views see André Malet, *Personne et amour dans la théologie trinitaire de saint Thomas d'Aquin* (Paris: Vrin, 1956) 37–42. Richard, *On the Grace of Contemplation* or *Benjamin major* 5.7; PL 196.176: *Natura interrogata vel Scriptura consulta unum eumdemque sensum pari loquuntur concordia.* Gaston Salet, "Introduction," *Richard of St. Victor, De Trinitate*; SC 63.26. Überweg and Geyer 267, 268.

[13] *On the Trinity* 3.1; SC 63.166. Dante, *Paradiso*, canto 10.

fore contemplation comes philosophical speculation. Contemplation coming out of adoration does not dispense one from intellectual rigor. In order to prepare for contemplation, one needs a deep and progressive understanding of the world, the soul, and God. In this he followed his master Hugh of St. Victor, who wrote in a manual for students on the study of the *artes* and the scriptures: "Learn everything: you will see afterwards that nothing is superfluous and that there is no joy in a knowledge that is cramped and narrow."[14]

FROM IMPERSONAL DOXOLOGY TO PERSONAL CONTEMPLATION

For trinitarian theology, the Cappadocians in the fourth century and Richard of St. Victor in the twelfth are important witnesses to the unity of theology, the spiritual quest, and mysticism. To transpose Richard's dictum with regard to contemplation, *ubi amor, ibi oculus* (where love, there the eye),[15] *ubi doxologia, ibi theologia* (where there is doxology, there is theology). The Cappadocians wrote before theology became divorced from spirituality and Richard wrote while the unity of theology and spirituality were within living memory. When they wrote on the Trinity they were writing on prayer and doxology. When reading even their more technical works, one is aware that before the doctrines of Trinity and the incarnation were given dogmatic formulation they were experienced mystically in doxology.[16] These dogmas are transpositions of their experience of doxology, but for them the pursuit of God in worship did not compromise the seriousness of the intellectual pursuit.

Basil and Gregory of Nyssa in the East and Augustine and Richard of St. Victor in the West are aware that all their marshaling of arguments, all their logical and linguistic skills, have a boundary. A different kind of clarity dwells on the other side of the border they cannot pass. The only road across the border is praise. To use the

[14] *Didascalicon* 6.1; PL 176.800–01. Jean Leclercq, "The Schoolmen of the Twelfth Century," *The Spirituality of the Middle Ages*, Leclercq, François Vandenbroucke, Louis Bouyer, eds. (New York: Desclée, 1968) 237.

[15] *On the Preparation of the Soul for Contemplation* or *Benjamin Minor* 13; PL 196.10.

[16] Andrew Louth, *The Origins of the Mystical Tradition* (Oxford: Clarendon, 1981) xi.

image dear to Gregory of Nyssa: doxology, like Moses, climbs the mountain of divine knowledge, and on attaining the impenetrable cloud at the peak, enters into the "luminous darkness," there to see God. "This is the seeing that consists in not seeing." Only astonishment seizes something. Or in the modern formulation of John Meyendorff: "The Unknowable . . . is deepest for the one who sees it."[17] Here one goes beyond the limit by giving back to God God's own glory.

In speech one is addressed as a "Thou," not as a "She" or "He." There is a first form of doxology, a personal address, when one says "I (we) give you glory, O God!" But the more usual liturgical form is the impersonal: "Glory be to the Father." In this second form what is said is greater than in the first form. In the second case I am ascribing to God, not the glory I recognize as belonging to God, the glory I carry in my heart and in my life, but also the glory of which I have no comprehension, which my poor mind cannot grasp, the glory which is God's before and beyond any possibility of my knowing. Also, it is a glory anterior to the church, a glory even the church at its holiest and purest does not suspect. This splendor belongs to God before the church bends the knee or the believer bows down. In this doxology not a new glory, but the circle of glory eternally old, is again ascribed to God in awe and adoration.[18]

To say this, one stands outside the usual personal grammar of address, and adopts a doxological, objective, impersonal grammar to say what the personal categories cannot carry. This is why the person addressed, God, is addressed clumsily in the third person singular, not as a "Thou." Desire, the heart of doxology, stumbles ahead of reason and penetrates where virtuous knowing and seeing cannot go. Eager, bleary-eyed, club-footed desire adopts a linguistically crude form of speech so that it can touch what it cannot see. "Never to reach satiety of desiring is truly to see God." Impersonal doxology and personal delight bow down together, bound together in an endless hymn determined only by the inexhaustible life of God. Ultimately, not definitions, not dialectics, but doxology brings the

---

[17] *Life of Moses* 162; SC 1bis.81. Meyendorff, *St. Gregory Palamas and Orthodox Spirituality* (Crestwood, N.Y.: St. Vladimir's, 1974) 43.

[18] Edmund Schlink, *The Coming Christ and the Coming Church* (Philadelphia: Fortress, 1967) 18–34.

theological task to fulfillment. That is why both confession *(homologia)* and theology *(theologia)* end where they start, in doxology *(doxologia)*.[19]

Doxology is, however, more than words and prostrations; it is that whole realm of thought, feeling, action—including feeding the hungry and clothing the naked—gathered in the hymn sung to God, opening the community to the living reality of God.[20] No less than this is gathered up in the Spirit, who is glory, to bring all through Christ to the Father.

THE WAY BACK:
REEXPERIENCING BIBLE AND LITURGY

Neither the emergence of trinitarian doctrine, nor its defense, originated in pure theory or abstract speculation. Rather, their origins are to be found in hearing again the revealed word in the liturgical glorification of God in the ordinary Christian community as it expresses its simple faith.[21] If we are looking for a way to construct a contemporary trinitarian theology reflecting these doxological and personalist themes, Basil's *On the Holy Spirit* and Richard's *On the Trinity* could serve as models. To use these models could not mean a simple return to the patristic/monastic theology of the early church and medieval period. Today it would have its own character, done in a contemporary mode, losing nothing of its philosophical discipline, but cast in personalist, experiential, biblical, and doxological categories. This is a return to origins, to the original experience, that is, to the praise and adoration in which the doxological community, the church, gathers to hear the Word of God and celebrate the mysteries. Also it is a return to the liturgical praxis where the church first experienced and recognized God as Father, Son, and Holy Spirit.

This reexperiencing of early ecclesial consciousness would enable

[19] Gregory of Nyssa, *The Life of Moses* 239; SC 1bis.108-09. Franz Courth, *Trinität in der Schrift und Patristik (Handbuch der Dogmengeschichte)* (Freiburg: Herder, 1988) II/1a.207.

[20] "The *Filioque* Clause in Ecumenical Perspective" (the "Klingenthal Memorandum")," in *Spirit of God, Spirit of Christ: Ecumenical Reflections on the Filioque Controversy*, Lukas Vischer, ed. (London: SPCK, 1981) 10.

[21] Walter Kasper, *The God of Jesus Christ* (New York: Crossroad, 1986) 242.

us to recover more of the biblical riches, sometimes lost because the development of trinitarian doctrine was often determined by christological controversies dominated by a quite necessary technical vocabulary. Would not retrieval of the biblical and liturgical experience of the early church help restore theology, especially trinitarian theology and pneumatology, to its role as a normal preparation for contemplation?

In 1960 Leo Scheffczyk, historian of trinitarian doctrine, well aware of the range and riches of thought in this field, suggested that "speculative trinitarian theology cannot easily develop itself further; it has reached near to the boundaries." On this, he declared, there was general agreement. On the other hand, there is that other agreement, namely, that trinitarian doctrine is essentially doxological in its origins and character.[22]

Could we not go beyond these two observations and develop a new style of doing trinitarian theology, including pneumatology, that would gather up the fruits of the long history of trinitarian speculation—retaining philosophical categories and argumentation, but casting trinitarian thought also in aesthetic, hymnodic, and doxological images, so that one can pray and preach and celebrate it? Doxology alone speaks the language of this contemplative country. The very objectivity of most liturgical doxology signals an attempt to breach the border. The impersonal vocabulary tries to say into that unknowing night what cannot be said in the knowing light. Doxology is the way to sing, in the phrase of poet John Berryman, "the unsayable center."

---

[22] "Die heilsökonomische Trinitätslehre des Rupert von Deutz und ihre dogmatische Bedeutung," *Kirche und Überlieferung*, Johannes Betz and Heinrich Fries, eds. (Freiburg: Herder, 1960) 90. Schlink, *Coming Christ and Coming Church*, 16–45. Wolfhart Pannenberg, "Analogy and Doxology," in Pannenberg, *Basic Questions in Theology* (London: SCM, 1970) 1.211–38. Dietrich Ritschl, "Historical Development and Implications of the *Filioque* Controversy," *Spirit of God, Spirit of Christ*, 64–65; Pia Luislampe, "Die doxologische Struktur der basilianischen Pneumatologie," in Luislampe, *Spiritus vivificans*, 32–40. William J. Hill, *The Three-Personed God: The Trinity as a Mystery of Salvation* (Washington, D.C.: Catholic University, 1982) 162. Catherine Mowry LaCugna, *God for Us: The Trinity and Christian Life* (San Francisco: HarperSanFrancisco, 1991), 319–75.

Chapter 4

To Do Pneumatology Is to Do Eschatology

The study of eschatology is a mine field, and the unwary can easily be blown away, especially if oblivious to the history of the term and the confusions associated with it. As a specialized field of study called "eschatology," it is not found in the Fathers, in medieval theologians, or in the Scholastics, though all wrote of the reality referred to by the term. Eschatology as a technical term appeared late in theological reflection—indeed, not until 1804 in a work by Karl Gottlieb Bretschneider. English usage is found for the first time in the book *Anastasis, or the Doctrine of the Resurrection of the Body, Rationally and Scripturally Considered,* published in London in 1845 by a certain George Bush.[1]

Besides the exegetical difficulties, there is confusion as to the content of eschatology. Sometimes messianism and apocalyptic are confused with eschatology. Messianism is concerned with the coming and the activity of the Messiah, and while messianism is related to the end times, it is not coterminus with it. Apocalyptic is a literary genre in which the future is described with the aid of revelations more or less symbolic. If apocalyptic is limited to the end of the world, it is easy to assimilate apocalyptic to eschatology. Some philosophers use the term eschatology in relation to the end of history, and for others it has a supra-historical and a-temporal sense.[2]

[1] Jean Carmignac, "Les dangers de l'eschatologie," *New Testament Studies* 17 (1971) 365–90, calls attention to Bretschneider's *Versuch einer systematischen Entwickelung aller in der Dogmatik vorkommenden Begriffe,* which went through many editions, and to Bush's book.

[2] Carmignac, *Le mirage de l'eschatologie* (Paris: Letouzey et Ane, 1979) 13–14.

As understood here, eschatology is the study of the final age of salvation history. It has as its object the events through which God orients human beings and the world to that end for which they were created. In the definition of Jean Giblet, to whom these first pages on eschatology are indebted, the final phase includes, negatively, the final judgment, and positively, the coming of the kingdom of God in which the elect believers enter into the fullness of life unfolded in the kingdom. These events come about by the intervention of the Messiah, whom God has invested with the sovereign power and also the mission of communicating the blessings of the kingdom to the elect.[3]

THE SPIRIT IN THE OLD TESTAMENT:
THE ORIENTATION TO THE FUTURE

Both Walter Eichrodt and Gerhard von Rad, major twentieth-century theologians of the Old Testament, saw spirit/charisma as central in the history of Israel. Eichrodt: "At the very beginning of Israelite religion we find the charisma, the special individual endowment of a person; and to such an extent is the whole structure based on it that without it, it would be inconceivable." Von Rad: "It is therefore evident that the charismatic was an absolutely constitutive factor in Jahwism."[4]

If spirit is to be found in the beginnings, so is eschatological awareness. Eschatology as a radical orientation to the future developed early in Old Testament prophecy in conjunction with the patriarchal promise, the monarchy, and the Sinai covenant. Though the spirit in the Old Testament is not restricted to eschatology, whenever *ruach* is associated with an outpouring it is always eschatological in nature. From the beginning, Israel's faith was oriented to promise and the future it contained. Chief among the proponents were the prophets, though even when they hailed the coming of God upon a new earth, rarely did their utterances concern a specifically messianic hope. In Joel 2:28-32 the message of hope in the midst of devastation is manifested in a universal charismatic out-

[3] Giblet, "Pneumatologie et eschatologie," *CSS* 2.899.
[4] Eichrodt, *Theology of the Old Testament*, 2 vols. (Philadelphia: Westminster, 1961) 1.292. Von Rad, *Old Testament Theology*, 2 vols. (New York: Harper & Row, 1962) 1.102.

pouring of the spirit touching Israel's present and future. Isaiah (32:15) and Ezekiel (11:19; 36:26-27) link the spirit to Israel's glory, which is not in the past but in the future.[5]

The true locus of Israel's identity, then, is in the future, but the fulfillment of the promise is not at the end of history. None of the prophets thought that history would end or break off. This reach to the future from within history is essential, because for Israel to lose the eschatological dimension would be to lose its identity. The Priestly source document (P) of the Pentateuch preserves this identity when it mentions the divine spirit at three crucial points of history: creation of the world (Gen 1:2), the construction of the sanctuary (Exod 31:3; 35:31), and the commissioning of Joshua (Num 27:18; Deut 34:9). But these are the only mentions of the spirit in the entire P source. In its present form the P document dates from exilic or post-exilic times, but has elements dating from the Mosaic period. Having a sacerdotal imprint, it is naturally concerned with the legitimation of sacred rites and orders. The authors of the P document wanted "a stable cult in a stable cosmos," in the midst of the disorienting conditions of the exile and the restoration.[6]

Not surprisingly, "the charismatic element has absolutely no place" in the priestly strategy. The priests had no interest in the destabilizing spirit disrupting good order. But because theirs is a non-eschatological cultic theology, and because it is the spirit which moves Israel to its future, the priestly influence moved Israel toward a consistent elimination of eschatological ideas. There are exceptions. Haggai (2:3-9; 20-23) and Zechariah (4:6-10; 6:15; 8:20-23; 12:1–14:21), both of whom may have been priests, saw the rebuilding of the temple as a great eschatological event related to the presence of the spirit. But the priestly aristocracy in Jerusalem tended to neglect the spirit and to push eschatological expectation more and more to the side, finally forcing it into separation from

---

[5] Arthur E. Sekki, *The Meaning of Ruach at Qumran* (Atlanta: Scholars, 1989) 82, n. 35. Samuel Terrien, *The Elusive Presence* (New York: Harper & Row, 1978) 66. Von Rad, *Theology of the Old Testament*, 2.320.

[6] Klaus Koch, *The Prophets: The Babylonian and Persian Periods* (Philadelphia: Fortress, 1982) 199. Joseph Blenkinsopp, *Prophecy and Canon* (Notre Dame: University of Notre Dame, 1977) 115. Norman K. Gottwald, *The Hebrew Bible: A Socio-Literary Introduction* (Philadelphia: Fortress, 1985) 473.

the religious consciousness.[7]

Though priests and prophets were often found collaborating during the monarchy and the exile, the priestly class, which established its claim to authority during the exile and gave us the Pentateuch in the form we now have it, tended to find the glory of Israel in its past. Focusing on cult and oracles, the priests turned Israel's look backward to its origins in marked contrast to the prophetic reach to the future.[8] Under priestly guidance, the march to the future ended in observance of the priestly law. Eschatology was lost and Israel's identity threatened.

PAUL: DOWN PAYMENT ON THE FUTURE

Paul, who identified himself as "a Hebrew born of Hebrews" (Phil 3:5), was an heir and developer of this essentially Israelite reach to the future. As Jean Giblet has noted, in 1 Thessalonians, probably the earliest of his extant letters, Paul expresses himself within the framework of a world in which the Father's raising of Jesus Christ from the dead has made him Lord, the one who will come to bring both judgment on those who have not believed the gospel and the resurrected life for those who have believed. The apostolic proclamation of the gospel is not like other impartings of information, nor like any other announcement of propositional truths, however exalted, but is made "in power and in the Holy Spirit and with full conviction" (1 Thess 1:5). The power comes from God (2:2, 4). Paul recognizes as the elect those in whom the power of the Spirit operates (1:4). In the relatively short period between the event of the resurrection and the return of Christ at the end of time together with the resurrection of the dead, the Spirit determines both the new existence of believers and the demands of holiness preparing them to meet with the Lord, the object of their hope (1:3; 3:13; 4:17). The whole of reality is sanctified in view of the move to the future.

In Paul's later epistles there is less talk of cosmic upheavals, and a recognition of the likelihood of personal death before the Lord returns, but Paul pays more attention to the present experience of

---

[7] Von Rad, *Theology of the Old Testament*, 1.99, 297.

[8] Blenkinsopp, *Prophecy and Canon*, 70, 75, 79.

union with Christ, who unites believers to him and makes them partakers of the Spirit. By linking the Spirit with the risen, exalted Lord, Paul orients the Spirit to the future. If the Spirit inaugurated and sustains the life of the resurrected Lord, then the Spirit will also inaugurate and sustain the life of believers in their resurrection. Paul sees in the resurrected Lord the realization of the believers' future. "The gospel concerning his Son, who was descended from David according to the flesh and was declared to be Son of God with power according to the spirit of holiness by resurrection from the dead, Jesus Christ" (Rom 1:3-4) may be a pre-Pauline formulation, making it the earliest witness to the resurrection. "Spirit" here is intrinsic to the resurrection, but in the Old Testament sense, where Ezekiel 37:14 attributes the resurrection of the whole of Israel—not of individuals—to the spirit of God.

Nonetheless, there are not two spirits. The phrase "spirit of holiness" seems to reflect the early Christian belief that Jesus' resurrection was actually part of the general resurrection, and that the spirit was intrinsic to it.[9] The orientation is future, but anchored in the death of Christ in such a way that as believers were co-crucified with Christ (Rom 6:6), and co-buried with him (6:4), so they also co-rise with him. Because the spirit/Spirit is the principle of the co-rising

[9] Joseph Fitzmyer, *Romans: A New Translation with Introduction and Commentary* (New York: Doubleday, 1993) 236. Fitzmyer (125) contends that the phrase "spirit of holiness" is not the Holy Spirit, the Third Person of the Trinity, but that "'Spirit of holiness' is a Palestinian Jewish equivalent of "holy Spirit." Though the Jewish "holy Spirit" and the Christian "Holy Spirit" are not the same, nevertheless, there are not two Spirits. Fitzmyer (115) points out that Paul ascribes the efficiency of the resurrection to the Father (Rom 4:24; 6:4; 8:11; 10:9; 1 Thess 1:10; Gal 1:1; 1 Cor 6:14; 15:15; 2 Cor 4:14). The phrase "spirit of holiness" has received a wide variety of interpretations. See Otto Kuss, *Der Römerbrief* (Regensburg: Pustet, 1963–78) 6–7. The Holy Spirit, as the Third Person of the Trinity, is surely an over-interpretation made in the light of later theological developments. Ernst Käsemann, *Commentary on Romans* (London: SCM, 1980) 12–13, 225, believes that "the Spirit of holiness is the power in virtue of which Jesus is appointed Son of God, just as the oral tradition of Jesus' baptism spoke of his messianic appointment by the Holy Spirit." Käsemann relates spirit in Romans 1:4 to the "motif of the messianic king and his enthronement," with special reference to "the singular function of the Spirit." In reference to Romans 6:11 Käsemann writes, "Here the Spirit is obviously regarded as the true resurrecting force, as is evident in Ephesians 1:19f." James D. G. Dunn, *Christology in the Making: A New Testament Inquiry*

with Christ, the Spirit represents a permanent power which cannot be undone.[10] Therefore believers "walk in newness of life" (6:4), a life which is directed to that future where the same Spirit which raised Jesus will fulfill his resurrection by raising the bodies of those believing in that resurrection (Rom 8:11). Christians possess the Spirit as the "down payment" of future glory (2 Cor 1:22; 5:5). To the extent they receive the Spirit, Christians are returned to the state of Adam and Eve before they sinned (Rom 8:18-25, 28-30, 38-39).

MARK AND MATTHEW:
AFTER THE LONG DROUGHT

Both Mark and Matthew have little to say about the Spirit in explicit terms. Mark mentions the Spirit in only six places, and Matthew in twelve.[11] But both mention the Spirit at the beginning of their gospels (Mark 1:10, 12; Matt 1:18, 20), which would raise eschatological expectations at least in Jewish readers. After the long absence or drought, the Spirit is back. Matthew, in fact, stands at the end of a long theological reflection backward from resurrection to conception. Raymond Brown has pointed out that in a pre-gospel period, as attested by Paul and the sermons in Acts, the resurrection dominated Christian awareness. It was the principal event associated with the divine proclamation of the identity of Jesus. When God raised Jesus from the grave and/or elevated Jesus to the right hand of God, God at the same time made or proclaimed him Lord, Messiah, and the Son of God.[12] In this retro-development, the Spirit

into the Origins of the Doctrine of the Incarnation (Philadelphia: Westminster, 1980) 144, believes that the context calls for the Spirit as the resurrecting power, but Paul does not take that step. Brendan Byrne, *Romans* (Collegeville: The Liturgical Press, 1996) 45, holds that in this text Spirit of holiness "almost certainly refers to the Spirit of God." Later in his commentary on Romans (394, 398), Fitzmyer admits that 1:4 refers "indirectly to the holy Spirit," a theme which Paul will treat extensively in chapter 8, and contends that Paul understands the Spirit as the divine presence to the justified Christian.

[10] Giblet, "Pneumatologie et eschatologie," 2.899. Käsemann, *Romans*, 166. Fitzmyer, *Romans*, 491–92.

[11] Mark 1:8, 10, 12; 3:29; 12:36; 13:11. Matthew 1:18, 20; 3:11, 16; 4:1; 10:20; 12:18, 28, 31, 32; 22:43; 28:19. Joseph Fitzmyer, *The Gospel According to Luke I–IX* (Garden City: Doubleday, 1981) 227.

[12] Raymond E. Brown, *The Birth of the Messiah* (Garden City: Doubleday, 1977) 29–32.

is the principle of Jesus' identity, beginning with the resurrection (Rom 1:4), moving back to the beginning of his public ministry (Luke 4:14-22), then moving further back to his baptism (Matt 3:16, 17), and finally to the conception of Jesus in the infancy narrative (Matt 1:18, 20). At every stage, the Spirit identifies who Jesus is, a fact of major significance for christology and its relationship to pneumatology.

Within Mark's community there was a heightened expectation of the coming end, fueled by the destruction of the temple and the influx of Christians from Judaea into Mark's community outside of Judaea (possibly Syria). This eschatological expectation is evident in the prophets within Mark's community who spoke in the name of Jesus (Mark 13:1-36). But there was simultaneously an opposing tendency, namely, a retarding of eschatological hope. Mark tries to move the community away from eschatological exultation back to the way of the cross. Matthew does not adopt this move to the cross; rather, he heightens the expectation. In the canonical gospels only Matthew uses the word *parousia* (24:3, 27, 37, 39), a detail suggesting the importance to the narrative of Jesus' future coming. Matthew preserves the eschatological material of Mark, adds more from other sources (10:32; 13:24-30, 37-40; 25:1-13), and heightens visionary and theophanic elements associated with apocalyptic (17:2, 6; 27:51; 28:2-4). Though the delay of the parousia was a crucial issue in the early church, the delay was a motif rather than a current problem by the time Matthew wrote.[13]

In both Mark and Matthew the narrative of Jesus' baptism in the Jordan and the temptation have messianic colorings (Mark 1:8-13; Matt 3:13-17; 4:1). Both evangelists have Jesus exorcising unclean spirits in the power of the Spirit, and the related blasphemy against the Spirit (Mark 3:22-29; Matt 12:25-28), and Mark records Jesus' promise of the Spirit to disciples when accused before tribunals (Mark 13:11-13). Presupposing that these texts belong to a pre-Markan stratum, Jean Giblet asks, What does this tell us about the

[13] Vicky Balabanski, *Eschatology in the Making: Mark, Matthew and the Didache* (Cambridge: Cambridge University, 1997) 206–07. John T. Carroll, "The Parousia of Jesus in the Synoptic Gospels and Acts," *The Return of Jesus in Early Christianity*, Carroll, ed. (Peabody, Mass.: Hendrickson, 2000) 13. Raymond E. Brown et al., "Eschatology and Apocalypticism," *The New Jerome Biblical Commentary*, 1363.

preaching of Jesus? Does this mean that neither in his apocalyptic teaching nor in his moral teaching does Jesus specify the Spirit as such? While neither Mark nor Matthew uses Spirit categories in a way that seems habitual for Luke, Paul, and John, even this minimum is significant for a Jewish milieu in which the Spirit is scarcely mentioned at all. To have the Spirit descend on Jesus at the beginning of his activity, to have a voice from heaven say "You are my Son, the Beloved; with you I am well pleased" (Mark 1:11; Matt 3:16, 17), is, indeed, to announce that the Spirit has returned.[14] To announce the Spirit that came down on Mary (Matt 1:18, 20), proclaim the Spirit that descended on Jesus at the Jordan, and assert that the Spirit drove him into the desert to be tempted (Mark 1:12; Matt 4:1) is, in Jewish ears, to signify that the messianic period has begun, the eschatological kingdom of God is present in power.

The exorcisms of Jesus belong to the earliest strata of New Testament witness and are of undoubted historicity. To exorcise unclean spirits by the Holy Spirit is to inaugurate the eschatological kingdom of God. The person who rejects the power of the Spirit by which Jesus exorcises, is thereby placed beyond forgiveness (Mark 3:29; Matt 12:31). All other sins, even blasphemy and profaning the name of God, could be forgiven. This is an index of how seriously Jesus took the efficacy of his binding of the strong man (Satan) by the Spirit. "Here is a consciousness of Spirit without real parallel at the time."[15]

LUKE/ACTS: THE SPIRIT IS EVERYWHERE

Mark and Matthew are sparing in the number of times they mention the Spirit; Luke is prodigal. In his gospel Luke mentions the Spirit seventeen, possibly eighteen times, and in Acts fifty-seven times. In spite of the attention to the Spirit, though, the Word of God, stimulated and accompanied by the Spirit, is in the forefront.[16]

In the extensive debate about Lukan theology, eschatology remains one of the most difficult aspects, partly because Luke has a sequel to

[14] Giblet, "Pneumatologie et eschatologie," 2.897–98.

[15] James D. G. Dunn, *Jesus and the Spirit* (Philadelphia: Westminster, 1975) 44, 53.

[16] Fitzmyer, *Luke I–IX*, 227. Francois Bovon, *Luke the Theologian: Thirty-three Years of Research (1950–1983)* (Allison Park, Pa.: Pickwick, 1987) 238.

his Jesus-story, suggesting that he has a distinctive eschatological position. Because Luke reinterprets sayings about the coming of the kingdom and the coming of the Son of Man in glory, and of the wrath to come, some, including Hans Conzelmann, have concluded that Luke has "definitely" abandoned the idea of the parousia. In the same tradition, Erich Grässer suggests that the Spirit is an element of a realizing eschatology, and is, in fact, an ersatz for the parousia. Joseph Fitzmyer notes the reasons for such conclusions. Luke has at times omitted sayings expressing an imminent eschaton, or modified them to blunt the eschatological edge. Some sayings (e.g., 12:38, 45; 13:8) imply delay or postponement of the end time. Also, some of the apocalyptic stage props in Mark 13 have been reduced or eliminated. Nevertheless, Luke has retained from the primitive gospel tradition a number of sayings of either John the Baptist or Jesus about imminent judgment or coming of the kingdom (3:7, 17; 10:9; 21:32). Not satisfied with this, Luke has added eschatological material. To the mission of the seventy (-two) disciples, Luke adds the warning that the kingdom has drawn near (10:11; see also 18:7-8).[17]

Within this broad eschatological framework Luke uses the Spirit to initiate important stages: first in the Period of Israel, then in the Period of Jesus (baptism, temptation, and the Nazareth scenes), and, finally, in the stages in the Period of the Church (ascension, Pentecost). The Spirit links the Period of Israel first to the Period of Jesus through Isaiah 61:1-2 ("The spirit of the Lord God is upon me") in Luke 4:18-19, and then to the Period of the Church through Joel 2:28-29 ("I will pour out my spirit") in Acts 2:17 and Joel 3:1-2 ("I will gather all the nations") in Acts 2:5. The same eschatological Spirit promised in the Period of Israel is active in the infancy accounts, and at the beginning of the ministry in the Period of Jesus when John the Baptist announces the imminent arrival of the One who will baptize with the Holy Spirit. The descent of the Spirit on Jesus at the Jordan inaugurates the public ministry under the power of the Spirit (3:21-22). By the Spirit Jesus is led into the

---

[17] Conzelmann, *The Theology of Luke* (New York: Harper & Row, 1961) 135. Grässer, *Das Problem der Parusievergöserung in den synoptischen Evangelien und in der Apostelgeschichte*, 3rd ed. (Berlin: Walter de Gruyter, 1977) 209. Fitzmyer, *Luke I–IX*, 231-35.

desert to be tempted (4:1) and later returns from the desert "with the power of the Spirit" (4:14). The whole of the ministry of Jesus is under the power and leading of the Spirit, making it clear that the role of the Spirit at the beginning of the Period of the Church in Acts is organically linked to the Spirit in the Period of Jesus. Luke carefully crafts the end of the Period of Jesus by twice mentioning "the promise of the Father" (Acts 1:4; Luke 24:49). This "promise" is to be poured out at the beginning of the Period of the Church, when the New Israel is renewed. During the church's beginnings the Spirit is the creative and prophetic presence of God (Acts 5:9; 8:39).[18]

Just as the Spirit initiated the Period of Christ, so in Acts 2 the Spirit initiates the Period of the Church, during which the Spirit is the very presence of Christ among the people of God. The reconstituted Twelve (Acts 1:15-26) is the preamble to the outpouring of the Spirit (2:1-4). As a consequence of the specifically eschatological outpouring prophesied by Joel and recounted by Luke (Acts 2:17-21), a whole series of Spirit events is presented: the choice of the seven "deacons" (actually more like presbyters or bishops) (6:2-6), Philip evangelizing Samaria (8:5-13), the reception of the Spirit in Ephesus (19:1-6), and the bestowal of the Spirit on Paul (9:17-18). During the initial Period of the Church the Spirit guides the Christian community. The parousia motif is not prominent in Acts, yet believers know the Lord may come in the near future, but in the meantime the mission of the church must go on.[19]

What Mark and Matthew see as promise, Luke sees as fulfillment. Instead of seeing Jesus just as a prophet, and therefore a bearer of the Spirit, Luke sees the Spirit as given to the whole people of God. As in Luke's Gospel the Spirit is the power of Jesus in baptism and ministry, so in Acts the Spirit assures the growth of the church and is the power of the disciples' proclamation, all this in the dynamic of Joel's prophetic eschatological outpouring. The delay of the parousia is not opposed to, but supports the expectation of an imminent end as the church carries on its mission. Luke, in fact, marries eschatological expectation with the task of carrying the good news to the

18 Fitzmyer, *Luke I–IX*, 227–30.
19 Ibid., 231. Carroll, "Parousia," 41–42, 45.

ends of the world—or at least to Rome.[20]

THE JOHANNINE CORPUS:
JESUS PRESENT IN THE SPIRIT

If it is true that Mark is the most future oriented of the four gospels, and John the most present oriented, it remains true that the "already" in John is complemented by the "not yet." In John there is a contrast between two spheres: one belongs to the Spirit, the other to the flesh (John 3:6; 6:63). The coming of Jesus represents the triumph of the Spirit over flesh, so that all worship of God is in the Spirit (4:21-23). Still, the full gift of life does not come during the ministry of Jesus, but only after the resurrection. And when Jesus speaks in the gospel of a present opportunity to receive life, we need to keep in mind the intention of the author—Jesus is speaking through the pages of the gospel to a post-resurrection audience.[21] When Jesus says that "It is the Spirit that gives life" (6:63), he is telling the post-resurrection audience that they have a chance to obtain life through faith in Jesus because they have received the principle of life, the Spirit. But the fullness of that Spirit is given only after Jesus is lifted up to the Father.

John's formulation is somewhat startling. Speaking of the "rivers of living water," the evangelist comments: "Now he said this about the Spirit, which believers in him were to receive [note the future], for as yet there was no Spirit" (7:39). John is not saying that the Spirit did not exist before the death and resurrection of Jesus; much less is he speculating on the Third Person of the Trinity. The evangelist is not concerned about the inner life of the Trinity, but about God's relation to us. Some manuscripts, possibly seeing theological difficulties, seek to soften the scandal of the biblical text with more accommodating formulations, e.g., "the Spirit was not yet *given*," or "the Spirit was not yet *on them*." But the unusual wording only means that the Spirit is not a reality for believers until

---

[20] Edward Schweizer, "pneuma," *The Theological Dictionary of the New Testament*, 6.410; Fitzmyer, *Luke I–IX*, 231. John T. Carroll, *Response to the End of History: Eschatology Situation in Luke-Acts* (Decatur, Ga.: Scholars, 1988) 166.

[21] Brown, et al., "Eschatology and Apocalypticism," 1364. Brown, *The Gospel According to John I–XII* (Garden City: Doubleday, 1966) cxv, cxviii.

To Do Pneumatology Is to Do Eschatology

43

the glorified Lord communicates it to them (20:22).[22] Only after Jesus is lifted up to the Father is the Spirit given (16:7; 19:30; 20:22).

The delay of the parousia was not an issue for John. He was writing after the fall of Jerusalem in 70 when the immediate hopes of the parousia faded. The reasons given why the parousia did not occur were various. A rather naïve answer is given in 2 Peter 3:3-8, namely, one day for the Lord is like a thousand years. But the Johannine answer goes deeper, and the answer is found in John's presentation of the Spirit/Paraclete. One can argue that it was the experience of the Spirit in the primitive church, and not the delay of the parousia, that pushed John in the direction of a "realized" eschatology. The future objective eschatology is not eliminated, but, as C. K. Barrett remarks, the Spirit is the means by which "the historical past and the historical future (in the two 'comings' of Jesus) are brought to bear upon the present in such a way as to determine the immediate spiritual presence of Jesus."[23]

[22] Brown, *John I–XII*, 324.

[23] Barrett, "The Place of Eschatology in the Fourth Gospel," *The Expository Times* 59 (1947–1948) 304. David E. Aune, "The Significance of the Delay of the Parousia for Early Christianity," *Current Issues in Biblical and Patristic Interpretation*, Gerald F. Hawthorne, ed. (Grand Rapids: Eerdmans, 1975) 109, questions whether the delay of the parousia was perceived as a problem by the early Christians. The gradual diminution of emphasis on the parousia "may be ascribed to the fact that it was functionally replaced by the conception of personal immortality upon death."

Chapter 5

Movement Toward Fixity:
Holy Spirit in Patristic Eschatology

There is a curious disparity between the eschatological character of the Spirit and the paucity of pneumatological content in much post-biblical eschatological thought. There is more pneumatology in the early post-biblical documents than is sometimes granted, though what there is has, with some notable exceptions, only a diminished relationship to eschatology. The postponement of the parousia did not produce the disastrous results sometimes attributed to it by modern authors, but the delay of the Lord's return seems to have contributed, not to a diminished pneumatology, but to a diminished role for the Spirit in the eschatology when measured against the New Testament witness.[1]

In the early post-biblical teaching there are four moments to eschatological expectation: the return of Christ, the general resurrection, the final judgment, and the apocalyptic, catastrophic end of the world as we know it. In this earliest period these four moments are expressed in an unreflective, non-systematic way, without attempting to resolve problems the issues raise.[2] The Spirit was part

[1] Wolf-Dieter Hauschild, *Gottes Geist und der Mensch: Studien zur frühchristlichen Pneumatologie* (Munich: C. Kaiser, 1972) 11. George Florovsky, "Eschatology in the Patristic Age: An Introduction," *Studia Patristica* 2, part 2 (1955) 235–50. Giovanni Filoramo, "Eschatology," *Encyclopedia of the Early Church*, Angelo Di Berardino, ed., 2 vols. (New York: Oxford University Press, 1992) 1.284–86. Christian Schütz, *Einführung in die Pneumatologie* (Darmstadt: Wissenschaftliche Buchgesellschaft, 1985) 34.

[2] Kelly, *Doctrines*, 462.

of the eschatological awareness, but was not singled out as an impelling force in the manner found in the New Testament.

The *Didache,* a short manual on Christian morals and church practice, likely dating from Syria in the first century, shows some pneumatological awareness, significant given its nature and brevity. Scholars recognize that the document was compiled in stages, with the eschatological chapter 16 added at the end, influenced by the Gospel of Matthew. But in contrast to Matthew, the author of the *Didache* did not think his era was part of the "last days" (as we have seen, parousia was still a motif for Matthew, but not a burning issue). If there is also late Jewish influence on the Didache, this may account for the absence of the Spirit, in the Christian sense, in the eschatological apocalyptic chapter where we might expect otherwise to find it.[3]

What is called the *Second Letter of Clement* is actually a homily delivered some time before 150, and attributed to an anonymous author, distinct from the author of the *First Letter of Clement.* The homily has a pronounced eschatology, indeed strong apocalypticism, which is the motivation for stern moral exhortations. Only in chapter 14 is there mention of the Spirit. Here the author differentiates between the fleshly and the spiritual church. The reader is exhorted to "guard the flesh, so that you may share the Spirit. . . . The flesh is able to share in this great life and immortality, provided the Holy Spirit is joined to it." The author of the letter has difficulty differentiating between Christ and the Spirit—not an uncommon problem in these early years.[4]

The principal aim of the *Shepherd of Hermas,* dated variously late

[3] *Didache* 4.7 (twice), 11 (four times); SC 248.162, 170, 171, 184, 186, 188. Vicky Balabanski, *Eschatology in the Making: Mark, Matthew and the Didache* (Cambridge: Cambridge University, 1997) 208. Ernst Bammel, "Schema und Vorlage von Didache 16," *Studia Patristica* 4, part 2 (1961) (*Texte und Untersuchungen* 79) 253–62.

[4] *Second Letter of Clement* 3, 5, 13, in *Die apostolischen Väter,* Karl Bihlmeyer, ed. (Tübingen: Mohr [Siebeck], 1956) 76–78. Harry A. Wolfson, *The Philosophy of the Church Fathers,* 2nd ed. (Cambridge: Harvard, 1964) 1.242.

first century to mid-second century, is to preach reform and the possibility of forgiveness at least once after baptism, a doctrine that made Tertullian, during his rigorist Montanist period, identify the author as "the Shepherd of those who love adultery." The text's pneumatology is embedded in a dualism characteristic of a particular strand of Jewish thought, namely, that of Qumran and the *Testaments of the Twelve Patriarchs*. The treatise contains two distinct pneumatologies, one dualistic, the other non-dualistic, but in both cases the Spirit comes from God and dwells in human beings. The eschaton has been realized in the present and this gives urgency to reform. In fact, the tract is more a call for reform than it is about the future moving toward the present. The Spirit is related to eschatology only in general terms. As Christ was the bearer of the Spirit, so the Christian as a bearer of Christ must also be a bearer of the Spirit. Whoever belongs to the "Tower," a symbol of the church, and remains in the church until the end, is clothed with the Spirit. The stones which make up the Tower are one with the rock, Christ. "There is only one Spirit and only one body." The Tower is in process, the building going on, with pauses, and will only be complete when the Lord comes to inspect, indeed test, the Tower. But test time is approaching.[5]

WITNESS FROM THE UNCORRUPTED SYRIAC TRADITION

Tatian, born in Syria about 120, represents a strong anti-Roman and anti-Greek bias, in favor of the pure Syrian tradition. Other early authors found it difficult to distinguish between the Logos and the Spirit. Tatian marks a development, though it would be too much to say that the Spirit attains the clarity of a distinct personal being. In his *Oration to the Greeks* he never mentions Jesus Christ, though neither did Theophilus and Athenagoras, which is symptomatic of their concern to refute scoffers, not set forth Christian doctrine. Speaking specifically of immortality, Tatian teaches that a person

---

[5] Tertullian, *On Modesty* 10.12; CCh 2.1301. Norbert Brox, *Der Hirt des Hermas* (Göttingen: Vandenhoeck & Ruprecht, 1991) 62. J. Christian Wilson, *Toward a Reassessment of the Shepherd of Hermas: Its Date and Its Pneumatology* (Lewiston, Me.: Mellen Biblical Press, 1993) 165. *Shepherd of Hermas* 90.5, 7; SC 53bis.320; 82.1–3, 7; SC 53bis.298–300.

without the Spirit is only "a torso." The divine Spirit belongs to the condition of humanity before the fall. Pointing to the end of history, Tatian declares that "if the Soul enters into union with the divine Spirit, it is no longer helpless, but ascends to the regions whither the Spirit guides it."[6]

Aphrahat belongs to the same pure Syrian tradition, still untouched by Greek categories. He writes about 345 out of a Jewish-Christian community dealing with the agonies of war and persecution. In touching on the resurrection of the dead, Aphrahat starts with baptism: "We have received the Spirit of the Messiah by baptism. In the hour that the priests call the Spirit, the Spirit opens the heaven, descends and covers the water—and those who are baptized put on the Spirit." When a believer dies and comes to the moment of the general resurrection, "the Spirit will be in the body in order to raise it up, and the glory will be exterior to the body in order to adorn it. The animated [human] spirit will be devoured by the Spirit. . . . Ravished by the Spirit this person will fly to meet its king and will be received with joy. The Messiah will receive with kindness the body which has kept the Spirit in purity." Not only is the Spirit the power of the resurrection, but "the Holy Spirit compels the Messiah to raise the bodies of those who had kept it [the Spirit] in purity."[7]

Unlike Tatian, who limits the saving function of the Spirit, Aphrahat has the Spirit taking the initiative and "forcing" the eschatological consummation. "In all haste the Spirit will open the tombs, and he will make the bodies to rise . . . and [the Spirit] will re-clothe [the one who has kept the Spirit in purity] with glory." Also significant is the parallel Aphrahat builds between the eschatological resurrection and the Genesis account of the creation of Adam.[8] Aphrahat, as no other post-biblical author, recaptures the intimate relation between pneumatology and eschatology.

---

[6] Winfrid Cramer, *Der Geist Gottes und des Menschen in frühsyrischer Theologie* (Münster: Aschendorff, 1979) 47, 52; here Cramer differs from Wolfson, *Philosophy of Church Fathers*, 237, who thinks Tatian identifies Logos and Spirit. L. W. Barnard, "The Heresy of Tatian–Once Again," *Journal of Ecclesiastical History* 19 (1968) 10. *Oration to the Greeks* 13; *Tatiani, Oratio ad Graecos*, Miroslav Marcovich, ed. (Berlin: Walter de Gruyter, 1995) 30.

[7] Aphrahat, *Demonstrations* 6.14; SC 349.400–03.

[8] Ibid. 8.5; SC 349.446. Cramer, *Der Geist Gottes*, 82.

"crass flesh"

IRENAEUS:
THE TRINITARIAN ORDER OF SALVATION

Irenaeus, Tertullian, and Hippolytus fought against the eschatological corruptions of gnosticism. The gnostics taught that matter was intrinsically evil and that therefore crass flesh could not have a share in salvation. Salvation must be purely spiritual. This was to attack Christian theology at its incarnational root. Irenaeus countered by affirming that the body was subject to the Word who became flesh, and that salvation is not just for the soul but necessarily includes the body.

Irenaeus sets this in the framework of a history of salvation, a growth process within history toward an ultimate end in a future that is about to dawn. Beginning with Genesis, he sketches this movement to the future in biblical terms. "Such is the order, rhythm, and movement through which a human being is created and modeled in the image and the resemblance of the uncreated God: the Father decides and commands, the Son executes and models, and the Spirit nourishes and gives the growth, the human person progressing thus, little by little, as an elevated being coming to perfection, that is, approaching the Uncreated."[9]

Already in the Old Testament God prepares the prophets "in order that human beings might become accustomed to carry the Spirit and to possess communion with God." But it is especially in the rhythms of trinitarian life that history moves toward its end: "God is able to do all things; [what God is capable of] is sometimes seen through the intervention of the Spirit according to the prophetic mode, sometimes viewed through the intervention of the Son according to [the mode of] adoption. Beyond this one can see [what God intends] in the kingdom of heaven according to the paternity: the Spirit preparing human beings for the Son in advance, and the Son conducting human beings to the Father, and the Father giving them incorruptibility and eternal life, so it comes about that each one sees God." Human beings in the whole expanse of history are being formed and molded "by the hands of God, that is, by the Son and the Spirit."[10]

[9] *Against Heresies* 4.38.3; SC 100.954–56. Jaschke, *Der Heilige Geist im Bekenntnis der Kirche* (Münster: Aschendorff, 1976) 194–97.

[10] *Against Heresies* 4.14.2; SC 100.542–44; 4, 20, 5; SC 100.638–40; 5, 28, 4; SC 153.360.

When Irenaeus wrote of humankind's new foundation at the end of the ages, a foundation in God through Christ and the Spirit,[11] he was anticipating some of the features of Origen's doctrine of the restoration of all things to an original state *(apocatastasis)*. Whether Origen really taught universal restoration of everything is disputed. Some texts seem to support such a view, but his expansive vision very likely did not include Satan and the damned.[12]

With great daring Origen postulates a theological system in which the end will be like the beginning, with the reestablishment in creation of the original harmony and unity. The vast cosmic evolution will end when "through the goodness of God, the submission of Christ [and the kingdom to the Father], and the unity of the Holy Spirit, all are led to an end like to the beginning." That the end is always like the beginning is a theological organizing principle. Within this eschatological vision Origen's pneumatology is greatly influenced by his ascetic goals. In the traditional manner the imparting of the Spirit has its basis in baptism (and foot washing), but his focus is more on the asceticism related to conversion than on sacramental action.[13] Through ascetical striving a believer, who has received the Spirit and is sanctified by the Spirit, participates in the death of Jesus, the Spirit making the believer capable of the heavenly sphere. In fact, the wings of the Spirit bear the pneumatic believer on high. In this context the Spirit-filled believer shares in the full glory of the great restoration at the end of the ages.

TERTULLIAN AND THE NEW PROPHECY

An explosion of the prophetic Spirit surfaced in Asia Minor, in the area of Phrygia, in the second half of the second century. This was

[11] Ibid., 5, 12, 1–4; SC 153.140–57; 4, 4, 1–10; SC 268.400–29.

[12] Kelly, *Doctrines*, 474 thinks that even though Origen protested that he did not include Satan and the damned, his system seems to demand their inclusion. But see Henri Crouzel, *Origen* (San Francisco: Harper & Row, 1989) 262–66. Brian Daley, *The Hope of the Early Church: A Handbook of Patristic Eschatology* (New York: Cambridge University, 1991) 60–64.

[13] *Homilies on Jeremiah* 14.18; SC 238.108. *On First Principles* 1, 6, 2; SC 252.196; 3.6.1, 3; SC 268.234–42. *Commentary on John* 32.7, 8; SC 385.218, 224. Hauschild, *Gottes Geist*, 122–27.

not the survival from the New Testament period of communities around the Mediterranean in which the Spirit as an end-time gift had never died out, but a new outbreak of prophecy together with apocalyptic expectations. Those involved believed that the inspired prophets were, in fact, the first fruits of the final days, a concrete proof that Christ's promise to send the Spirit was actually being realized in their midst.[14]

In the initial stages of Montanism, its adherents portrayed the end of the world in images taken from the Apocalypse. But when the end did not come, Montanists turned from being apocalyptic enthusiasts to rigoristic sectarians. Even Hippolytus and that dedicated heresy hunter, Epiphanius of Salamis, said that Montanists were not heretics, that they were in agreement with the great church in matters of dogma.[15] But because the Montanists posed a threat to the great church in their use of apocalyptic images, a reaction set in against the book of the Apocalypse, and for hundreds of years its canonicity was disputed in the East.

Tertullian does not have the grand, cosmic design of Origen, but rather sees the final eschatological event as the moment when accounts are settled: reward for the just and punishment for the unjust. He presents "the fast approaching coming of our Lord" as a spectacle terrible and magnificent, surpassing the games of the circus.[16] His pneumatology meets eschatology mostly in relation to the resurrection of the flesh.

When Tertullian wrote his treatise *On the Resurrection* he was a committed Montanist. Indeed, he invokes the New Prophecy [Montanism] which dispels all the obscurities concerning the resurrection of the dead by pouring out the prophetic Paraclete anew. Tertullian reminds us to read, in addition to the scriptures in which the flesh is brought under judgment, those pages in which the flesh is made glorious in the fulfillment of the prophecy of Joel. The full

[14] Georg Kretschmar, "Le développement de la doctrine du Saint-Esprit du Nouveau Testament à Nicée," *Verbum Caro* 22 (1968) 29.

[15] William Tabbernee, "Revelation 21 and the Montanist 'New Jerusalem,'" *Australian Biblical Review* 37 (1989) 52–60. Hippolytus, *Refutation of All Heresies* 8.19, in *Refutatio Omnium Haeresium*, Miroslav Marcovich, ed. (New York: De Gruyter, 1986) 338. Epiphanius, *Panarion*, 2.1; PG 41.856.

[16] *On Penitence* 2.11; SC 316.150. *On the Spectacles* 30.1; SC 332.316.

blossoming of that hope is rooted in the Spirit, but the Spirit also assures believers that they know neither the time nor the hour of that unfolding. Though the works of the flesh are condemned, the flesh is not, because of the Spirit dwelling within. Those who have put on Christ and have the indwelling Spirit become a holy land, "truly flowing with milk and honey," because of the hope that is theirs. The hope of the resurrection is sure because the flesh is the bride, but through the blood of Christ the Spirit is the bridegroom.[17] The bridegroom, the Spirit, is in charge.

THE DIVORCE OF PNEUMATOLOGY FROM ESCHATOLOGY

What conclusions can be drawn from the much abbreviated review in these chapters of Old and New Testament evidence and early post-biblical witness about the relation of pneumatology to eschatology? In broadest terms, the relation has historically been under threat. And the threat is not simply to a theological category, but to the nature of Old and New Testament faith, the identity of Jesus Christ, the church.

The radical orientation toward the future developed early in Old Testament prophecy, the patriarchal promise, the monarchy, and the Sinai covenant—all linked to the spirit. One starts with eschatology before one ends with it. Of great importance is the insight that this link between spirit and eschatology does not belong to a later development, but to Israel's deepest roots and its earliest history, as found in its self-understanding. The true identity of Israel is found not in the past but in the future to which the spirit moves it. In that future, identity is to be found not at the end of history, but at the beginning and within a history which, by the presence of the Spirit, moves to a consummation beyond history.

In the New Testament, Spirit is linked to Messiah and resurrection. The Spirit is the principle of identity of the Messiah, tells us who Jesus is. The Spirit identifies the son of Mary, inaugurates the public ministry of Jesus, raises Jesus from the dead, and is the pledge of the resurrection of the faithful. As the Spirit inaugurated

---

[17] *On the Resurrection* 63.9; 10.1; 23.7; 24.9; 46.7, 8; 26.11; 50.4; 53.18; 63.3; CCh 2.1012, 933, 950, 952, 983, 955, 992, 1000, 1011.

the period of Jesus, so the Spirit inaugurates the period of the church, which itself is on the way. As the Spirit is essential to the identity of Jesus, so also for the church, which, as the New Israel, is on the move to a future consummation.

The post-biblical evidence indicates that the link between Spirit and eschatology was fragile. Though both the doctrine of the Spirit and eschatology will continue to develop along separate lines, they lose their relationship to one another from about the third century onward. This loss constitutes a threat to the identity of the church, because the Spirit is the principle of the church's identity. If the Spirit is divided from eschatology, then awareness that the church is on the move to a God-given goal is lost. Without the principle of movement, the church is in danger of turning from a pilgrimage people into a structure standing still. When this happens, glory is in stasis. In the splendor of its institutions, in the beauty of its liturgies, in the radiance of its saints, the earthly church is its own static end—in a word, triumphalism. The parousia has a sign hanging around its neck stamped not "delayed," but "canceled."

Chapter 6

To Do Pneumatology Is to Start at the Beginning: Pentecost?

It would be difficult to exaggerate the importance Paul attributes to the work of the Spirit. For him, the experience of the Spirit is vivid in its external accompaniments (Gal 3:5; 1 Cor 1:4-9), moral transformation (1 Thess 2:13; 1 Cor 6:9-11), enlightenment (1 Cor 2:12), joy (1 Thess 1:5-9), love (Gal 5:22; Rom 5:5), awareness of being children of God (Gal 4:6; Rom 8:15), freedom (2 Cor 3:17; Rom 8:2), salvation (2 Thess 2:13; Eph 1:13; Titus 3:5-7), consciousness of the Spirit's presence and power (1 Thess 1:5; Gal 3:1-5; 1 Cor 2:4-16; 6:15-19). The recipient of the Spirit could not be unaware of the event. "In the earliest days of Christianity possession of the Spirit was a fact of immediate perception."[1] Given this extensive evidence, how is it that Paul, along with other New Testament authors, apparently knows nothing about the transforming Pentecost experience that Luke, in Acts 2:1-4, describes with remarkable discipline but still vividly and in some detail?

A PLURALITY OF PENTECOSTS?

Luke undoubtedly sees monumental, even epochal, significance in the coming of the Spirit narrated in Acts 2. More than that, his narration shapes the succeeding story. Luke wants all the extraordinary power and dynamism to issue from Jerusalem. There was one

[1] Lucien Cerfaux, *The Christian in the Theology of St. Paul* (New York: Herder and Herder, 1967) 239. James D. G. Dunn, *Baptism in the Holy Spirit* (Naperville, Ill.: Allenson, 1970) 174, 149.

Pentecost, not many; there is one source, Jerusalem, not many.[2]

But looking narrowly at Luke's account, the exegete faces at least two possibilities. One is to see Luke's Pentecost as an overly enthusiastic account of an event of dubious historicity. Even if one is drawn to the conclusion that the passage is a theological construction, it is unwise simply to reject the core as without any possible basis in history. The Lukan account might well represent an authentic Christian memory of the first manifestation of the Spirit to the community on the feast of Pentecost. The other possibility is that Luke gathered together into one graphic narrative a series of experiences of the Spirit's presence in the community.[3]

A different account is given in the "Johannine Pentecost" (John 20:19-23). It is dubious methodology to harmonize John with Acts by assuming that one treats of an earlier historical giving of the Spirit and the other of a later. There is no evidence that either Luke or John knew of the other's manner of presenting the event or events, nor did either make allowance for the

---

[2] Dunn, *Jesus and the Spirit: A Study of the Religious and Charismatic Experience of Jesus and the First Christians as Reflected in the New Testament* (Grand Rapids: Eerdmans, 1997) 138. Jerome Murphy-O'Connor, *Paul: A Critical Life* (Oxford: Clarendon, 1996) 53.

[3] Ernst Haenchen, *The Acts of the Apostles: A Commentary* (Philadelphia: Westminster, 1971) 172–75, outlines the various positions exegetes have taken. He takes the position that Luke's narrative is wholly a theological construction. Richard F. Zehnle, *Peter's Pentecost Discourse* (Nashville: Abingdon, 1971) 112, contends that "the cumulative evidence of the rest of early Christian literature renders improbable any spectacular intervention of the Spirit at all in the early days of the community." Luke Timothy Johnson, *The Acts of the Apostles* (Collegeville: The Liturgical Press, 1992) 45–47, is circumspect in speaking of a theological construction, referring to "narrative suspense," "symbolism," and "Moses typology." Dunn, *Jesus and the Spirit,* 142, is also careful: "In short, it is by no means certain, but not at all unlikely, that the historical events underlying Acts 2.1–13 took place on the first Pentecost after Jesus' death." Raymond E. Brown, *The Gospel According to John XIII–XXI* (Garden City: Doubleday, 1970) 1039. Barrett, *The Holy Spirit and the Gospel Tradition* (London: SPCK, 1966) 159–60, thinks there may be two accounts of "Pentecost" in Acts, namely, 2:1-4 and 4:31. Eduard Schweizer, *The Theological Dictionary of the New Testament,* Gerhard Kittel, ed. (Grand Rapids: Eerdmans, 1964–1976) 6.410. John J. McNamee, "The Role of the Spirit in Pentecostalism: A Comparative Study" (Ph.D. diss.: University of Tübingen, 1974) 171.

other's presentation.[4]

In the Johannine Pentecost the risen Christ breathes on his disciples (20:22). For any Jew this would recall the act of Yahweh in the first creation, forming Adam from the dust of the earth and breathing life into his nostrils (Gen 2:7). By breathing on the disciples, the risen Lord imparts to them the Holy Spirit. In John's account there is nothing partial or provisional about the imparting of the Spirit. This is a total fulfilment of passages promising the giving of the Spirit (7:39) or the coming of the Paraclete (14:26). And the imparting of the Spirit is neither purely personal nor individual, but is specifically related to the sending of the disciples into the world (20:21). For John this event took place on the evening of Easter day. Luke's chronology is different, determined by the Sinai covenant associated in the Jewish mind with Pentecost. Possibly he wanted the coming of the Spirit to coincide with the next feast, Pentecost.

The two accounts reflect different agendas, not unusual in dealing with biblical events recounted by different authors. John differs from Luke in the date for the giving of the Spirit, and in John's account there are no immediate signs of transformation that one finds in Acts. John gives us no mighty wind, no tongues of fire, no charismatic expressions (speaking in tongues), no three thousand converts. Both Luke and John place the coming of the Spirit after the ascension, while having different views of the ascension. Paul, too, sees the imparting of the Spirit as an immediate consequence of the ascension.[5]

But what of Galilee? Ernst Haenchen believes that Luke apparently had no sources concerning the Christianization of Galilee. But Ernst Lohmeyer believes there were two earliest churches, one in Jerusalem and one in Galilee. Even though Luke wants to stress the centrality of Jerusalem in the church's mission, he seems to indicate that besides the Pentecost in Jerusalem recounted in Acts 2 there were other "Pentecosts" elsewhere. Apollos, a Jew from Alexandria who was on fire with the Spirit (Acts 18:25), did not derive his

---

[4] Brown, *John XIII–XXI*, 1038–39.

[5] Dunn, *Baptism in the Holy Spirit*, 174. Rudolf Bultmann, *The Gospel of John* (Philadelphia: Westminster, 1971) 691.

To Do Pneumatology Is to Start at the Beginning: Pentecost?

experience from a Jerusalem source.[6] Other groups existed, apparently independent of Jerusalem, at least initially (Mark 9:38-40; Matt 7:15-23). The community at Damascus was a scene of charismatic events (Acts 9:17), so Jerusalem could not claim exclusive rights to an outpouring of the Spirit.

Further, Mark gives evidence that the post-resurrection events were to take place not in Jerusalem but in Galilee (16:7). Matthew (28:16-20) also shifts the focus to Galilee, away from Jerusalem. Raymond E. Brown suggests that Galilee has a better claim than Judaea (Jerusalem) to be the original site of Jesus' first appearance to the disciples. Walter Schmithals believes that Galilee, not Jerusalem, is "the home of Christianity," contending that "an original church remained active in Galilee and disseminated its influence not only to Jerusalem by way of Samaria, but also to Syria, Damascus, Antioch, all places where Acts takes early Christian churches for granted." The evidence from Mark and Matthew persuades Hans Conzelmann that "there was in Galilee a second 'original congregation' or group of congregations. This conjecture has every likelihood in its favor. From the very outset the church was not limited to the city of Jerusalem."[7]

This biblical evidence of other churches initially independent of Jerusalem does not invalidate Jerusalem as the dominant center of Christianity. Dunn likens the first years to a brush fire, with the major conflagration in Jerusalem, speading gradually and engulfing other smaller fires started independently.[8]

Given the disparity of the evidence, no unified tradition seems to have been handed on, but it is clear that the Christian imagination has been dominated by the Lukan account of events in Jerusalem to the detriment of Galilee, as though Galilee were off the map.

[6] Haenchen, *The Acts of the Apostles: A Commentary* (Philadelphia: Westminster, 1971) 174. Lohmeyer, *Galiläa und Jerusalem* (Göttingen: Vandenhoeck & Ruprecht, 1936). Dunn, *Jesus and the Spirit*, 137–38.

[7] Brown, *John XIII–XXI*, 1039. Schmithals, *Paul and James* (Naperville, Ill.: Allenson, 1965) 33. Conzelmann, *History of Primitive Christianity* (Naperville, Ill.: Abingdon, 1973) 33. See also L. E. Elliott-Binns, *Galilean Christianity* (Naperville, Ill.: Allenson, 1956).

[8] *Jesus and the Spirit*, 139.

Rudolf Schnackenburg believes that the "Lukan Pentecost" ought to be regarded "not as a norm but as an exception, namely, as a special manifestation of the Spirit, which assisted the primitive Church to make a break-through," that is, the growth of the ecclesial community beyond Jerusalem.[9] With this difference in mind one can hold that the messages of Luke and John are functionally one: the glorified Christ pours out the prophetic Spirit, an outpouring universal in scope, for the empowering of the community's mission. Both see the Spirit as a continuation of the work of Jesus, whose place the Spirit takes. The "Johannine Pentecost" and the event Luke narrates in Acts 2 have the same purpose—to tell of the bestowing of the one gift of the Spirit on the church by the risen and ascended Lord.

Exegetes are shy of many questions of historicity. But the disparity of the evidence forces the question. We are pushed to distinguish between the historicity of an outpouring of the Spirit on the one hand and the historicity of the outpouring of the Spirit in the precise terms given by Luke in Acts 2 on the other hand. If the second is somewhat in doubt, the evidence assures the first. An event or events of great significance for the life of the church happened. The undoubted message is: the Spirit is above all a gift to the church, belonging constitutively to the church's deepest identity, as the spirit belongs constitutively to the identity of Israel, as the Spirit belongs constitutively to the identity of Jesus.

The narrative of Acts 2 is inspired and canonical. It forms a major New Testament image of the transformative power of the Spirit and cannot be dispensed with without impoverishing ecclesiology and spirituality. Along with the incarnational feasts of the Annunciation and Christmas, the feast of Pentecost represents a central liturgical celebration. The calendar is unthinkable without it. The event of Acts 2 is an essential part of the church's proclamation.

PENTECOST:
NOT THE SPIRIT'S FIRST ENTRANCE INTO HISTORY
In the West there has been a tendency to take the Pentecost event of

[9] *The Gospel According to St. John* (New York: Herder & Herder, 1968) 3.325.

Acts 2 as the point of departure for pneumatology. But in the early church there was an awareness that Pentecost posed a particular problem, promoting the supposition that the Spirit came for the first time after the resurrection of Jesus. Irenaeus seems aware of the danger, as are Origen, Basil, Gregory of Nazianzus, and the fifth- or sixth-century Armenian document, the *Teaching of St. Gregory*.[10]

If pneumatology takes its point of departure only from the Pentecost event, the whole previous history is impoverished, the life and preaching and miracles of Jesus are "Spirit-less." The Spirit, a principle of identity for Jesus, is the power by which Jesus is conceived and raised from the dead.[11] Further, the early Christians understood that it was the Spirit-endowed Jesus who promised the sending of the Spirit. Pentecost is the fulfilment of that promise.

Beyond this there is an implicit Marcionism (rejection of the Old Testament) in the pragmatic denial that the spirit of Yahweh, which is constitutive of the history and identity of Israel, witnesses to the power of God in the wonders of Israel's saga. While the understanding of the spirit of Yahweh in the Old Testament is not identical with the Holy Spirit in the New, there are not, as has been said, two spirits. Origen is clear: "It is, however, certainly taught . . . that there is not one Spirit in the men of the Old [Testament] and another in those [New Testament prophets] who were inspired at the coming of Christ." Jews and Christians are deprived of their full history if excessive place is given to the Pentecost event as the point of departure for pneumatology, as though the spirit/Spirit then entered history for the first time. Such a truncating imperils the unity of the plan of salvation. Gregory of Nazianzus writes: "Christ

---

[10] Irenaeus, *Against Heresies* 3.12.5; SC 211.196. Origen, *On First Principles* 1, Preface, 4; SC 252.82. Basil, *On the Holy Spirit* 16.39; SC 17bis.384, 386. Gregory of Nazianzus, *Discourse* 31.29; SC 250.332–36. *The Teaching of Saint Gregory: An Early Armenian Catechism*, Robert W. Thomson, ed. (Cambridge: Harvard, 1970) 115–18.

[11] Schweizer, "pneuma," *The Theological Dictionary of the New Testament*, 6.416–17; Joseph Fitzmyer, *Romans* (New York: Doubleday, 1993) 124–25. Otto Kuss, *Der Römerbrief* (Regensburg: Pustet, 1963–78) 1.6–7. "The *Filioque* Clause in Ecumenical Perspective" (the "Klingenthal Memorandum"), in *Spirit of God, Spirit of Christ: Ecumenical Reflections on the Filioque Controversy*, Lukas Vischer, ed. (London: SPCK, 1981) 9.

is born; the Spirit is the forerunner."[12] The history of the Spirit does not start at Pentecost.

The role of the Spirit in the conception of Jesus, in his baptism, and in the whole of his ministry, as well as the role of the spirit in the history of Israel, is safeguarded by insisting that Pentecost is not the first appearance of the Spirit in history, much less the first decisive appearance. This is no diminution of the importance of Pentecost. The disciples were drunk with no ordinary wine on that day, because the Spirit is not given in measure, not determined by the limitations of need, but poured out extravagantly, in such a way that the Spirit cannot be manipulated, programmed, or controlled, pointing to a new claim of universalism in which the Spirit acts as God's secret in history. In the Pentecost event the Spirit is the breath in history that cannot be exhaustively grasped, the power within history that cannot be ultimately domesticated, even by the church. In fact, the event of Pentecost is a decisive new epiphany of the triune God, as important as the epiphany of the triune God in the incarnation, from which the mystery of Pentecost must not be separated.[13]

The Spirit is not a minor person in relation to the Father and the Son, not a junior grade person. Pentecost and incarnation have an intimate, interior relationship to one another, related by the mutuality and reciprocity with which each mystery is present to the other. Without the coming of the Spirit on Mary, the descent of the Spirit upon the disciples in the upper room would not have been possible. Without Pentecost, the promise of the incarnation would be unfulfilled. From the mutuality and reciprocity of Pentecost and incarnation the new phase of the one divine economy begins in the mystery and the splendor of the church.

[12] Origen, *On First Principles* 1, Preface, 4; SC 252.82. Gregory of Nazianzus, *Fifth Theological Oration* 31.29; SC 250.332.

[13] Charles Lee Graves, "The Holy Spirit in the Theology of Sergius Bulgakov" (Ph.D. diss.: University of Basel, 1970) 89. Nikos Nissiotis, "Pneumatological Christology as a Presupposition of Ecclesiology," *Oecumenica: Jahrbuch für ökumenische Forschung* 2 (1967) 249–50.

Chapter 7

No Unified Vision in the New Testament

Both the Hebrew *ruach* and the Greek *pneuma*, which we translate as spirit, mean, among other things, a movement of air, primarily breath or wind. Writing on the Old Testament spirit or the New Testament Holy Spirit is as difficult as laying hold of breath or grasping the wind. This elusive quality of the biblical spirit/Spirit is reinforced in the first years of the sub-apostolic period, in the later patristic and scholastic writings, and remains with us today.

Niceta of Remesiana at the end of the fourth century states the problem directly: "That there is much about the Holy Spirit we cannot understand is clear from the Gospel." In modern times Albert Outler noted that "despite heroic hermeneutical efforts by recent exegetes, the biblical notions of pneumatology are far from simple and clear," and Jules Lebreton remarked that "in the question of the Holy Spirit revelation furnished little material."[1]

Both Arthur W. Wainwright and Hans Conzelmann, basing themselves on the work of Rudolf Bultmann, note the wide variety of views of the Spirit, views that are not easily harmonized. At times the view is more animistic (an independent, personal power which can fall on a person and take possession), and at other times more dynamic (an impersonal power, which, like a fluid, fills a person). Bultmann thinks that "Spirit" is used in both senses in Acts and

---

[1] Niceta, *The Power of the Holy Spirit* 5; PL 52.855. Outler, "Veni Creator Spiritus: The Doctrine of the Holy Spirit," in Martin E. Marty and Dean G. Peerman, eds., *New Theology* 4 (London: Macmillan, 1967) 195–96. Lebreton, *Histoire du dogme de la Trinité: des origines au concile de Nicée*, 2 vols. (Paris: Beauchesne, 1928) 2.561.

Paul. Wainwright does not believe that dynamistic descriptions of the Spirit actually imply the Spirit is impersonal.[2]

LITTLE IN THE SYNOPTICS,
MUCH IN PAUL AND JOHN

Besides the lack of a unified view of the Spirit, there is the disparity in the amount of attention given to the Spirit. In the earliest New Testament writings, the letters of Paul, the material on the Spirit is extensive, showing us the Spirit in a variety of contexts. But Paul makes his contribution to the lack of concreteness, to a kind of Spirit anonymity. "Now the Lord is the Spirit" (2 Cor 3:17) was widely interpreted as fuzzing the identity of the Spirit. The text was often read as identifying the exalted Christ with the Spirit, though it is more likely a midrash on Exodus 34:29-35.[3]

Paul speaks extensively of the Spirit, but it is another matter with

[2] Wainwright, *The Trinity in the New Testament* (London: SPCK, 1962) 203. Conzelmann, *An Outline of the Theology of the New Testament* (London: SCM, 1969) 39. Bultmann, *Theology of the New Testament*, 2 vols. (New York: Scribner, 1951) 2.155. See also Walter Schmithals, "Geisterfahrung als Christuserfahrung," *Erfahrung und Theologie des Heiligen Geistes*, Claus Heitmann and Heribert Mühlen, eds. (Munich: Kösel, 1974) 101, who thinks "there is hardly a New Testament concept more difficult to grasp than the concept of '*Pneuma*.'" In the Greek tradition *pneuma* had indicated a material substance. According to Martien Parmentier, "The Doctrine of the Holy Spirit in the Works of Gregory of Nyssa," *Ekklesiastikos Pharos* 58 (1956) 439, the de-materialization of *pneuma* and its spiritualization was a Jewish and Christian task, begun in the Book of Wisdom and in Philo, completed in the New Testament. Not all of the New Testament impulses were decisive for the post-biblical development of pneumatology. Theodor Rüsch, *Die Entstehung der Lehre vom Heiligen Geist* (Zurich: Zwingli, 1952) 39–44, identifies the following themes: the movement of the *Pneuma* to the Word, power, the work of Jesus in proclamation and praise, a person possessed by the Spirit remains in full control of the faculties, communion between the *Pneuma* and the human spirit, edification, love as the context in which *Pneuma* is made manifest, eschatology, discernment of spirits, confession of Jesus as Lord, presence of the Spirit = the presence of God. Even locating the issues within the New Testament is a problem because exegetes have not always been attentive to the role of the Spirit in their research. Xavier Léon-Dufour, "Bulletin d'exégèse du nouveau testament," *Recherches de science religieuse* 55 (1967) 575–79, criticizes both Rudolf Schnackenburg and Raymond Brown for giving insufficient attention to the Spirit in their exegetical writings.

[3] James D. G. Dunn, *Christology in the Making: A New Testament Inquiry into the Origins of the Doctrine of the Incarnation* (Philadelphia: Westminster, 1980) 143.

the synoptic gospels. Exegetes are in general agreement that Jesus himself seldom spoke of the Spirit, but the texts present Jesus as impelled by the Spirit (Luke 4:1), as one who acts in the Spirit (Luke 4:18-21; 6:19). He was very likely conscious of being a Spirit-bearer (Mark 1:12; 3:22-29; also perhaps 3:11). Further, Gerald O'Collins suggests that Jesus never seems to have pointed unambiguously to his deeds as signs of the Spirit's power. Jesus does not seem to possess the kind of intense awareness of the Spirit that he had of the God whom he called "Abba."[4]

The synoptics describe the Spirit in a way the Jewish tradition had long done, that is, the dynamic power of God, the act of God, touching Jesus and touching others through him. Jesus is conceived by the power of the Holy Spirit (Luke 1:35), the Spirit descends on Jesus at his baptism (Matt 3:16). Jesus who is full of the Spirit is led by the Spirit to the place of temptation (Matt 4:1). Jesus, "filled with the power of the Spirit" (Luke 4:14), engages in his ministry. However, only after the resurrection and exaltation did a new and more intimate way of speaking of the Spirit and of Jesus' relationship to the Spirit appear.[5]

The synoptic teaching on the Spirit has its affinities to that of the Fourth Gospel. If one follows the clear outline of the apostolic preaching in Mark, and even more clearly in Matthew and Luke, there is a fixed outline of the apostolic proclamation as seen in Acts 10 and 13, including the messianic anointing of Jesus with the Holy Spirit, to which, in Mark, John the Baptist bears witness. This outline is followed by the Fourth Gospel.[6] The Fourth Gospel stands in close affinity to the early preaching, including the role ascribed to the Spirit.

Though John gives great importance to Jesus as the incarnate Logos, he is seemingly unafraid of adoptionist interpretations, for he gives firm place to the tradition of Jesus being anointed with the Spirit at the Jordan (John 1:32-33; 3:34), which could

---

[4] Eduard Schweizer, "The Spirit of Power," *Interpretation* 6 (1952) 264; *The Spirit of God* (Philadelphia: Fortress, 1980) 35. O'Collins, *Christology* (Oxford: University Press, 1995) 148.

[5] Ibid.

[6] C. H. Dodd, *The Apostolic Preaching and its Developments* (New York: Harper & Row, 1964) 69–70.

be understood to mean that Jesus became divine at that moment. More than any other evangelist, John ties the giving of the Spirit to Jesus' death. It is from the side of Jesus that the Spirit flows (7:38-39). Virtually everything said about the Paraclete in the Fourth Gospel has been said elsewhere in the gospel about Jesus. "Thus, the one whom John calls 'another Paraclete' is another Jesus . . . the Paraclete is the presence of Jesus when Jesus is absent."[7]

Though Hans Windisch believes that Jesus himself was a pneumatic personality, a primary carrier of the Spirit, he contends that no references to the Spirit attributed to Jesus in the synoptics or in John are genuine. C. K. Barrett asks a different question, namely, whether Jesus could have spoken of the Spirit at all, because the accounts presuppose the considerable perspective of a continuing Christian history.[8]

Whether the evidence is sparse, as in the case of the synoptics, or abundant, as in John, the question of level of the evidence arises. Do the references to the Spirit represent the earliest primary experience, or are they secondary theological formulations of the evangelists? While it is true that the New Testament books were written through the prism of the early church's experience of Pentecost and the Spirit, the descent of the Spirit on Jesus at the Jordan testifies to the role of the Spirit in identifying who Jesus is and what constitutes his mission.[9] Only with the greatest difficulty could one say that such an event, testified to in all four gospels, is simply a theological construction of the evangelists.

The question raised by the synoptics and John about whether Jesus himself ever spoke of the Spirit may not be all that significant. Even some major Old Testament prophets did not claim the title

[7] Raymond E. Brown, *The Gospel According to John XIII–XXI* (Garden City: Doubleday, 1970) 1140–41. Dunn, "Spirit and Holy Spirit in the New Testament," in his *The Christ and the Spirit: Collected Essays*, 2 vols. (Grand Rapids: Eerdmans, 1991) 1.17.

[8] Windisch, *The Spirit-Paraclete in the Fourth Gospel* (Philadelphia: Fortress, 1968). Jacob Kremer, "Jesu Verheissung des Geistes," *Die Kirche des Anfangs: Festschrift für Heinz Schürmann*, Rudolf Schnackenburg, Josef Ernst, and Joachim Wanke, eds. (Freiburg im Breisgau: Herder, 1978) 272–73, believes that Jesus' implicit promise of the Spirit was interpreted explicitly in light of the Easter experience. Barrett, *The Gospel According to St. John*, 2nd ed. (London: SPCK, 1978) 88.

[9] Kilian McDonnell, *The Baptism of Jesus in the Jordan: The Trinitarian and Cosmic Order of Salvation* (Collegeville: The Liturgical Press, 1996) 1–14.

prophet or claim the spirit as their authority, in large part because the excesses of the ecstatic prophets brought the spirit into disrepute—"the man of the spirit is mad" (Hos 9:7). If one follows Rudolph Bultmann, one is not surprised at the paucity of references in the synoptics. Bultmann asks whether the tradition suppressed the prophetic apocalyptic character of Jesus' preaching in order to present him as a less threatening teaching rabbi. Or did Jesus not wish to proclaim himself as a bearer of the Spirit, and therefore a prophet, because his claim was that he was more than a prophet? Or is the reason for the paucity of references in the synoptics to be found in the messianic secret, that is, were Jesus to speak more of the Spirit he would reveal himself prematurely as the Messiah, something it was his express purpose, at least in Mark, to keep secret until the resurrection (Mark 9:9)? In Luke/Acts Jesus is the one who possesses the Spirit in fullness from the beginning, being Lord of the Spirit. After the resurrection, the Christ imparts the Spirit to the community. Whatever one says of the role of the Spirit in Jesus' Jordan experience, John Meier concludes that one can take "the baptism of Jesus by John as the firm historical starting point for any treatment of Jesus' public ministry."[10]

THE SPIRIT IN THE TRIADIC AWARENESS

For the immediate problem, the elusive quality of the Spirit, the baptismal event at the Jordan is helpful because it relates the Spirit

[10] Barrett, "Why Do the Gospels Say So Little about the Spirit?" in his *The Holy Spirit and the Gospel Tradition* (London: SPCK, 1966) 148. Bultmann, *The History of the Synoptic Tradition* (New York: Harper & Row, 1968) 108–30. Martin Hengel, *The Charismatic Leader and His Followers* (New York: Crossroad, 1981) 64. William Wrede, *The Messianic Secret* (Cambridge: Clarke, 1971). There has been much discussion on the messianic secret since Wrede first published his work in 1901. Dunn, *The Christ and the Spirit*, 1.77, re-examines the discussion and says that "the so-called 'messianic secret' originated in the life-situation of Jesus and is in essence at least wholly historical." C. M. Tuckett, "Messianic Secret," *The Anchor Bible Dictionary* (New York: Doubleday, 1992) 4.800, concludes that probably no one today would wholeheartedly support all that Wrede said about the texts in Mark: "Many of these elements are due to Mark himself, and hence are not to be traced to Jesus, and their interpretation is vital for a proper understanding of Mark's gospel." Meier, *A Marginal Jew: Rethinking the Historical Jesus*, 2 vols. (New York: Doubleday, 1991–1994) 2.105.

to the triadic perspective of the New Testament. All three persons are named, the voice of the Father, the descent of the dove, and, of course, the Son standing in the waters of the Jordan. In John's Gospel there is no direct report of Jesus' baptism, but rather an allusion to the baptismal tradition (John 1:29-34). John is not interested in historical details, but rather focuses on the theological meaning, recording "the mature Christian reflection" of the community. Already in the prologue the evangelist has identified Jesus as the eternal Son of God (1:1, 18). So the preexistence of the Son is already established. John's narrative of the baptism sums up the content of the prologue.[11] The relationship of the Spirit to the Son of God, who will baptize in the Holy Spirit (1:33) at the beginning of John's Gospel, gives the Spirit a small measure of concreteness. This is not an isolated atomistic Spirit, but precisely the Spirit of God sent upon the Son. Here, as in Matthew, the Spirit belongs to the triadic awareness of the New Testament.

No one doubts the great significance that the baptismal commission of Matthew 28:16-20 had in the development of pneumatology in general and the divinity of the Spirit in particular, keeping the Spirit in a triadic context. The text can be seen as a summary of the whole gospel. The Father has given Jesus supreme and universal authority—no boundaries. The disciples are commanded to share their discipleship not only with their fellow Jews, but also universally, with non-Jews. The universality of the command embraces all peoples, all cultures. The Spirit will guide and protect the church until God's kingdom comes into its fullness.[12] The text very likely reflects the liturgical practice of the apostolic church and became embodied in the sacramental life of the post-apostolic church. No single text was so weighty in shaping pneumatology as Jesus' command to baptize in the name of the Father, Son, and Holy Spirit. Yet it does not stand alone.

Without suggesting dependence, the triadic teaching of the Matthean text is reinforced by the Corinthian texts (1 Cor 12:3-5; 2 Cor 13:13). Also significant is the Spirit as a central fact of Jesus'

[11] Schnackenburg, *The Gospel According to St. John*, 3 vols. (New York: Crossroad, 1982) 1.297. Barrett, *John*, 170.

[12] Daniel J. Harrington, *The Gospel of Matthew* (Collegeville: The Liturgical Press, 1991) 416–17.

life—conception (Luke 1:35), baptism (Luke 3:22), miracles, ministry (Luke 4:14, 18; Matt 12:28), resurrection (Rom 1:4), and sending of the Spirit (John 15:26). The constant relation between Christ and the Spirit in the New Testament helped create the climate in which the divinity of the Spirit would be recognized with clarity at a later date, as the theological elaboration of the Son's divinity emerged. The Spirit is regularly called "the Spirit of God" (Rom 8:9, 11, 14; 1 Cor 2:11, 14; 3:16; Eph 3:16). The Spirit does divine works, such as raising the believers from the dead (Rom 8:11). Paul equates the Yahweh of the Old Testament with the Spirit the believers are now experiencing: Yahweh (Lord) = Spirit = Spirit of Yahweh (Lord) (2 Cor 3:12-18).[13] The Spirit of God is the Spirit of Christ (Rom 8:9; Gal 4:6). The Spirit enables the believer to say, as Christ did, "Abba! Father!" (Rom 8:15; Gal 4:4).

The relation of the Spirit to the christological texts makes it evident that the first pneumatological reflections could find their basis in the christological texts. In the infancy narrative, Luke builds Jesus' divine sonship on the same themes that Paul draws on in Romans 1:3-4. Luke 1:35 reads, "The Holy Spirit will come upon you, and the power of the Most High will overshadow you; therefore the child to be born will be holy; he will be called Son of God." The Romans text reads (using Brown's translation), "Born of the seed of David according to the flesh, designated Son of God in power according to the Holy Spirit as of the resurrection from the dead." Both go back to the common theological tradition which ascribed the conception of the Son of God in Mary's womb to the creative act of God's Spirit. Even in the enthusiasm of the Pentecost event, Luke has Peter preach a sermon (Acts 2:14-36) not about a Spirit-centered kingdom but about Jesus crucified and risen. When the Spirit is mentioned it is to point out to the audience that Jesus, "having received from the Father the promise of the Holy Spirit . . . has poured out this that you both see and hear." The early christological reflections are already the beginnings of pneumatology, and are related to the cross and resurrection even in the enthusiastic moment of Pentecost.[14]

[13] Dunn, *Christology in the Making*, 143–44.
[14] Brown, *The Birth of the Messiah* (Garden City: Doubleday, 1977) 311–16; also 50–54 and 133–43. Heribert Mühlen, "Das Christusereignis als Tat des Heiligen Geistes," *MS*, 3/2:515.

No Unified Vision in the New Testament

Though the first christology was likely not a specific Spirit christology, the understanding of the mediation between Christ and humankind is uniquely the work—indeed, an event—of the Holy Spirit, and this leads to a "pneumatically oriented Christology." Such a christology was not aided by an explicit New Testament teaching on the Trinity, which did not exist. Not even the roots of the trinitarian doctrine are present in the New Testament, if one is speaking of a three-personed God. What do exist are the explicit triadic formulas, suggesting that threeness of this kind was implicit from the beginning.[15] The triadic emphasis in the New Testament forms the point of departure for the trajectory that develops into trinitarian doctrine as we understand it. And within that triadic mentality the relationship of "in Christ" and "in the Spirit" was worked out.

The relation of the Spirit to God and to the Son, Jesus Christ, will be decisive as the post-biblical period struggles, given the scarcity of evidence in some of the canonical traditions and the lack of a unified coherent teaching on the Spirit in the New Testament. Though the issue in the immediate post-biblical period was not the divinity of the Spirit—divinity was generally assumed—the struggle to come to terms with the Trinity meant coming to terms with the divinity of the Spirit in a more explicit formulation.

[15] Walter Kasper, *Jesus the Christ* (New York: Paulist, 1976) 249. Franz J. Schierse, "Die neutestamentliche Trinitätsoffenbarung," *MS*, 2.85. Kelly, *Creeds*, 12.

Chapter 8

Losing the Battle to Stay with the Imprecision of Scripture

The lack of a unified vision and the inherent ambiguity of the Spirit made it difficult to assert the divinity of the Spirit and yet stay within the bounds of scripture, which was silent on this point. Even for those with orthodox views it was difficult to find the theological language to express the divinity of the Spirit and the personal distinction of the Spirit within the Trinity. The words of Gregory of Nazianzus were no exaggeration: "To be only slightly in error was to be orthodox."[1]

The move beyond scripture was tortuous. Because the Spirit was not an issue in 325, the Council of Nicaea was content to restrict itself to asserting, "[We believe] in the Holy Spirit." However, Nicaea places the Spirit in a decisive trinitarian context, thus determining (along with the biblical baptismal commission, which is its source) future theological developments.

The same Nicene reticence is manifest some twenty-five years later in Cyril of Jerusalem, writing before the major debate over the Spirit. Cyril takes refuge in the words of scripture, not moving beyond them: "Let us assert of the Holy Spirit . . . only what is written; let us not busy ourselves about what is not written. The

---

[1] André de Halleux, "Towards an Ecumenical Agreement on the Procession of the Holy Spirit and the Addition of the *Filioque* to the Creed," *Spirit of God, Spirit of Christ: Ecumenical Reflections on the Filioque Controversy*, Lukas Vischer, ed. (London: SPCK, 1981) 75. Gregory of Nazianzus, *Discourse in Honor of Athanasius, Bishop of Alexandria* 21.33; SC 270.182.

Holy Spirit has authored the scriptures; he has spoken of himself all that he wished, or all that we could grasp; let us confine ourselves to what he has said, for it is reckless to do otherwise." Cyril discourages prying into the nature *(physis)* and person *(hypostasis)* of the Spirit because the scriptures are silent.[2]

Hilary of Poitiers displays the same reticence as others of his age, partly because he knows that both the Father and the Son are "holy" and "spirit." He touches on the Spirit rarely, and then the exposition remains undeveloped. He believes in the divinity and consubstantiality of the Spirit, in the Spirit as power and in the charisms of the Spirit, but even when the context calls for words like "God," "divinity," "consubstantiality," he does not use them. Of course, since the controversies concerning the Spirit had not yet arisen, he had small need to be either assertive or defensive. In abstaining from a bold assertion of the divinity of the Spirit, Hilary was keeping to the central tradition of being no more explicit in this matter than the scriptures themselves. Yet, as his work *On the Synods* shows, he was not ignorant of the vocabulary of "divinity" and "consubstantiality." He responds to the Arians' objection that the word *homoousios* is not in scripture by saying that new developments demand new words. To one who says, "I do not wish to speak words which are not in scripture," Hilary retorts that "ingenerate" *(innascibilis)* for the Son and "like" *(homoiousios)* for relating the Son to the Father—both favorite Arian words—are not in the Bible.[3] Still, the Arians use them. Hilary, therefore, demonstrates both his hesitation to move beyond the scriptures and his simultaneous recognition that sometimes necessity pushes one across borders.

[2] Cyril of Jerusalem, *Catechetical Lectures* 16.2, 24, in *Cyrilli Hierosolymarum Archiepiscopi Opera Quae Supersunt Omnia*, W. C. Reischl and J. Rupp, eds.; 2 vols. (Munich: Keck, 1848/1850) 2.206, 236.

[3] Hilary of Poitiers, *On the Trinity* 2.30; CCSL 62.65. He touches on the Spirit in 1.29–35, written in 356–357; 7.19–32, written at the end of 359; and 12.55–57, written also at the end of 359. Comparatively, this is not much. Louis Doutreleau, "Introduction," Didymus the Blind, *Treatise on the Holy Spirit* SC 386.23–24. Hilary, *Against Constantius* 16; PL 10.594. R. P. C. Hanson, *The Search for the Christian Doctrine of God* (Edinburgh: T. & T. Clark, 1988) 891.

Athanasius will show himself extremely reluctant to walk across the scriptural boundaries fixed in the central tradition. But one is not master of a history which raises questions not raised before. In solving them one must grasp the intention *(dianoia)* and the direction or range of the biblical text.[4] Congruence with the intention of the sacred text is the assurance that what is said beyond scripture is in accordance with the sacred text, that is, the intention of scripture controls doctrinal statements that move beyond scripture. This principle is operative in Athanasius's *Letters to Serapion,* composed in 359, the first extended treatment of the Spirit since Origen's *On First Principles,* written about a century and a quarter earlier. Athanasius vigorously responds to the threat raised by the deniers of the Spirit some thirty years after Nicaea.

For Athanasius, the crisis over the divinity of the Spirit was set within the broader Arian dispute concerning the divinity of Jesus Christ—it was a "crisis within a crisis." As in his defense of the divinity of Christ, his first argument is the divinization the Spirit effects. The Spirit makes us like God. If the Spirit makes us divine, it cannot be a creature. Here Athanasius anticipates an argument that will be dear to Gregory of Nazianzus. And like Gregory's, Athanasius's argument is aggressively determined by trinitarian categories: the Spirit is intimately related to Father and Son. Athanasius wants to defend the divinity of the Spirit, but is hesitant, as is Basil, to be too explicit. "It is enough to know that the Spirit is not a creature, and is not listed along with created things, for nothing alien is associated with the Trinity, but is inseparable and consistent in itself. This doctrine is enough. Beyond that, the cherubim cover with their wings." Where the cherubim do not pry, we do not pry.[5]

When Athanasius approaches the doctrine of the Spirit in a formal way, he uses negative statements in keeping with his desire to adhere to the scriptures: the Holy Spirit is not a creature, not an angel. In the first seven sections of the third of his *Letters to Serapion,* Athanasius seven times repeats "the Spirit is not a creature." Never

---

[4] Hanson, *Search,* 871.

[5] C.R.B. Shapland, "Introduction," *The Letters of Saint Athanasius Concerning the Holy Spirit* (London: Epworth, 1951) 35. Athanasius, *Letters to Serapion* 1.23–24; SC 15.124–28; 1.2; SC 15.80–82; 1.17; SC 15.112.

Losing the Battle to Stay with the Imprecision of Scripture

does Athanasius use God *(theos)* of the Spirit. The closest he comes is to say that the Spirit "is confessed as God." He labels as presumptuous the coining of new words, though he twice uses the non-biblical *homoousios* of the Spirit in the *Letters to Serapion.*[6]

If the Council of Nicaea, pressed by the challenge of heresy, had used a word not found in scripture, Athanasius feels he is justified, pressed by heresy, to apply *homoousios* to the Spirit, though he does this reluctantly. During the three decades after Nicaea he did not use *homoousios.* Even when he returned to *homoousios* he, like Hilary, was not willing to die for the word itself. Rather he wanted to treat as brothers those who accepted the doctrine, but had objections to the word.[7] This is truly the sign of a great mind and a magnanimous spirit. (To this we will return later.) A great noise had been made about *homoousios* by the defenders of Nicaea, but the issue at Nicaea was not a technical term, it was a doctrine: Jesus is one with the Father and divine. Athanasius avoids going into the question of the Spirit's origin. He really wants simply to affirm the negative: The Spirit is not a creature.

But Athanasius was being pushed by another necessity which involved concreteness of a sort. In the *Letters to Serapion* Athanasius's opponents, men of culture, claimed to be themselves adversaries of the Arians because they were one with tradition which accords divinity to the Son. Even though they denied divinity to the Spirit, they considered themselves orthodox. In his broader debate with those who were more strictly Arian, Athanasius had opponents who were not prepared to allow that God could or would communicate the divine self. The Arian doctrine of the Son was a safeguard against God the Father coming into too close proximity with the world. The strict Arians posited a radical disjunction between the Father and the Son. The Son was not coeternal with the Father;

---

[6] Joseph Lebon, "Introduction," *Letters to Serapion*, SC 15.57. Doutreleau, "Introduction," SC 386.28. Athanasius, *Letters to Serapion* 1.31; SC 15.139; 1.27; 3.1; SC 17.133, 165.

[7] Athanasius, *Letter on the Synods of Arminum and Seleucia* 41; PG 26.764d–65a. Hilary, *From an Historical Work*, Fragment 3.28; PL 10.655a, while looking upon the creed of Nicaea as "full and perfect," and while defending *homoousios*, felt that true faith could be had without the use of this one word. C.F.A. Borchardt, *Hilary of Poitiers' Role in the Arian Struggle* (The Hague: Nijhoff, 1966) 37, 159–65.

though the Son exists before all time and all creation, the Son is later than the Father, from whom the Son is derived. To support their view they could call on a long and respectable tradition of Logos theology. To this extent they were conservatives, married to the past.

Athanasius, however, was quite sure that God had done precisely what the Arians feared, namely, God had made the most intimate contact with the created order in the Spirit through Christ. More than that, the incarnate Son in the Spirit was the greatest guarantee that God had the most immediate personal contact with the world and humankind. In a phrase similar to that of Theophilus of Antioch and Irenaeus, who spoke of the two hands of God, Athanasius held that the Son and the Spirit were the two eyes of God.[8] Besides celebrating the bridging of the Creator/creature gap, this was an expression of the intimate relation between the doctrine of the Spirit and that of the Son. If the Son made contact with creation, so did the Spirit.

Athanasius enunciates a principle that will guide his pneumatology: "The Spirit bears the same relation to the Son as the Son to the Father."[9] By this principle of correlativity—what is true of the Son in relation to the Father is also true, in its own proper mode, of the Spirit in relation to the Son—the Spirit, too, broke out of the Godhead and made awe-inspiring contact with creation and with the most interior life of humankind. Among other things, this makes holiness possible. The Spirit divinizes.

[8] Hanson, *Search*, 426. Athanasius, *Commentary on the Psalms* 32.18; PG 27.165d.
[9] *Letters to Serapion* 1.21; SC 15.120. Athanasius has a twentieth-century counterpart in Karl Barth, *Church Dogmatics* (Edinburgh: T. & T. Clark, 1936) 1/1.354–55, who also had to confront those who said that Trinity (one nature, three hypostases) is not found in scripture. He answered that if one has to remain entirely and completely with the words of scripture, then all theological reflection is impossible. Franz J. Schierse, "Die neutestamentliche Trinitätsoffenbarung," *MS* 2.87–88, thinks that the New Testament itself is not surpassed by subsequent trinitarian development. "We are working with a false optic when we think that the trinitarian theology of the later time has pushed forward to decisively new and deeper knowledge, while in reality only a few undiscussed supposed points of view of the New Testament have been more sharply expressed and so translated into speech understandable to *their* [later] time."

Losing the Battle to Stay with the Imprecision of Scripture

The lack of an articulated doctrine of the Spirit in the New Testament and the reluctance to go beyond the clear words of scripture in the early post-biblical period meant that, though there was reflection on the Spirit, it was not extensive, except in Irenaeus and Origen. An impetus to further development, to be more explicit and concrete, was given by those who denied the divinity of the Spirit. These groups emerged between 355 and 361, but they were not prominent until about 373. These deniers of the Spirit's divinity are variously called Pneumatomachoi, Tropici, and Macedonians. It would be a mistake to suppose that any of the three represented a defined theological position. Rather, they constituted a loose grouping, holding one suspicion in common: that the pro-Nicene theologians were scandalously going beyond scripture. Standing on the word of scripture, they moved the Spirit to the center of discussion for a comparatively short period of time, twenty-five years. Seen from the standpoint of further church history, this discussion "left behind almost no trace."[10]

The deniers of the Spirit confronted theologians again with the trinitarian problem, namely, the unity and threeness of Father, Son, and Holy Spirit. If the Spirit is not divine, not a *hypostasis*, then there is no Trinity. In 360 Eunomius, an Arian, said that the Paraclete was "the first creature of the First Born, the greatest of all and the only one such." Obviously this was not yet seen as the center of the battle, because when Basil was writing his *Against Eunomius* the question of the Spirit had just begun to be raised and the attention given to the Third Person was comparatively small. At the end of the treatise Basil admits, "Without blushing we confess our ignorance of the Holy Spirit." But when he became a bishop in 370, Basil's preaching and correspondence show more intense focus on the Spirit.[11]

In Egypt, three Alexandrian synods (362, 363, 369) defended the

---

[10] Hanson, *Search*, 766. Georg Kretschmar, *Studien zur frühchristlichen Trinitätstheologie* (Tübingen: Mohr, 1956) 1.

[11] Basil, *Apology* 25; SC 305.286. Milton Anastos, "Basil's *Kata Eunomiou*, A Critical Analysis," in *Basil of Caesarea: Christian, Humanist, Ascetic*, Paul J. Fedwick, ed. (Toronto: Pontifical Institute of Mediaeval Studies, 1981) 117–18. Basil, *Against Eunomius* 3.6; SC 305.166. Jean Gribomont, "Intransigence and Irenicism in Saint Basil's 'De Spiritu Sancto,'" *Word and Spirit* 1 (1979) 110.

divinity of the Spirit. The 362 synod, with Athanasius presiding, insists that the Spirit is "not a creature, nor a stranger [to the divinity], but is proper [to the divinity], and, as regards substance, is indivisible from the Father and the Son." The 363 synod returns to the trinitarian argument, accusing those who deny the divinity of the Spirit of blaspheming the Trinity because they separate the Spirit from the Father and the Son. The 369 synod refutes those who wish to distort the naked brevity of "[we believe] in the Holy Spirit" of Nicaea's creed, as though the Fathers of that council had any doubts about the divinity of the Spirit. The eighty-six bishops in the Alexandrian Council of 369 reaffirm the divinity of the Spirit because the Spirit is integral to trinitarian life.[12] In the highly disciplined abruptness of "[we believe] in the Holy Spirit," Nicaea was at least maintaining the tradition of not going beyond the Bible, while at the same time associating the Spirit integrally with the Trinity. If associated with the Father and the Son, on the same level with them, then the Spirit must be divine.

In 376 Amphilochius, cousin of Gregory of Nazianzus, and the bishop to whom Basil dedicated *On the Holy Spirit,* rose to defend the divinity of the Spirit in the Synod of Iconium (in Cappadocia), over which he likely presided. What appears to be a synodal letter under Amphilochius's name calls for an end to a reticence that does not take the appropriate necessities of the moment into account. This was a decided departure from Basil's position, and Basil was still alive at the time of the synod. Even in the midst of the heated controversy about the divinity of the Spirit, even in the very act of defending and protesting the divinity of the Spirit, Basil still thought, "Perhaps this is a time for silence," and he appeals to the authority of Solomon: "For everything there is a season, and a time for every matter under heaven . . . a time to keep silence, and a time to speak" (Eccl 3:1, 7).[13] We will return to Basil later.

Though Nicaea had associated the Spirit with the Trinity, it had not gone beyond scripture to explicitly say the Spirit is divine. But now, since groups have arisen explicitly denying the Spirit's divinity,

[12] Athanasius, *Tome to the People of Antioch* 5; PG 26.802b; *Letter to the Emperor Jovian* 1 and 4; PG 26, 815b, 819a; *Letter to the African Bishops* 11; PG 26.1047b. Doutreleau, "Introduction," SC 386.30–31.

[13] *On the Holy Spirit* 29.75; SC 17bis.518.

the situation is different. To paraphrase Amphilochius: "What was sufficient for Nicaea is not sufficient for us. Nicaea committed us to a trinitarian doctrine, but no trinitarian doctrine is possible if the Spirit is not recognized as trinitarian and therefore divine."[14]

DIDYMUS THE BLIND:
TREAD SOFTLY AND REMAIN WITHIN SCRIPTURE

The times had changed also in Alexandria. There was a different climate twenty years after Athanasius wrote his *Letters to Serapion* in 359, when Didymus the Blind (c. 313–398) wrote his *Treatise on the Holy Spirit*. Didymus was writing in the latter half of the 370s, possibly within two years after Athanasius's death in 373 and a few years before the Council of Constantinople in 381. Though Didymus was intimately acquainted with Athanasius's *Letters to Serapion,* he neither mentions nor cites Athanasius—an anomaly, given Athanasius's eminence and authority and his having been Didymus's bishop for many years. Didymus perhaps felt it necessary to distance himself from the combative, aggressive tenor of Athanasius's writings on the Spirit. In the calmer atmosphere the late 370s Didymus is serene, less bellicose, more given than Athanasius to laying out positive argumentation.[15]

The blind scholar, together with Augustine, thought that the pagan philosophers, though they knew of the Father and the Son, were totally ignorant of the Holy Spirit because they did not know the scriptures. So secret and veiled is the Spirit! This position had been held by Origen, who wrote, "No one except those who are familiar with the law and the prophets, or those who profess their belief in Christ, could have even a suspicion of the personal existence of the Holy Spirit."[16] Didymus, a teacher in the school *(didaskaleion)* of Alexandria and thus a successor to Origen, returns to this teaching of the great master on the necessity of knowing the scriptures if one is to know the Holy Spirit.

Even if one possesses the scriptures, one does not boldly approach

---

[14] *Synodal Letter* PG 39.93–98.

[15] Doutreleau, "Introduction," SC 386.40.

[16] Didymus, *Treatise on the Holy Spirit* 3; SC 386.144. Augustine, *Questions on the Heptateuch* 7.2.25; CSEL 28/2.106. Origen, *On First Principles* 1.3.1; SC 252.144.

the doctrine of the Spirit. Didymus prefaces his remarks on the divinity of the Spirit with a caution: "It is necessary to approach divine things with reverence and extreme care, but especially in that which concerns the divinity of the Spirit." One needs to take care not to blaspheme against the Spirit, because the punishment for such an offense extends for eternity (Matt 12:31-32). The humble Christian "will measure his capacity, guarding silence in the face of a question in which one assumes responsibility only when one knows it is full of danger."[17]

Didymus has it both ways. While remaining within the biblical word he asserts the logic of scripture, declaring the divinity of the Spirit: "Since therefore the Holy Scripture does not say more about the Trinity, except that God is the Father of the Savior and that the Son is begotten by the Father, we should believe no more than what is written, namely, that the Holy Spirit is uncreated, whereupon it follows that the uncreated substance has full communion with the Father and the Son."[18]

In all this groping we see how the strange abruptness of the creed of the Council of Nicaea paid off. All the council could manage for the Spirit was "[we believe] in the Holy Spirit." However, the trinitarian logic of the creed, reflecting the Great Commission (Matt 28:19), with its focus on discipleship and baptism, and the historic faith of the church, proved helpful during the years when the divinity of the Spirit was at issue, when the church was struggling with the text of scripture—not wanting to go beyond it while still wanting to be more concrete, but afraid that the concreteness would tear away the necessary veil of mystery which scripture itself had placed there.

[17] Didymus, *Treatise on the Holy Spirit* 1–2; SC 386.142–44.
[18] Ibid., 271; SC 386.386.

Chapter 9

The Mission of the Spirit: Junior Grade?

If beginnings are decisive for what follows—indeed, if they contain the future—how one approaches pneumatology will make a difference in how the doctrine of God is perceived and formed. Of the many Old Testament traditions, the Deuteronomic vision carried special weight. Here everything is interrelated in a unified theological vision: one Yahweh, one (comprehensive) Israel, one revelation, one promised land, one place of worship, one prophet. Christian monotheism inherited this unified vision and, while recognizing the differences, is at pains to stay in "perfect harmony" with the history of Israel by saying that "there is only one and the same God" in both testaments, one and the same Father, Son, and Spirit in both covenants. This is one reason the early church saw itself as belonging to the story that began with Abraham and Sarah. Even the Old Testament becomes gospel. The new understanding of God begins with the experience Jesus has of the Spirit and the Father.[1]

[1] Ernst Käsemann, "The Beginnings of Christian Theology," in his *New Testament Questions of Today* (Philadelphia: Fortress, 1969) 82. Gerhard von Rad, *Old Testament Theology*, 2 vols. (New York: Harper & Row, 1962) 1.229. Irenaeus, *Against Heresies* 3.12.13; 4.21.2; 4.36.8; 4.33.1; SC 100.678, 914, 846. Origen, *On First Principles* 1, Preface 4; SC 253.13. See also Cyril of Jerusalem, *Catechetical Lectures* 17.18, in *Cyrilli Hierosolymarum Archiepiscopi Opera Quae Supersunt Omnia*, W. C. Reischl and J. Rupp, eds.; 2 vols. (Munich: Keck, 1848/1850) 2.272. In Irenaeus–Father: *Against Heresies* 4.36.8; SC 100.914; Son: *Against Heresies* 4.20.7; SC 100.647, 649; Spirit: *Against Heresies* 4.20.6; SC 100.645, 647. Origen, *Commentary on John* 1, 6, 36; SC 120.78, 80. *The Teaching of Saint Gregory: An Early Armenian Catechism* 298–99, Robert W. Thomson, ed. (Cambridge: Harvard, 1970) 56–57.

The newness of the New Testament is in the missions of the Son and the Spirit from the Father. The biblical basis of the Son's mission from the Father is clearly stated (Gal 4:6; John 3:17; 5:23; 6:57; 17:18), as is the Spirit's being sent by the Father (Gal 4:6; John 14:16, 26) and also the Spirit's being sent by the Son (Luke 24:49; John 15:26; 16:7). So the Father sends the Son, and the Father and the Son send the Spirit (in Eastern theology the Father alone sends the Spirit because the Father alone is the source of the Spirit).

THE RELATION OF ETERNAL PROCESSIONS TO TEMPORAL MISSIONS

For Thomas Aquinas, a mission includes an eternal procession with something added, namely, a temporal effect. One speaks of visible and invisible missions. In the visible missions the effect is visible (the human nature of Christ at the incarnation, the dove at the Jordan, and the tongues of fire at Pentecost, the latter two symbolizing the Spirit). The visible mission is ordered to the visible manifestation of the person who is sent. The mission of the Son is said to be visible because the sending of the Son from the Father terminates in the incarnation, which has a dimension of visibility. In the invisible missions the effect is invisible, namely, the interior sanctification of a human person through justification and grace. The mission of the Spirit which ends in the indwelling of the Spirit (1 Cor 3:16; 6:19; Rom 5:5; 8:11) is invisible, but not necessarily beyond the realm of experience. The invisible mission is ordered to the self-giving of the uncreated person, the Son and the Spirit, to the human created person in the justifying process. The effect of the visible missions (human nature of Christ, tongues of fire) reveals and is ordered to the invisible missions, such as interior transformation by sharing in the life of God.[2]

When considering the missions of the Son and the Spirit in history, one can start with the processions in the immanent Trinity, that is, God considered in God's own self, prior to God's relation to history. Processions mean that from all eternity the Son proceeds, or issues forth from the Father (God from God) and the Holy Spirit

---

[2] *Summa theologiae* I, q43, a2, ad3. Bertrand de Margerie, *The Christian Trinity in History* (Still River, Mass.: St. Bede's, 1982) 329.

from the Father and the Son (or from the Father alone, if one follows the Greek tradition). These eternal processions belong to God's inner life. Starting with these processions interior to God's life has been the traditional theological manual approach, which stands behind the exposition of the visible and invisible missions given above. The temporal missions of the Son and the Spirit in history were seen as extensions of the eternal processions from the Father. But one can also start, not at the interior of God's life, but with the historical and salvific experience of the Son and the Spirit, which is the way chosen here, though the two ways are not completely separable.[3]

THE WAY OF EXPERIENCE

From the experience of the Son and the Spirit as sent by the Father, one can arrive at the "sense" of the Trinity in the missions. The Father sends and is not sent, and the Son and Spirit are sent. The two sendings and the two sent are the self-communication of God. In Christ and the Spirit, God reveals the divine Self in the two "hands of God."[4] We make a quasi-experiential journey back to Christian beginnings to recapture the immediacy of the first experience. The journey is quasi-experiential because it is made not in a void but in harmony with the living tradition. The experience may start again from square one in the biblical witness (insofar as that is possible), but it is not a hermit's journey.

The teaching on the eternal processions and their relation to the temporal missions is based on the biblical witness. And in that witness there is one tradition, as John Zizioulas points out, in which the Spirit appears to depend on Christ—the mission of the Spirit is to make effective the work of Christ and to glorify Christ.[5] Christ

---

[3] No attempt is made here to give a complete theology of divine missions. See the standard exposition in Walter Kasper, *The God of Jesus Christ* (New York: Crossroad, 1984) 277–79.

[4] Irenaeus, *Against Heresies* 5.6.1; SC 153.72. For the eleventh-century Symeon the New Theologian, *Ethics* 3.103–12; SC 122.398, the Spirit is "the mouth of God" because the Son, the Word of God, "needs to be expressed or revealed by the Holy Spirit, as if by a mouth, or he (the Son) cannot be known or understood."

[5] "Implications ecclésiologiques de deux types de pneumatologie," *Communio Sanctorum: Mélanges offerts à Jean Jacques von Allmen* (Geneva: Labor et Fides, 1982) 141.

The Mission of the Spirit: Junior Grade?

sends the Spirit (John 15:26; 16:7), who appears as an agent of Christ (the Spirit will "remind you of all that I have said to you" [John 14:26]; the Spirit "will take what is mine and declare it to you" [16:14]). This biblical perspective places Christ in a temporal priority to the Spirit.

A second tradition in the New Testament gives temporal priority to the Spirit over the Son.[6] Here again, one starts, not in the immanent Trinity (God in God's own self, divorced from history) but in the economy of salvation. Here the Spirit is the forerunner of the Son. Through the prophets the Spirit announces the coming of Christ (Luke 24:27). The Spirit overshadows Mary (Luke 1:35; Matt 1:20), the Holy Spirit comes down on Christ in the Jordan and is the power of his ministry (Matt 3:16; Mark 1:12; Luke 3:22). And, if Romans 1:3-4 can be used ("declared to be Son of God with power according to the spirit of holiness by resurrection from the dead"), as some exegetes claim, the Spirit (together with the Father) is the power of the resurrection.

In this vision of the economy of salvation, the Son seems to depend on the Spirit. Basil writes, "When we speak of the plan of salvation, accomplished in God's goodness by our Great God and Savior, Jesus Christ, who would deny that it was all made possible through the grace of the Spirit? . . . Everything that happened since the Lord's coming in the flesh, it all comes to pass through the Spirit. In the first place, the Lord was anointed with the Holy Spirit [at his baptism]. After his baptism, the Holy Spirit was present in every action he performed."[7] At no point in the plan of salvation is the Spirit absent as the one who announces ahead of time

[6] Zizioulas, "The Teaching of the 2nd Ecumenical Council on the Holy Spirit in Historical and Ecumenical Perspective," *CSS*, 1.38–39. See also Zizioulas, *Being as Communion: Studies in Personhood and the Church* (Crestwood: St. Vladimir's, 1985) 128. Martien Parmentier, "The Doctrine of the Holy Spirit in the Works of Gregory of Nyssa," *Ekklesiastikos Pharos* 58 (1976) 425–28, calls attention to the same tradition expressed in Gregory. See also Emmanuel Pataq Siman, *L'expérience de l'Esprit par l'église d'après la tradition syrienne d'Antioche* (Paris: Beauchesne, 1971) 132–34, and Jean Daniélou, "Chrismation prébaptismale et divinité de l'Esprit chez Grégoire de Nysse," *Recherches de sciences religieuses* 56 (1968) 184–92. Daniélou notes Gregory's dependence on Basil, *On the Holy Spirit* 11.27; SC 17bis.340, 342.

[7] *On the Holy Spirit* 16:39; SC 17bis.384–86.

and precedes.

This approach finds expression in old liturgical rites in Palestine and Syria, where chrismation, the imparting of the Spirit, preceded baptism. This suggests that there is another way of looking at precedence—the Spirit moment precedes the Christ moment, and the Christ moment depends on the Spirit moment.[8] This is the order of history, and of experience.

A QUESTION OF PRIORITY

Heribert Mühlen, standing in the long tradition where the point of departure is the immanent Trinity, says that the mission of the Son has a logical priority over that of the Spirit by reason of the inner-trinitarian order of processions.[9] The procession of the Son from the Father is logically prior to that of the Spirit. In Western theology the eternal procession of the Spirit is from the Father and the Son as from one principle. In Eastern theology the Spirit proceeds from the Father alone. To the logical priority of the eternal procession of the Son about which Mühlen speaks is added a temporal priority, that is, the incarnation comes before Pentecost. Part of the Eastern polemic against the *filioque* is the contention that it makes the mission of the Spirit a junior-grade mission, not of equal importance with that of the Son—and this in spite of all Western protests to the contrary.

Examining the theologies of East and West, an unbiased judge

---

[8] A third perspective is that of Tom F. Driver, *Christ in a Changing World: Toward an Ethical Christology* (New York: Crossroad, 1981), mentioned here as a curiosity. Driver is opposed to a christocentric theology (principally because of gender issues), and gives priority to the Spirit in a schema: Spirit–God–Christ. He prefers this pattern to the hierarchically ordered Father, Son, and Holy Spirit. "I shall bluntly say that I do not think we may any longer pretend that Jesus is our starting point" (35). "When Christian theology put Christ at the center of time, regarding his unity with God as forever decisive, it put a frame around the divine/human context, setting limits to the Spirit" (111–12). And in *Patterns of Grace* (San Francisco: Harper & Row, 1977) 34, Driver writes, "The theological doctrine of the Word, I fear, has preened itself into an outrageous male chauvinism." One can critique Driver in two ways. First, he has the human agenda determine revelation. Second, though one can sympathize with his strictures against christomonism, his solution is not viable because not truly trinitarian.

[9] *Der Heilige Geist als Person: Beitrag zur Frage nach der dem heiligen Geistes eigentumlichen Funktion in der Trinität, bei der Inkarnation und im Gnadenbund* (Münster: Aschendorff, 1963) 260.

would have to say that the East has been more successful than the West in giving the Spirit and the mission of the Spirit due equality. Further, the East has been more successful in integrating the Holy Spirit into the whole theological process, which is not to deny that Eastern theologians also have their problems with pneumatology. This is not a matter of hubris, of the East scorning the West. This goes deeper than human pride. If the person of the Spirit is not equal to that of the Son, if the mission of the Spirit is not as important as that of the Son, then the Trinity collapses. The Trinity cannot support imbalanced, unequal persons or missions.

The East is not protesting all subordination, all dependence of the mission of the Spirit on that of Christ. What is problematic is when the Spirit never attains the age of majority, never reaches the kind of "autonomy" recognized in the Second Person, even though it is admitted that the modalities of this "autonomy" or "maturity" are different for each person.

CAUTIONS ON THE THEOLOGY OF MISSIONS

The missions of the two persons (the Father sends but is not sent) are two modalities of God's self-communication of the Son and the Spirit (the Son in the Spirit and the Spirit through the Son). A methodological caution: a generic conception of mission ignores the specificity of the person who is sent and the modality of each one's presence in narrative time—the Son is historical in the flesh; the Spirit, not hypostatically incarnated, is transhistorical in grace. A generic conception of mission also ignores the formal purpose of each sending—the Son to die and rise for our salvation; the Spirit to make the mystery of the Son effective in the church. The determination of the character of mission is not only the Father who sends but also who is sent and why.[10]

The question remains whether the missions of the Son and the Spirit are two distinct economies, as Vladimir Lossky would have it, or two moments of one operation of God's revealing and saving action, as John Zizioulas, Nikos Nissiotis, and David Coffey hold.[11]

[10] Wilhelm Breuning, "Pneumatologie," in Herbert Vorgrimler, ed., *Bilan de la théologie du XXe siècle* (Paris: Casterman, 1970) 2.345–46.

[11] Lossky, *The Mystical Theology of the Eastern Church* (Crestwood, N.Y.: St. Vladimir's, 1976) 156–73. Zizioulas, *Being as Communion*, 129. Nissiotis,

Lossky, whose christology is more trinitarian and moves with more dispatch to the Father and to the whole dynamic of inner-trinitarian life than is typical of the West, proceeds from the distinct hypostatic being of the Spirit to a distinct economy and independent mission of the Spirit. The larger framework for this is the Eastern view that the Spirit eternally proceeds from the Father alone. Also operative is the Eastern tendency to opt for that biblical tradition in which christology is dependent on pneumatology. Both positions lend themselves to giving more prominence to the role of the Spirit, a prominence that is proper and appropriate.

However, another way of avoiding an improper subordination of the Spirit to the Son is to emphasize the distinction between the two missions. To this one adds the conviction of the equality of the Son and the Spirit, and the equality of each person's mission. At the same time, one recognizes in the *perichoresis* of equal persons—the inter-penetrating dance of the persons of the Son and the Spirit—the mutual interpenetrating of their missions, equal missions that remain unmixed and without confusion. This mutual penetration of equal persons and missions in no way subordinates the Spirit to the Son in an improper way. Not even a dominant soteriological christology is necessarily opposed to the mutual penetration of equal persons and missions.[12]

Behind Lossky's teaching on the special economy of the Spirit is the larger Orthodox emphasis on the "independent" mission of the Spirit flowing out of teaching that the Spirit eternally proceeds from the Father alone as from a principle. The Orthodox recognize that the Spirit comes from the Son, but not as from a principle, because they consider principle to mean ultimate origin. The Father is the single ultimate origin.[13]

"Pneumatological Christology as a Presupposition of Ecclesiology," *Oecumenica: Jahrbuch für ökumenische Forschung* 2 (1967) 235–51. Coffey, *Grace: The Gift of the Holy Spirit* (Manly, Australia: Catholic Institute of Sydney, 1979) 54–71.

[12] Molly T. Marshall, *Joining the Dance: A Theology of the Spirit* (Valley Forge, Pa.: Judson, 2003), develops the image of *perichoresis* in a fully trinitarian manner.

[13] Markos A. Orphanos, "The Procession of the Holy Spirit According to Certain Later Greek Fathers," and Dietrich Ritschl, "Historical Development and Implications of the Filioque Controversy," in *Spirit of God, Spirit of Christ: Ecumenical Reflections on the Filioque Controversy*, Lukas Vischer, ed. (London: SPCK, 1981) 21–45, 46–65.

The Mission of the Spirit: Junior Grade?

Perhaps one can get at the problem of the improper subordination of the Spirit to the Son by recognizing that the invisible missions of the Son and the Spirit in justification and grace are simultaneous. Basil seems to be pointing to the synchronous character of the two missions when he writes, "The Holy Spirit cannot be divided from the Father and the Son in worship. If you remain outside the Spirit, you cannot worship at all. . . . Light cannot be separated from what it makes visible, and it is impossible for you to recognize Christ, the Image of the invisible God, unless the Spirit enlightens you. Once you see the Image, you cannot ignore the Light; you see Light and Image simultaneously."[14]

The simultaneity of the two invisible missions entails that all christology is pneumatologically determined and all pneumatology is christologically determined: "The Spirit is never separated from him [Christ]." One could add, "Christ is never separated from the Spirit." The one is not just a duplicate of the other, because the modality of the relationship is determined by the dynamic of Christ being sent in the power of the Spirit, and in grace we go "in the Spirit through Christ to the Father." The one is no more the reverse of the other than the "How" (Spirit) of the gospel is the reverse of the "What" (Christ, the Son) of the gospel.[15]

The visible missions are viewed sequentially—the Son's visible mission in the incarnation is anterior to the Spirit's visible mission at Jesus' baptism and at Pentecost. In the West, the sequential character of the Spirit's visible mission has been interpreted as a second order mission. This is not said in explicit terms, but exposes itself in an attitude, in the way pneumatology is related to christology. In theological terms this means that one builds up the church, sacraments, and grace in constitutive christological terms in the first moment, and then adds the Spirit in a second, later, non-constitutive moment. In this perspective, the Spirit is tinsel added to an already existing

[14] *On the Holy Spirit* 26.64; SC 17bis.476.

[15] Ibid., 19.49; SC 17bis.418. The vocabulary of the Spirit as the "How" and the Son as the "What" has been borrowed from Nikos Nissiotis, "Pneumatological Christology." The "How" and the "What" should be used with discretion because the coming of the Spirit is also integral to the content of the gospel proclamation.

The Other Hand of God

tree. Here being second in a sequence results in giving the Spirit something of a junior status.

It is true that the "visible" mission of the Spirit at Pentecost is ordered to the visible mission of the Son in carrying out the work of redemption in the church. But the incarnation and Jesus' public ministry have a dependence on the Spirit and an inbuilt impulse toward Pentecost. The church is not the body of the Spirit, but the Spirit makes the eternal Son take on human nature, and the Spirit gives birth to the church at Pentecost. This takes nothing away from the Spirit's role of not speaking "on his own . . . he will take what is mine and declare it to you" (John 16:13–14).

For a truly biblical theology, both perspectives are necessary— christology dependent on pneumatology, and pneumatology dependent on christology. Because the West has espoused too one-sidedly a pneumatology dependent on christology, it has an excessively instrumental understanding of the visible and invisible missions of the Spirit. This instrumental understanding has been criticized in the East for its imbalance. Though the West would want to retain the instrumental understanding, one must grant that the East's critique has a point. The instrumental understanding, poorly constructed or presented, can lead to distortion, namely, the mission of the Spirit is subordinated to that of the Son in an improper way. Then the mission of the Spirit becomes a junior grade mission of a junior grade person.

Instrumentality improperly understood can turn the Spirit into a person outside of and beyond the mystery the Spirit makes present, that is, the Spirit is not operative within the mission of the Son but makes sorties into history. When correctly interpreted, however, the Spirit's mission is at the interior of the Son's mission. Even when the Spirit acts "instrumentally," the Spirit acts from the inside, and its instrumentality is interior.

In addition to making the Spirit stand after and exterior to the mystery of the Son, the instrumentality of the "How" of the gospel can be presented as less substantive and less important than the "What" of the gospel. Jesus Christ is the material center of the gospel, but this undisputed fact can lead to a kind of christomonism in theology and preaching that squeezes out the Spirit moment of the economy. The remedy is not more books on the Holy Spirit or

The Mission of the Spirit: Junior Grade?

more sermons dedicated specifically to the Spirit or equal time given to the Spirit in theology and preaching. Rather, the remedy is the recognition that the "How" of the Spirit is as important as the "What" of the Son, that both are central in different modalities, even while the Son remains the material center of the proclamation. The correction is in the recognition of the perichoretic character of the two missions of the Son and the Spirit (the one present and active at the interior of the other), which means that the Spirit's role, including its implicit trinitarian dynamic, is more clearly integrated into theology and proclamation. This does not rule out a certain proper subordination of the Spirit to the Son, as the Son is subordinate to the Father, though it is not ontological subordination.

And finally, the Spirit as the "How" of the gospel should be evident when preaching on the "What" of the gospel. The "How" of the Spirit also belongs in some way to the material content of proclamation, namely, to the "What" of the Son. In short, the descent of the Spirit on Mary (Matt 1:20; Luke 1:35) and the descent of the Spirit on the Apostles and Mary at Pentecost (Acts 2:1-4) also belong to the material center of the gospel.

If beginnings contain the future, then the new understanding of God, beginning with the experience of the Son and the Spirit as sent by the Father, means that one of the tasks of theology is to re-appropriate the original experience so we can understand and judge how the church has been faithful to it. The whole of Christian theology should be a thematizing of that experience. This re-appropriation will mean recapturing the pneumatological moment in its christological context, the baptism of Jesus in the Jordan, the role of the Spirit in the ministry of Jesus, the surrender of the Spirit on the cross, the Spirit as a resurrecting power (together with the Father), and the Spirit descending on the early Christian community as sent by the Risen Christ. But the experience, personal and ecclesial, cannot be appropriated only conceptually or in dogmatic formulas. We need to go beyond words, categories, and dogmas. "Without our experience of Father, Son, and Spirit in salvation history, we would ultimately be unable to conceive at all of their subsisting distinctly as one God."[16]

[16] Karl Rahner, *The Trinity* (New York: Seabury, 1974) 110–11.

Chapter 10

God Beyond the Self of God

Contemporary writers often use a rhetoric of "reality" when speaking of the Spirit. Karl Barth can say that the Spirit is "*actus purus,* pure reality . . . what is intangible and impossible, unknown and unknowable, becomes concrete and possible, known and observable." For Alexander Schmemann the Spirit is "*Reality* itself in which all that exists finds its fulfillment." Wolfhart Pannenberg calls the Spirit "the present reality of God." For Sergius Bulgakov, the Spirit "is the principle of reality."[1] In these pages this rhetoric of "reality" is manifested by speaking of the contact function of the Spirit. The Father sends the Son in the Spirit to touch and transform the world and church, leading them in the Spirit, through the Son/Christ to the Father.

Biblical confessions of the names do not yet express the full trinitarian confession of three distinct persons as in the fourth century. For instance, in Paul *to hagion pneuma,* the holy Spirit, is not yet a personal being distinct from the Father and the Son. Paul may personify the Spirit, that is, he may personify the Old Testament understanding of the spirit, but this is not yet conceiving of the Spirit as a person. For Paul the Spirit is the dynamic presence of God in the justified Christian.[2] In the Johannine writings there is a stronger

[1] Barth, *The Epistle to the Romans* (Oxford: University Press, 1933) 274. Schmemann, *Of Water and the Spirit* (London: SPCK, 1974) 108. Pannenberg, *The Apostle's Creed* (Philadelphia: Westminster, 1972) 140. Bulgakov, *Le Paraclet,* 58, quoted in Martien Parmentier, "Saint Gregory of Nyssa's Doctrine of the Holy Spirit," *Ekklesiastikos Pharos* 59 (1977) 424.

[2] Joseph Fitzmyer, *Romans* (New York: Doubleday, 1993) 480.

move toward personification, but here too we are still a long way from the fourth century.

In biblical times confessions differed considerably; some were one-membered ("Jesus is Lord," 1 Cor 12:3), others two-membered (God and Christ as in 1 Tim 6:13), and still others three-membered (Father, Son, and Holy Spirit, as in Matt 28:19), and they flourished side by side as expressions of one kerygma.[3] There was considerable freedom, as seen in the biblical order of the names in the three-membered texts:

God–Holy Spirit–Son/Christ (Gal 4:6; Mark 1:9-11; Matt 1:18-25; Luke 1:26-38; 4:1, 14-19; John 3:34).

Jesus/Christ–God–Holy Spirit (2 Cor 13:13; Acts 2:32-33). Spirit–Christ–God (1 Cor 12:4-6; Eph 4:4-7).

God–Son/Christ–Holy Spirit (1 Cor 12:4-6; 2 Cor 1:21-22; Rom 8:3-17; Eph 1:3-14; 2:4-5, 18-22; 4:4-7; Acts 5:32; 15:7-11).[4]

The synoptic pattern is clearly God–Holy Spirit–Son/Christ. In addition there are the "to the Father" texts in Paul and John: "Do everything in the name of the Lord Jesus, giving thanks to God the Father through him" (Col 3:17; cf. Rom 1:8-10; 5:9-11; 7:25; 8:34; 1 Cor 15:24; 2 Cor 1:20; Heb 7:25; Gal 4:4-7; Eph 1:3-14; Col 1:3; 3:17; John 20:17; 1 John 2:1). The biblical tradition, especially the liturgy, has seen in Father–Holy Spirit–Son/Christ (the entire scheme would add the return, that is, Spirit–Father) a dominant, though not an exclusive, pattern of the way God relates to humankind: From the Father through the Son in the Holy Spirit, and the return in the Spirit through Christ back to the Father. This is not a mere numbering, but an indication of a rhythm of trinitarian life as it reaches out in history. It is the triune quest for communion so we can share in the dynamic of that life.[5]

[3] Kelly, *Creeds*, 24.
[4] The patterns are open to some debate, for instance John 3:34, depending on the exegesis of the text.
[5] Cyprian Vagaggini, *Theological Dimensions of the Liturgy* (Collegeville: The Liturgical Press, 1976) 198–202. David Coffey, "From the Biblical to the Immanent Trinity," in his *Deus Trinitas: The Doctrine of the Triune God* (New York: Oxford University Press, 1999) 33–45, discusses the patterns.

The synoptic pattern is incorporated into some aspects of Syrian liturgical practice, is dear to Orthodox theology, and represents a christology dependent on pneumatology. Orthodox theologians could argue that the reason they give preference to the Father–Holy Spirit–Son model is that they want to say the Spirit is present not only in the incarnation but also in the whole mission of Christ. One reason for this, though not the only one, might be to counteract a Western pneumatology that takes its point of departure too exclusively from Pentecost and can compromise the range of the Spirit.

Looking at how the Eastern tradition relates to this pattern, one notices that the Spirit serves the same contact function. The Spirit effects the incarnation of Christ, anoints Jesus at the Jordan, and is the power of his ministry. In Christian baptism it is the Spirit who joins believers to the mystery of Christ and makes believers sons and daughters of God. The function of the Spirit is the same in both the God–Son/Christ–Holy Spirit model and in the God–Holy Spirit–Son/Christ model, though the configuration and emphases are different. What is of interest is not the specific order of names but what the model says about the function of the Spirit (as well as of the Father and the Son). Function, not order *(taxis)*, is the control.

Exegetically, the God–Spirit–Son/Christ model of Galatians 4:6 seems to be saying this: God has sent the Spirit, which is verified in the Galatians' experience (3:2-5), and *therefore* they are children of God. Likewise Romans 8:15-16, a parallel passage, does not suppose the gift of being children of God is prior to the gift of the Spirit. The very gift of the Spirit makes them God's sons and daughters.[6]

In 1 Corinthians 12:4-6 Paul is dealing with the underlying unity in diversity of the charisms, progressing from the charisms of the Spirit to the service of Christ to the ultimate origin and creative force, God. In Ephesians 4:4-6, where the issue is again unity of spirit, the pattern is Spirit, Christ, God, with the author suggesting that he is proceeding from "body–Spirit–hope" to "Lord–faith–baptism" and finally "God and Father of all," an unfolding triad.

---

[6] Hans-Dieter Betz, *Galatians* (Philadelphia: Fortress, 1979) 210. Acts 15:7-11 ascribes instrumentality to the Spirit, namely, "by giving them (the Gentiles) the Holy Spirit" (a reference back to 10:44, the Cornelius account) God has demonstrated his will. Luke Timothy Johnson, *The Acts of the Apostles* (Collegeville: The Liturgical Press, 1992) 262. Fitzmyer, *Romans*, 498.

God Beyond the Self of God

The church's journey of hope to God begins in the Spirit, passes through faith in the Lord manifested in baptism, to God as the goal. This is possibly the logic of experience, proceeding from the experience of the Spirit.[7]

THE DOUBLE MOVEMENT FROM
THE FATHER TO THE FATHER

The post-biblical period was quick to pick up the God–Son/Christ–Spirit pattern. Irenaeus in the second century writes, "The baptism of our rebirth comes through these three articles, granting us rebirth unto God the Father, through His Son, by the Holy Spirit. For those who are bearers of the Spirit of God are led to the Word, that is, to the Son; but the Son takes them and presents them to the Father; and the Father confers incorruptibility. So without the Spirit there is no seeing the Word of God, and without the Son there is no approaching the Father; for the Son is the knowledge of the Father, and knowledge of the Son is through the Holy Spirit."[8] For Irenaeus this is a matter of order and rhythm of successive stages on the progressive journey toward God for those being saved.

Irenaeus sees a double movement, out or down from God: Father–Son–Spirit; and back or up to God: Spirit–Son–Father. Though this pattern in Irenaeus should not be exaggerated, it does constitute the key to his theology. Irenaeus does not present fully developed trinitarian thought, but already he is well aware that this double movement does not mean a strict and exclusive temporal periodization.[9]

The Father is the origin of the downward (outward) movement and the goal of the ascending (returning) movement. Creation and the church are the intermediate goal of the outward movement,

[7] Markus Barth, *Ephesians*, 2 vols. (Garden City: Doubleday, 1974) 2.463. R. R. Williams, "Logic versus Experience in the Order of Credal Formulae," *New Testament Studies* 1 (1954) 44, suggests, without demonstration, that Spirit, Christ, God is the original order, with the more metaphysical order of God, Christ/Son, Spirit deriving "its power from a previous experiential contact with the realities it tries to explain." Though attractive, the thesis is not compelling.

[8] *Demonstration of the Apostolic Preaching* 7; SC 406.92.

[9] Basil Studer, *Trinity and Incarnation* (Collegeville: The Liturgical Press, 1993) 60. Hans-Jochen Jaschke, *Der Heilige Geist im Bekenntnis der Kirche* (Münster: Aschendorff, 1976) 330.

achieved in the Spirit. The Father is the point of departure and ultimate goal of the two movements. The Spirit is both the point of contact with the world and the church on the downward movement and the turning around point on the journey back from world and church to the Father.[10] The primary earthly locus of this movement is baptism and the church, in which believers are touched and transformed by the Spirit, and made bearers of the prophetic Spirit who leads to the Son, bringing them to the Father.

For Origen in the third century, those the Father creates for eternal life are moving toward purity, the Son instructing them, but the process is brought to perfection by the Holy Spirit, "through whom alone they can receive God." By the reception of the Spirit one can have communion *(koinonia)* in the Son and the Father. Origen also uses the Son–Spirit–Father model, where salvation leads from the objective revelation of the Son, through the subjective appropriation in the Spirit—the point of touching, the contact of immediacy—to a life made perfect in the Father.[11]

The pattern of a two-fold movement appears clearly in Basil in the fourth century: "The way of divine knowledge ascends from one Spirit through the one Son to the one Father. Likewise, in the opposite direction, natural goodness, the holiness of nature and the royal dignity flow from the Father, through the Only-Begotten to the Spirit." Basing himself first on 1 Corinthians 13:13 and then possibly on Athanasius, Basil speaks of the way of knowledge, ascending not only by way of the Spirit but in the divine Spirit: "[The Holy Spirit] gives true knowledge of God in God's self," but it is a knowledge gained by walking the trinitarian road through the Son to the Father. "One cannot see the Father without the Spirit."[12]

[10] Ibid., 165–66.

[11] Origen, *On First Principles* 1.3.8; SC 252.164. Hans Urs von Balthasar, *Origen: Spirit and Fire* (Washington, D.C.: Catholic University, 1984) 14.

[12] *On the Holy Spirit* 18.45, 47; SC 17bis.412; 16.38; SC 17bis.382. Basil, *Letters* 226.3, in *Saint Basile: Lettres*, Yves Courtonne, ed.; 3 vols. (Paris: Société d'Édition 'Les Belles Lettres,' 1966) 3.27: "Our Spirit *(nous)* illumined by the Holy Spirit, looks to the Son, and in him, as in an image, contemplates the Father." Commenting on 1 Corinthians 13:13, Athanasius, *Letters to Serapion* 1.30; SC 15.38–39, says, "For this grace and gift given is bestowed in the Triad, from the Father, through the Son, in the Holy Spirit. As the grace given is from the Father through the Son, so we can have no communion in the gift except in the Holy Spirit. For it

Ephrem knew only a few Greek words, living as he did when Syriac Christianity was still in its purely Semitic phase.[13] In Ephrem one can see how the Syrians perceive the Spirit as the universal touch of God, the all-embracing divine efficacy in matters pertaining to salvation, using mostly, but not exclusively, the God–Spirit–Son/Christ model. The Spirit was present in the prophets before the incarnation, and afterwards, especially in the mystery of Christ:

Fire and Spirit are in the womb of her who bore You.
Fire and Spirit are in the river in which You were baptized.
Fire and Spirit are in our baptism,
and in the Bread and Cup is Fire and the Holy Spirit.[14]

The pneumatological roots of christology in the Syrian tradition, especially in the texts relating to the annunciation, the baptism of Jesus, and Pentecost, demonstrate how the mystery of the Spirit played a primary role in defining the mystery of Christ, especially with regard to the baptism of Jesus. We have Tatian's Diatessaron preserved in Ephrem's commentary, where the Spirit not only remains upon Jesus but rests upon him, following the account of the baptism in Mark 1:10.[15] Here the translation seems to have been influenced by the "rest" which Jesus promises ("Come to me . . . and I will give you rest" [Matt 11:28-29]).

Gabriele Winkler has shown that in the Syrian tradition the "rest" is the Spirit resting on Jesus at his baptism. This resting is the mutual knowledge of the Father and the Son, and is believers' participation in the inner divine knowledge between the Father and the Son. The Spirit, sent by the Father, rests on the Son. The broader framework is God's establishing Jesus' identity through the Spirit

is when we partake of him that we have the love of the Father and the grace of the Son and the communion of the Spirit himself."

[13] On the Semitic phase see Sebastian Brock, *The Holy Spirit in the Syrian Baptismal Tradition* (Kerala [India]: no publisher given, 1979) 2.

[14] *Hymns on Faith* 10.17; CSCO 155.35, 36.

[15] *Commentary on the Concordant Gospel or Diatessaron* 4.1.3; SC 121.94. See also 3.15 and 1.31; SC 121.90, 63.

The Other Hand of God

and resting upon him at the Jordan, as the Spirit rested on the waters of chaos in Genesis. The mother Spirit, which brings forth all life in the beginning, rests on Jesus at the Jordan, whereby Jesus becomes the Spirit-filled Son. Winkler claims that the christology in the earliest tradition is Spirit christology, "the Logos christology being entirely absent." This Syrian pneumatology is in large part a synoptic view: Father–Spirit–Son, though the Syrians were well acquainted also with the dynamic of Father–Son–Spirit.[16]

[16] "Ein bedeutsamer Zusammenhang zwischen der Erkenntnis und Ruhe in Matt 11, 27–29 und dem Ruhen des Geistes auf Jesus am Jordan. Eine Analyse zur Geist-Christologie in syrischen und armenischen Quellen," *Muséon* 96 (1983) 279, 315, 325. Winfrid Cramer, *Der Geist Gottes und des Menschen in frühsyrischer Theologie* (Münster: Aschendorff, 1979) 28–29, 33, 35, 71–73.

Chapter 11

The Return: The Highway Back to the Father

The synoptic view of the Spirit, which found a home in Syrian pneumatology, is also represented in Basil. In *On the Holy Spirit* Basil maintains this same order: "The road of the knowledge of God proceeds from the Spirit, who is one, by the Son, who is one, even to the Father, who is one." This way of knowing must be inverted in order to attain holiness: "The natural goodness, the holiness of nature and the royal dignity flows from the Father, through the Only-Begotten, even to the Spirit."[1]

What Basil in the East was saying about the Spirit as the point of departure for the return, Marius Victorinus was saying in the West. Like Augustine, he was a native of Africa, but made a living in Rome as a rhetor and vigorous proponent of paganism. Augustine reports that Victorinus defended Roman paganism "with the thunder of his eloquence." As an old man he converted to Christianity, causing a sensation in mid-fourth-century Rome. He promptly became an ardent defender of his newfound faith as he had formerly defended Roman paganism. Victorinus, who knew Platonic philosophy better than he knew Christian theology and became the leader of a spiritual movement of Platonic Christianity that gained full strength between 380 and 415, was the first Latin author to write a metaphysical treatise on the Trinity.[2]

[1] *On the Holy Spirit* 18.47; SC 17bis.412.
[2] Augustine, *Confessions* 8.2.3; CCSL 27.115. Mary Clark, "Introduction," *Marius Victorinus: Theological Treatises on the Trinity* (Washington, D.C.: Catholic University, 1981) 1–10. See also Peter Brown, *Augustine of Hippo: A Biography* (Berkeley: University of California, 1967) 92, 103, 151.

Well before the Council of Constantinople (381), and even before Basil, Victorinus recognized the full divinity and consubstantiality of the Holy Spirit, but like others before him, he failed to make a distinction between the Son and the Spirit. In pneumatology his was an original voice, conceiving of the Spirit as "the voice of the voice." The Spirit is the substance of all three persons, though there is a difference he does not explain. There is "a double potentiality of the Logos in reference to God, one revealed *(in manifesto)*, that is, Christ in the flesh, the other secret *(in occulto)*, the Holy Spirit. . . . So all Three are One: The Father silence which is not silent, but a voice in silence; the Son, next, the voice; the Paraclete, the voice of the voice."[3] The Spirit as the trinitarian "Voice of the Voice" is an attractive contemplative approach.

Victorinus conceives the Trinity as a double circular movement. In the "first movement of life," the Son goes forth from the Father and, circling back, advances toward the Father. The Spirit is the connecting bond *(copula)* between Father and Son, one of the few notions Augustine took in part from Victorinus. In the second circle of life, the Son descends from the Father to create the world, and the world is led back to the Father by the Spirit.[4] The Spirit is the third, who, as the one who links Father and Son, not only is the point of contact with creation but is named *regressus* (return). If the Spirit is the point of contact between the first movement and the second (and therefore with the redeemed world), the Spirit is also the turning around point on the way back to the Father.

Victorinus is using a vocabulary common to both East and West when he writes, "The Holy Spirit is consummation, perfection, and full liberation." The movement is from repose (Father) to progression (Son) to return (Holy Spirit), namely, *status, progressio, regressus*. The Father and the Son dialogue with the world through the Spirit. The Spirit constitutes the intersection between these two contiguous circles: (1) the Father and Son, and (2) Son/Christ and world. Unless the Spirit unites Father and Son, the Spirit cannot be the point of contact with all redeemed humanity, uniting it, and, as the return,

---

[3] "*Paraclitus vox vocis*," in *Against Arius* 1.13; CSEL 83/1.72. R.P.C. Hanson, *The Search for the Christian Doctrine of God* (Edinburgh: T. & T. Clark, 1988) 551.

[4] *Against Arius* 1.60, 4.7; CSEL 83/1.160, 233–35. "*Adesto, sancte spiritus, patris et filii copula*," *Hymn* 1.4; CSEL 83/1.285.

bringing it back to the Father, thus completing the trinitarian cycle of life. The circular movement has its beginning and ending in the Father, "from the Father to the Father."[5]

Cyril of Alexandria also represents this rhythm from the Father to the Father. "Our return *(epanalepsis)* to the Father is effected through Christ our savior only by means of the participation *(koinonia)* and sanctification of the Spirit. The Spirit it is who elevates us to the Son and so unites us to God. When we receive the Spirit we become sharers and partakers *(koinonia)* of the divine nature. But we receive the Spirit through the Son, and in the Son we receive the Father."[6] The point of entry into this rhythm of life is clearly the Holy Spirit; without the Spirit there is no supernatural elevation (as the Latins put it), no divinization (as the Greeks and Syrians put it), no participation in that movement from the Father through the Son and back to the Father. The movement from Spirit to Son is "a return" to the Father because the Father was the point of departure.

THE RETURN: NOT SIMPLY A REVERSAL OF THE WAY FROM THE FATHER

The truth that Basil, Marius Victorinus, and Cyril of Alexandria propose, when taken too simplistically, poses a threat to trinitarian understanding. Karl Rahner's epigram that we noted in Chapter 1—

---

[5] *On Ephesians* 1.13; CSEL 83/2.19. *Hymn* 3.72–74, 243–45; CSEL 83/1.297, 303. "*Erecta motio cyclica . . . hoc est a patre in patrem*," in *Against Arius* 1.61; CSEL 83/1.161.

[6] *Commentary on John* 11.10, in *Sancti Patris Nostri Cyrilli Archiepiscopi Alexandrini Opera*, Philip E. Pusey, ed.; 7 vols. (1868; Brussels: Culture et Civilisation, 1965), *In D. Joannis Evangelium* 2.722. Gerard Philips, in a review of Paul Galtier's *Le Saint Esprit en nous d'après les pères grecs* (Rome: Gregorian University, 1946) appearing in *Ephemerides Theologicae Lovaniensis* 24 (1948) 133, says that for the Greek Fathers the Spirit is the point of contact. Matthias Scheeben, *The Mysteries of Christianity* (St. Louis: Herder, 1947) 179, discerns a return movement to the Father which is the inversion of the eternal processional movement within God (Son and Spirit proceeding from the Father) and the temporal missions from the Father toward us (according to incarnation and Pentecost). In the inversion, the Holy Spirit, outpoured upon us, dwelling among us, elevates and divinizes us in our union with the Son, and through the Son with the Father. Because the Spirit joins us to the Son, his Father becomes our Father. The Father is the terminus because the temporal missions of the Son and the Spirit end where they began.

"The 'economic' Trinity is the 'immanent' Trinity and the 'immanent' Trinity is the 'economic' Trinity"—closes the gap between God in God's self and God as manifested in history. What is revealed, in fact given, in the coming of the Son and the Holy Spirit in the Paschal mysteries (including resurrection, Pentecost, and Ascension) is nothing else than the reality of God's self as it existed from all eternity. God as expressing the proper divine reality in history does not lie or deceive.[7]

Yves Congar basically agrees with Rahner, but wants to limit the absolute character of his dictum. "Even if God's creatures did not exist, God would still be Trinity." Congar rightly insists that the self-communication of God in history takes place in condescendence, humiliation, self-emptying, and the cross. There is distance between God in God's self and God as revealing and communicating the divine reality in history. God revealed in history does not exhaust the reality of the eternal God. So the way from us to God cannot be a simple reflection of the way from God to us.[8] Nor can it be a simple reversal. Though a two-way street, the way to God is not just an inversion of the way God traveled to us.

David Coffey accepts the order of the reversal (from God–Son/Christ–Spirit to Spirit–Son/Christ–God), noting that the reversal is the order in Galatians 4:6 and Ephesians 2:18. But he does not accept the traditional reasons given in support. In his own words, "a wrong reason is provided for the right answer."[9]

The return cannot be a simple reversal because the processional model (Father–Son/Christ–Spirit) coming to us is *ad extra*, the order of revelation, while the return to the Father is *ab intra*, the order of interior transformation or conformity to divine life. Though the return involves the same persons in reverse order, it is on an entirely different track, so it cannot be a simple reversal. Why? One reason has already been noted, namely, that the processional model is only revelatory (tells us who the triune God is), not transformative (conforming us to the life of God and effecting union),

[7] *The Trinity* (New York: Seabury, 1974) 22.
[8] *I Believe in the Holy Spirit* (New York: Seabury, 1983) 3.11–17. See also John Zizioulas, "The Teaching of the 2nd Ecumenical Council on the Holy Spirit in Historical and Ecumenical Relations," *CSS* 1.50–53.
[9] "A Proper Mission of the Holy Spirit," *Theological Studies* 47 (1986) 230.

while the return model is both revelatory and transformative. The processional model provides no proper explanation of how the Holy Spirit unites us to the Father, but the return model does offer clarification on the role of the Spirit in both incarnation and transformative grace. So the return model is comprehensive, while the processional is partial. Further, the return carries with it the mystery and history of Jesus' death, resurrection, and Pentecost, not contained in the processional model.[10]

IN THE CIRCULAR MOVEMENT OF REDEMPTION

Besides the descending and ascending model, and the inversion or reverse model, there is also a circular, revolving movement of redemption, which in its variations closely resembles the descending and ascending movement. The Spirit in the circular movement of redemption is the point at which church and world are caught up into trinitarian life.

Ingo Hermann and Wilhelm Thüsing both detect in Paul the circular movement from God to humankind, and likewise the return from humankind to God, as primarily a pneumatological dynamic (which does not exclude a kind of christological concentration). The Spirit crying "Abba! Father!" is specifically the Spirit of Christ. The Spirit orders Christ to the Father, a conviction implicit in the movement of the Spirit from the Father and to the Father, a movement characteristic of Paul. Thüsing concludes that the Spirit coming from God effects openness to God and joins to God.[11]

Hermann contends it is first in the Spirit that the revolving trinitarian life is evident. This circle of life takes the Father as its point of departure, passes through the *Kyrios,* and reaches humanity in the Spirit. Having attained this intermediate goal, then, by the Spirit-prompted cry of those who are children of God in the Son, namely,

---

[10] David Coffey, *Grace: The Gift of the Holy Spirit* (Manly, Australia: Catholic Institute of Sydney, 1979) 114; "A Proper Mission," 234; *Deus Trinitas: The Doctrine of the Triune God* (New York: Oxford University Press, 1999) 35–45; "The Holy Spirit as the Mutual Love of the Father and the Son," *Theological Studies* 51 (1990) 193–229.

[11] Hermann, *Kyrios und Pneuma* (Munich: Kösel, 1961) 98. Thüsing, *Per Christum in Deum: Studien zum Verhältnis von Christozentrik und Theozentrik in den paulinischen Hauptbriefen*, 2nd ed. (Munster: Aschendorff, 1968) 119, 155–59.

"Abba!" the circle returns to the Father. Only because the *Kyrios* possesses the Spirit can the Lord touch the interior spirit of redeemed humanity; only in the Spirit does the sovereignty and reign of the *Kyrios* become reality on the way to being handed over to the Father (1 Cor 15:24, 28). The Spirit is the miraculous divine power standing in absolute contrast to all that is human. This Spirit of the Father (Rom 8:9, 11), the manifestation of the Father's life-giving power and glory (Rom 6:4; 2 Cor 13:4), is the means by which the Father raises up Christ, makes Jesus "Lord" and "life-giving spirit" (1 Cor 15:45; cf. Rom 1:4). In this dynamic the Spirit is both the means of communication between redeemed humanity and the Lord (Gal 4:6), and, as the power of God, the medium of encounter between believers and the Father (Rom 5:5; Gal 5:5).[12]

MEDIATION AND HORIZON

By theological temperament Origen, the first theologian to thematize the Spirit, is Logos centered, even Logos dominated, so the Spirit does not come to full expression in *On First Principles* despite Origen's orthodoxy and admirable trinitarianism. He sees the Spirit as a dynamic creative force in the saints, binding God and humankind, joining those worthy to the transcendent God. The Spirit is decisively an expression of the divine operating in history as the mediation (not the mediator) between God and humankind. This view is also reflected in modern authors.[13]

---

[12] Rudolf Bultmann, *Theology of the New Testament*, 2 vols. (New York: Scribner, 1951) 2.153. Joseph Fitzmyer, "To Know Him and the Power of his Resurrection," in his *To Advance the Gospel: New Testament Studies* (New York: Crossroad, 1981) 202–13. Here I am following Fitzmyer, who clearly sees the Spirit as raising up Jesus, instead of James D. G. Dunn, *Christology in the Making: A New Testament Inquiry into the Origins of the Doctrine of the Incarnation* (Philadelphia: Westminster, 1980) 144, who thinks Paul tends, but hesitates, to make the Spirit the resurrecting force in the case of Jesus. Brendan Byrne, *Romans* (Collegeville: The Liturgical Press, 1996) 196, believes it possible that "glory" *(doxa)* of Romans 6:4 means the glory attendant on Christ's resurrection, or the likeness into which he rose. Hermann, *Kyrios und Pneuma*, 97–98, 111–13.

[13] Kilian McDonnell, "Does Origen Have a Trinitarian Doctrine of the Holy Spirit?" *Gregorianum* 75, 1 (1994). Wolf-Dieter Hauschild, *Gottes Geist und der Mensch: Studien zur frühchristlichen Pneumatologie* (Munich: Kaiser, 1972) 146–49. Otto Kuss, *Der Römerbrief* (Regensburg: Pustet, 1963–78) 593: "The

Though he thinks that Origen's doctrine of the Spirit "is not entirely healthy," Basil, too, works out of a similar conception. God turns toward humanity in the Spirit in order to give redeemed creation a participation in the holiness of God. Though the Spirit stands between humankind and God, when the line is drawn between the two the Spirit is always on the divine side. Basil, like Origen, conceives of the Spirit as the all-embracing mediation (not mediator) between God and humankind. A double movement typifies the Spirit: The divine movement toward the fully transcendent God and the sanctifying movement toward us. But the sanctifying movement toward us is deceptive. The movement toward us is Father–Son–Holy Spirit. Basil does not want the Spirit separated from the Father and the Son. He is concerned to maintain the deepest union between baptism, creed, and doxology. Because we celebrate a trinitarian baptism we confess a trinitarian faith, which determines the form of the doxology.[14]

For Basil and for the Cappadocians as a whole, it is within the context of the mediation that is the Spirit that we experience God. As R.P.C. Hanson says about the Cappadocians, "it would be in any circumstances mistaken to image that we could experience the Persons of the Trinity separately: this would inevitably result in a lapse into blatant tritheism (three gods). We experience God in God the Holy Spirit; indeed we experience God as God the Holy Spirit."[15] The reason why the Cappadocians can hold such a position is because the Spirit is that all embracing mediation, the universal horizon, the point of contact where the initiative of the Finger of God (Luke 11:20) from above touches our response from below.

Though Basil is concerned with the question of rank, lest the Arians grasp the formulation to make the Son and the Spirit

Spirit dominates the whole room between God and humanity." Walter Kasper, *Jesus the Christ* (New York: Paulist, 1976) 250: "The Spirit as mediation between Father and Son is at the same time the mediation of God into history."

[14] *On the Holy Spirit* 29.73; SC 17bis.506; 10.26; SC 17bis.338.3. Pia Luislampe, *Spiritus vivificans. Grundzüge einer Theologie des Heiligen Geistes nach Basilius von Caesarea* (Münster: Aschendorff, 1981) 169–70. J. M. Hornus, "La divinité du Saint-Esprit comme condition du salut personnel selon Basile," *Verbum Caro* 23 (1969) 37–38.

[15] "The Transformation of Images in the Trinitarian Theology of the Fourth Century," *Studia Patristica* 17/1 (1982) 112.

The Return: The Highway Back to the Father

ontologically inferior to the Father, he turns away from asking questions about the nature of the Spirit. This may be one reason he is reluctant to apply *homoousios* (of one substance) to the Spirit, preferring to speak of the oneness of the divinity by using communion language *(koinonia)*. We cannot know the nature of the Spirit; we only know the Spirit from the Spirit's works: "From the works comes knowledge, and from knowledge comes adoration."[16] The move is from experience of the Spirit to the Son to the Father. And one does not ask impertinent questions, does not pry.

GREGORY OF NYSSA: THE REVOLVING CIRCLE OF GLORY

One of Gregory of Nyssa's models of the Trinity is "the revolving circle of glory from like to like."[17] He is concerned to establish the equality of the three persons in this forceful circular movement that is continuous, indeed, eternal. This intra-trinitarian stream of glory begins from the Father, moves through the Son, in the Spirit, in whom it returns through the Son, and back to the Father, a movement from like (Father) through like (Son) in like (Spirit). The Spirit is the point in this circular movement where contact is made with humanity. The Spirit unites believers among themselves and with God in a way analogous to the way in which the Spirit unites the Father and the Son in the circle of glory. The Spirit can do this because the Spirit not only possesses glory but is glory.

The glory operates at three levels: (1) within the Trinity itself; (2) between God and humanity; and (3) within humanity itself. Within the Trinity: "The power of glory could never be displayed by one who was not glory, and honor, and majesty, and greatness. Now the Spirit does glorify the Father and the Son. . . . You see the revolving circle of the glory moving from Like to Like. The Son is glorified by the Spirit; the Father is glorified by the Son; again the Son has his glory from the Father." Between God and humanity in the Son: "The Only-begotten thus becomes the glory of the

---

[16] Zizioulas, "Teaching of the 2nd Ecumenical Council," 1.34. Basil, *Letter* 234.3, in *Lettres*, Yves Courtonne, ed., 3 vols. (Paris: Société d'Édition "Les Belles Lettres," 1957–1966) 3.43.

[17] *Against the Macedonians*, 22, in *Opera*, Werner Jaeger, ed. (Leiden: Brill, 1952–) 3/1.109.

Spirit"—an explicit expression of the glory operating between God and humanity in the Spirit. But other human beings have communion in this revolving circle of glory, and their point of entrance is the Spirit. Within humanity itself: "In no other way could they who are separated be united, unless they are joined together in the unity of the Spirit."[18]

Because the Spirit has glory and is glory, the Spirit can operate at all three levels. If the Spirit were not equal to the Father and Son, did not fully share in the divine glory, the Spirit would not unify the Father and the Son, and there would be no Trinity. Humankind could have no communion in God, and humans would be like a pile of rocks, having no interior relation to one another, no communion among themselves.[19]

[18] Ibid. *In That "When"* (Homily) PG 44.1320d.
[19] Martien Parmentier, "St. Gregory of Nyssa's Doctrine of the Holy Spirit," *Ekklesiastikos Pharos* 58 (1976) 423.

Chapter 12

The Spirit Is the Touch of God

In Chapter 9 we noted John Zizioulas's detection of two patterns in the biblical witness: pneumatology conditioned by christology, and christology conditioned by pneumatology. Zizioulas maintains that the former is tied to the mission of the church in the New Testament. The Spirit is given so that the church, previously constituted, can carry on its mission. In particular, Acts portrays the miraculous expansion of the church as a manifestation of the Spirit in history, a community on pilgrimage in the direction of the kingdom. The Spirit is obedient to Christ, and because the Spirit is sent by Christ, the Spirit constitutes the church as the body of Christ. The head of the body, Christ, precedes the church and leads the church (Acts 3:15; 5:31; Heb 2:10; 12:2).

The controlling idea of this type of ecclesiology is obedience to Christ. The obedience of the body (church) to the head (Christ) mandates a certain distance between the two. The view of the church in which the Spirit follows Christ is conducive to the kind of linear salvation history associated with the name of Oscar Cullmann. Because the Spirit is given by Christ, the Spirit appears to be an agent of Christ. In this perspective, christology is the source of pneumatology.

Parallel to the pneumatology conditioned by christology is a christology conditioned by pneumatology. Here the Spirit is not tied only to the mission and expansion of the church, but also to its eschatological nature (Acts 2:17; Rom 8:11, 23; 1 Cor 15:44, 45; 2 Cor 1:22; Eph 1:14). Instead of placing the emphasis on the risen Christ imparting the Spirit, the Spirit constitutes the identity of

Jesus from his conception through his baptism all the way to his resurrection. Zizioulas maintains that the New Testament synthesizes both types, sometimes in the same text, as in Luke/Acts, and that abandonment of the synthesis has had dire consequences. "In my opinion in the course of history the two types diverged in such a manner that a real fissure manifested itself at the base of the church. The greater part of the theological differences between the East and the West, if not all of them, are tied to this problem. Our ecumenical problems cannot be properly examined without a profound awareness of their roots in this divergence at the level of pneumatology."[1]

What is striking for our present purposes is what I call the touching, contacting function of the Spirit in both types. In christology conditioned by pneumatology, the risen Christ sends the Pentecostal Spirit upon the apostles to give birth to the church, leading it through salvation history to the eschatological consummation. The Spirit is the "Spirit of Christ," and is both the agent of Christ and the abiding presence of the risen Christ in his church.

But the contact function is even clearer in the second type, pneumatology conditioned by christology. It is the Spirit who constitutes the identity of Jesus in his birth (Matt 1:20; Luke 1:35), and the synoptics proclaim this identity in terms of the Spirit at the baptism (Matt 2:13-17; Mark 1:9-11; Luke 3:21, 22). It is the Spirit who drives Jesus into the desert to be tempted (Luke 4:1); in the power of the Spirit Jesus returns to Galilee. The Spirit goes before. John testifies first to a revelation and then to a theophany, namely, he saw the Spirit descending and remaining on Jesus. The Baptist who declares that he previously did not know him (John 1:31) now proclaims, "And I myself have seen and have testified that this is the Son of God" (John 1:34). The Spirit precedes Jesus.

In some fluid way there is a habit of mind that returns to a "touch function" or a "contact function" in these models, irrespective of the order of the names. I use contact and touch with some hesitation. Emil Brunner warns against false objectivizing, any formulation that "fixes the contact point for divine revelation and personal experience." And Catherine Mowry LaCugna is concerned

[1] "Implications ecclésiologiques de deux types de pneumatologie," *Communio Sanctorum: Mélanges offerts à Jean Jacques von Allmen* (Geneva: Labor et Fides, 1982) 141–54.

that such formulations can cause theological tarrying at one trinitarian site, thus interrupting the dynamic: "There is no reason to stop at any one point . . . , no reason to single out one point as if it could be fixed or frozen in time. Christology is no more and no less prominent than pneumatology."[2]

One can take a different approach to the question of contact or touch. Joseph Ratzinger proposes that the mission of the Spirit in history (in contrast to the person of the Spirit) was the object of the credal affirmation. The end of the creed reads, "I believe in the Holy Spirit." But Ratzinger contends that the insertion of the definite article "the" misplaces the meaning. Originally the phrase seems to have referred to salvation history, not primarily to Trinity.[3]

This emphasis on the Spirit in relation to history and the church has special theological significance. In functional terms (obviously not ontologically), the Spirit is the point of contact between God and humankind. Therefore when one builds a theology, one does not start with a consideration of God or with humankind in itself, but at the point where the one "touches" the other.[4] Or in Otto Kuss's words, "The Spirit dominates the whole room between God and humanity."[5] Or in Walter Kasper's formulation, "The Spirit as mediation between Father and Son is at the same time the mediation of God into history."[6] The Spirit who is experienced in history is that point of contact between God and humankind but, in the other "direction," the point of entry into the mystery of Christ through which the mystery of the Father is attained.

CRUDITY TAKEN SERIOUSLY NOT LITERALLY AS POINTER TO FUNCTION

Touching, contact, ascending, and descending have nothing to do with spatial movement or chronology. Nor do they have to do with

---

[2] Brunner, *Vom Werk des Heiligen Geistes* (Tübingen: Mohr [Siebeck], 1935) 8. LaCugna, *God For Us: The Trinity and Christian Life* (San Francisco: Harper, 1991) 223.

[3] *Introduction to Christianity* (New York: Herder and Herder, 1970) 255.

[4] Hans-Jurgen Goertz, *Geist und Wirklichkeit: Ein Studie zur Pneumatologie Erich Schaeders* (Göttingen: Vandenhoeck & Ruprecht, 1980) 34.

[5] *Der Römerbrief* (Regensburg: Postet, 1963–78) 593.

[6] *Jesus the Christ* (New York: Paulist, 1976) 250.

place, geography, frozen stasis, or with pausing along the highway, but with function and movement, expressed in the crudest possible terms so that the reader will take contact and touch seriously as function but not literally in a geographical or spatial sense. We neither shift the tarrying point from christology to pneumatology nor erect a new stop-over. Rather, we discern the movement without omitting any of the Son or Spirit moments from the Father, and bypassing none on the way back to God. The Spirit is not a pit stop along the trinitarian highway.

This seems to be what Heribert Mühlen means when he says that the Spirit is "itself the unmediated, mediating immediacy of our standing over against Christ." He is writing of the analogous character of the mediating functions of Jesus and of his Spirit. "One cannot say that the Logos is in the strict sense one and the same in the Father, in his human nature, and in us, for that would mean the 'extension' of the hypostatic union also to us. Still less can one say . . . that the Father is in the strict sense one and the same in the Son, in the Holy Spirit, and in us. The Holy Spirit, however, is, in the strictest sense, one and the same in the Father, in the Son, in the human nature of Jesus, and in us! The Spirit is, without qualification, the universal mediation which, on the basis of the Spirit going out from the Father and the Son, mediates all with all." There is no encounter or contact with God, no faith encounter with other Christians, outside of the Spirit.[7]

---

[7] "Das Christusereignis als Tat des Heiligen Geistes," *MS* 3/2.515; *Una Mystica Persona. Die Kirche als das Mysterium der heilsgeschichtlichen Identität des Heiligen Geistes in Christus und den Christen: Eine Person in vielen Personen*, 3rd ed. (Munich: Schöningh, 1968) 11.70–11.83. According to Bernard Sesboüé, "Bulletin de théologie dogmatique: Pneumatologie," *Recherches des sciences religieuses* 76 (1988) 123–24, Mühlen, during a colloquium in Strasbourg at Pentecost 1982, suggested that in using the phrase "mediating immediacy" of the Spirit's role, it might be advantageous to replace "immediate" with "direct." Commenting on this, Edward Kilmartin, "Summary of Bibliography" (diskette file: Kilmartin Archives, Jesuit Community at Boston College), notes: "Direct: The inspiration of Scripture is direct but mediate. A direct action with mediation (word and sacrament); direct action without mediation (vertical intervention of God received and exercised in a direct and actual dependence). By the mediation of Jesus he does not accord to us an encounter with himself, but with God directly. The Spirit is not a mediator between Christ and us. He is the mediation of the mediator, and in this sense it is he who permits a direct encounter with Jesus himself. The experience a

Edward Kilmartin takes over the category of "mediated immediacy" of the Spirit from Mühlen. "The unity between Christ and the Church is personal and immediate because it is mediated by the one Spirit. The Holy Spirit is not 'mediator' between Christ and us, but rather mediation of the mediator, because the Holy Spirit is the Spirit of Christ whom he shares with us." In less philosophical terms Walter Kasper again points to the mediation of the Spirit: "The Spirit is, therefore, in every respect the mediation, in freedom, of love, unity and distinction."[8]

For Karl Rahner, too, the Spirit is the mediation between God and humankind. Rahner contends that "in God's *self*-communication to the creature, radically understood, the mediation itself must be God and cannot amount to a creaturely mediation." Or more concretely: "God must mediate to himself and through himself," otherwise he remains in metaphysical remoteness. Through the mediated immediacy of the Spirit, the Gift of God, who is the Self of God, the Spirit removes this remoteness in a way which is proper to the Spirit, and is not merely an appropriation.[9] By reason of this mediation of the Spirit, real relations are established between human persons and God. The great chasm is bridged.

Karl Barth stands in this same tradition. In summarizing the way Barth gropes his way to a theological formulation, Philip Rosato writes, "Barth's own pneumatology is at its core a search for a theologically legitimate principle of mediation at the center of

priori of the Spirit categorializes itself in the mediations a posteriori of the word, sacraments and ministry. The direct character of the relation with God does not exclude mediation by the experience that man makes of himself, community and by the historical autotransmission of the Spirit in Jesus Christ." Jerome M. Hall, *We Have the Mind of Christ: The Holy Spirit and Liturgical Memory in the Thought of Edward J. Kilmartin* (Collegeville: The Liturgical Press, 2001) 96, n. 81.

[8] Kilmartin, "The Catholic Tradition of Eucharistic Theology: Towards the Third Millennium," *Theological Studies* 55 (1994) 435; *The Eucharist in the West*, Robert J. Daly, ed. (Collegeville: The Liturgical Press, 1998) 357. See also Hall, *We Have the Mind of Christ*, 83–84; 96–97; 118. Kasper, *Jesus the Christ* (New York: Paulist, 1976) 268.

[9] "Oneness and Threefoldness of God in Discussion with Islam," *Theological Investigations*, 23 vols. (New York: Crossroad, 1966–1992) 18.116, 118; "Some Implications of the Scholastic Concept of Uncreated Grace," *Theological Investigations*, 1.343–46.

Christian dogmatics—at the point where the transition is made between Christ and the Christian. Only the Holy Spirit, the divine mediator, can validly serve this function."[10]

The Greek Orthodox theologian Nikos Nissiotis approaches the role of the Spirit in Christ's relationship to the Father and to the church. He writes that "the 'how' of the realization of this double relationship should be examined with the 'what.'" Speaking more specifically of the "how," Nissiotis writes that "the Spirit creates the 'link' between God and man, through a chosen woman who gave birth to Jesus. . . . In the Incarnation and the historical life of Jesus the energy of the Spirit is the decisive element, because it is the Spirit who makes the 'link' possible and who maintains, by His work, the union between God and man in the historical person of Jesus."[11] Here again we meet the Spirit as the divine immediacy which is proper to the Spirit, the "how" by which the "what" is effected in history.

That the Spirit functions as the immediacy of God in a kind of *proprium,* something that distinguishes one person from another, is not offensive to trinitarian thinking. The three self-communications are the self-communication of the one God in three "relative" ways in which God subsists. The three-foldedness of this self-communication is not a merely verbally distinct communication, as though what was communicated was absolutely and in every respect the same but, because of our weakened understanding, named with different words. In salvation history the distinction of this self-communication is "real." Within the historical order the self-communication of the triune God takes place through a double mediation, corresponding to the missions of the Word and the Spirit.

The metaphors of touching, ascent, descent have nothing to do with one person being the means of reaching another person in some second moment.[12] If the Son is in the Spirit and the Spirit in the Son, the one is not a "second moment" for the other. Nor are the images of descent and ascent, of touching, in their deepest roots a reflection

---

[10] *The Spirit as Lord: The Pneumatology of Karl Barth* (Edinburgh: T. & T. Clark, 1981) 21. I believe it is better not to speak of the Spirit as mediator. That is Christ's role. The Spirit however is the very mediation of Christ the mediator.

[11] "Pneumatological Christology as a Presupposition of Ecclesiology," *Oecumenica: Jahrbuch für ökumenische Forschung* 2 (1967) 237, 240.

[12] Peter Fransen, *The New Life of Grace* (London: Chapman, 1969) 41.

on the eternal nature of God, though God betrays who God is by divine acts of self-communication. Rather, they are a primitive reflection on the lived experience of God's converting and sanctifying power as God reaches through and in the divine self to save.

And when speaking of the contact function or the function of touching, one must be on guard against taking contact or touch to represent a limited point. A pin or a nail or a touch of a hand has a limited extension. But the contact function of the Spirit extends as far as the mediatorial office of Jesus Christ—to the whole created order of nature and grace. If Jesus is the universal mediator, the Spirit is the universal mediation.

The personalist contact or touching function helps to avoid an abstract view of trinitarian outreach that would order trinitarian life in arid philosophical categories. The Trinity is about the personal force of God's love expressing itself in a reaching out beyond the divine Self to touch and transform humanity and creation and lead them back to their place of origin, the Father, in praise and wonder. Contact and touch are implicit in the lover/beloved relationship, and in any manifestation of communion. If there is no touch, can there be true love? When the person-to-person love relationship is forgotten, trinitarian doctrine becomes "technology, perverting the uncluttered simplicity and spontaneity of the faith," to employ the derogatory language Basil uses in a different context.[13]

The Spirit dominates the whole "space" between God and humankind, where the Spirit is God's decisive wonder, linking God and humankind, changing us by giving a share in divine knowledge, gifts, and life. Or the Spirit is "the turn around." The Spirit is the end point of God's journey to us; the Spirit is the point of departure of our journey to God. The texts also indicate this intent by suggesting that the Spirit acts as a bridge. Even after the redemption, there is no other bridge between the divine world and the human world. If the Spirit is not present and active, we are cut off from God. We go to God only in the Spirit through Christ. Everything that God effects must pass over this bridge. The Spirit is "the Absolute Nearness." The Spirit conveys the immanence of God, a creative active presence understood as being one with God's reality. Preparing

---

[13] *On the Holy Spirit* 6.13; SC 17bis.286–89.

for the Jubilee Year 2000, the Theological-Historical Commission issued the document *The Holy Spirit, Lord and Giver of Life,* which uses contact language to describe the role of the Spirit in God's nearness: "It is impossible to have any contact with God if not in the Spirit. . . . The Spirit is the place for experiencing God-in-us and God-for-us."[14]

CRANES, ROPES, AND LADDERS

As we have seen, early in the post-biblical period this contact image was picked up and expressed in various forms and with various orderings of the divine names. Freedom in formulation still persisted, but was exercised within a sense of discipline and order, especially in a liturgical context. The early church did not hesitate to use stereotyped formulae—two-membered (Father and Son) and three-membered (Father, Son, Holy Spirit). Theologians moved back and forth between them without noticing major problems. The two-membered formulae were not a trinitarian denial. Even Basil, firm trinitarian and defender of the divinity of the Spirit, still carried on some of his trinitarian argument in binitarian terms.[15]

But three-membered formulae remained strong, especially in the God, Son/Christ, Spirit form. Ignatius of Antioch addresses the Christians as "stones of the Father's temple made ready for the building of God the Father, carried up to the heights by the crane of Jesus Christ (which is his cross), using the Holy Spirit as a rope." Irenaeus writes of the Spirit as "the ladder of our ascent to God." Athanasius says the Father is the source, the Son is the river,

---

[14] Otto Kuss, *Der Römerbrief* (Regensburg: Pustet, 1963–78) 593. Hans Dietrich Wendland, *Die Briefe an die Korinther* (Göttingen: Vandenhoeck & Ruprecht, 1968) 30. Lucien Cerfaux, "L'église et le règne de Dieu d'après saint Paul," *Ephemerides Theologicae Lovanienses* 2 (1925) 192. Jacques Guillet, "Esprit," *Dictionnaire de Spiritualité* 4.1255. Mühlen, *Der Heilige Geist als Person: Beitrag zur Frage nach der dem heiligen Geistes eigentumlichen Funktion in der Trinität, bei der Inkarnation und im Gnadenbund* (Münster: Aschendorff, 1963) 328. William J. Hill, *The Three-Personed God: The Trinity as a Mystery of Salvation* (Washington, D.C.: Catholic University, 1982) 298. *The Holy Spirit, Lord and Giver of Life* (New York: Crossroad, 1997) 28.

[15] Oscar Cullmann, *Early Christian Worship* (London: SCM, 1953) 23. Basil, *On the Holy Spirit* 5.7–8.21, presents the argument mainly in terms of the Father and the Son.

and we are made to drink of the Spirit. Gregory of Nyssa, in a letter mistakenly attributed to Basil, says that "as he who grasps one end of a chain pulls along with the other end to himself, so he who draws the Spirit, draws both the Son and the Father along with it."[16]

Gregory uses the image of "touch," relating it to the creed. First, he announces the principle: As the Spirit is the unction with which Christ is anointed, "there is no interval of separation between the Son and the Holy Spirit." As a body is wholly covered with the oil of anointment, there is no space, no interval between the oil and the body. Therefore to touch Christ, you must first touch the oil/Spirit with which he is anointed: "Whosoever is to touch the Son by faith must needs first encounter the oil in the very act of touching; there is not a part of him devoid of the Holy Spirit. Therefore profession of the Lordship of the Son arises in those who entertain it by means of the Holy Spirit; on all sides the Holy Spirit is met by those who by faith approach the Son."[17]

Gregory is pointing to the universal character of the Spirit's role: "There is no part of him [Christ] devoid of the Holy Spirit." The role of the Spirit as a touch of God is not that of a certain point of entry, but "all sides." To change the image, the Spirit is the universal horizon, not a series of individual points. Or to change the vocabulary again: the Spirit is not another mediator, but is the very mediation

[16] Ignatius of Antioch, *Ephesians* 9.1; SC 10.64. Irenaeus, *Against Heresies* 3.24.15; SC 211.472. Basil, *Letters to Serapion* 1.19; SC 15.116. This took a great number of forms: Father is light, Son is radiance, Spirit is energy; Father is the root, the Son is the sprout, the Spirit is the fruit. Basil, *Letter* 38.4, in *Lettres*, Yves Courtonne, ed., 3 vols. (Paris: Société d'Édition "Les Belles Lettres," 1957–1966) 1.86. Reinhard Hübner, "Gregor von Nyssa als Verfasser der sog. Ep. 38 des Basilius," *Epektasis: mélanges patristiques offerts au cardinal Jean Daniélou*, Jacques Fontaine and Charles Kannengiesser, eds. (Paris: Beauchesne, 1972) 463–90.

[17] *Against the Macedonians*, 16, in *Opera*, Werner Jaeger, ed. (Leiden: Brill, 1952–) 3/1.103. Matthias Scheeben, *Die Mysterien des Christentums* in *Gesammelte Schriften*, Josef Höfer, ed., 8 vols. (Freiburg im Breisgau: Herder, 1941) 2.123, speaks of the Holy Spirit as the "conductor," as in a lightning rod. Scheeben was deeply influenced by the early Greek tradition. (This section of his book does not appear in the English translation, *The Mysteries of Christianity*.) David Coffey, *Deus Trinitas: The Doctrine of the Triune God* (New York: Oxford University Press, 1999) 36.

itself, and the mediation is as universal as the extent of the work of Christ the mediator.[18]

TAKE NUMBERS SERIOUSLY, NOT LITERALLY

If contact, touch, descent, ascent, and turn around, cranes, ropes, ladders, and circles are crude instruments, not to be taken literally, the same is true of the numbers 1 and 3. Basil, for instance, has the greatest hesitation to use numbers of the Trinity. Still, he is aware of our creaturely condition in which crude metaphors are the only way we can speak of God. When used of the Trinity, 1 (one) is not a number. It means "identity." Basil both protests against the use of numbers and uses them. "Count if you must, but do not dishonor the truth. One should honor the silence in those things which cannot be said. Or, at least, one uses numbers with piety [that is, bowing down before the mystery] when it concerns holy things." The truth of the Trinity is not honored when numbers are taken literally. When numbers are used of the Trinity, it is in a species of "meta-mathematics," because the divine persons do not exist alongside one another but in one another. "If we count, we do not add, increasing from one to many. We do not say, 'one, two, three,' or 'first, second, third.' Because 'I myself, that is, God, am the first and the last.'"[19]

Basil shows how he takes numbers seriously as a way of designating function when he exegetes 1 Corinthians 12:4-11: "Now there are varieties of gifts, but the same Spirit; and there are varieties of services, but the same Lord; and there are varieties of activities, but it is the same God who activates all of them in everyone." Basil explains: "Just because the apostle in the above passage mentions the Spirit first, the Son second, and God the Father third, do not assume that he has reversed the order [that is, the order given in the

---

[18] In terms of Paul's christology Ingo Hermann writes, "The Spirit is the medium of communication between the *Kyrios* and humankind"; "*Pneuma* is the medium of the encounter between God and humankind," *Kyrios und Pneuma* (Munich: Kösel, 1961) 98, 113.

[19] Maximus the Confessor, *On the Divine Names*, 13; PG 4:412, holds the same position: "Even if the Godhead, which is beyond all, is worshipped by us as Trinity and as unity, we know neither the three nor the one as numbers." Basil, *On the Holy Spirit* 18.44–45; SC 17bis.404.

great baptismal command of Matthew 28:19)." Paul mentions the Spirit first, says Basil, because it is through the Spirit that we receive the gifts of God. "For the apostle has been inspired by human relations: When one receives a gift, we thank first the one who brings the gift, then the one who sent the gift, and finally one ascends in thought to the source and the cause of the gift."[20] Here Basil uses the order Spirit, Son, Father to indicate first the contact function of the Spirit, or the order of experience; that is, the Spirit is the person who brings the gift, the Son being the one who sent the gift, and the Father is the ultimate source of the gift. In a word, Basil uses order to indicate theological function.

SPIRIT MAKES REAL IN US WHAT IS REAL IN CHRIST

God worked through the Son in the Spirit to make what was real in Jesus Christ become real in us. The Spirit is medium of communication between the *Kyrios* and humankind.[21] Without the Spirit one cannot know Christ; without the Spirit one cannot have access to the Father. "Through him [Christ] both of us [you who were far off and . . . those who were near] have access in one Spirit to the Father" (Eph 2:18).

Without the Spirit God remains a private self, an isolated glory, an island apart. In this sense the Spirit is sovereign and all inclusive, the universal horizon, the exclusive point where we touch God and God touches us from within. Without the Spirit, the church and world are left in their sin, the redemption Christ won on the cross never reaches us, and the way to the Father is barred. For us there is no sharing in God's glory, no eternal life.

The Spirit operates as the reality of the exalted Son, not alongside Christ but in Christ, in movement from the Father and back to the Father. It is not just as the Spirit, but precisely as the Spirit of Christ, that the Spirit is the all-embracing mediation, that is, the Spirit which made Christ an icon of the Father, giving believers participation in

[20] Ibid., 16.35; SC 17bis.376; at 26.62; SC 17bis.470 Basil indicates the contact function of the Spirit by acknowledging that the scriptures "often designate the Spirit as the place of those who are sanctified."

[21] Hermann, *Kyrios und Pneuma*, 398.

this iconic face of the Father (Rom 8:29), making them children of God in the Son, that believers might return to God. It is through this same Spirit—who is the Spirit of Christ—that believers call "Abba! Father!"

Chapter 13

The Tradition of Subordinationism

It is difficult to distinguish the subordinationism found in writers we now recognize as orthodox witnesses to the faith from erroneous speculation. The pre-Nicenes perceived that the Son and the Spirit come from the Father. To safeguard monotheism, they used a subordinating vocabulary. "With the exception of Athanasius virtually every theologian, East and West, accepted some form of subordinationism at least up to the year 355."[1] Note that Hanson extends this period up to thirty years after the *homoousios* of Nicaea in 325, indicating that those who considered Christ "of one substance" with the Father did not necessarily exclude all subordinating tendencies regarding the Son—which also has repercussions for the Spirit. The acceptable style of subordinationism has nothing to do with what was perceived as Arian rationalism and its conviction that impeccable logic, apart from ecclesial discernment, is enough. Based on biblical evidence, influenced by various philosophical streams, subordinationist formulations of the pre-Nicene era were cast in history of salvation categories, and therefore were generally economic in character, not essentialist and ontological.[2]

Origen continued to have enormous influence in the post-Nicene

---

[1] R.P.C. Hanson, *The Search for the Christian Doctrine of God* (Edinburgh: T. & T. Clark, 1988) xix. Henri Crouzel, *Origen* (San Francisco: Harper & Row, 1989) 203. Bernard Lonergan, *The Way to Nicaea: The Dialectical Development of Trinitarian Theology* (Philadelphia: Westminster, 1976) 41–42. Robert Grant, *Gods and the One God* (London: SPCK, 1986) 160.

[2] Wolfgang Marcus, "Subordinationismus," *Lexikon für Theologie und Kirche* 2nd ed., 9.1138–39.

period. The claim of the Arians that he is their chief supporter seems to demand ontological conclusions that he himself never drew. An injustice is done to Origen if his subordinationist formulations are attributed to metaphysical considerations; in their roots they are biblical. To judge pre-Nicene authors by the criteria of a later theology is anachronistic, and precludes correct historical understanding.[3]

ARIUS AND THE NICENE REACTION

The pneumatology of Arius presents formidable historical problems because this Libyan theologian wrote little, and of that the remains are small. Neither in the few surviving letters of Arius nor in the fragments of his *Thalia* (popular songs with doctrinal content) is there any direct and formal denial of the divinity of the Spirit. Arius mentions the Spirit only incidentally, and subordinates the Spirit to the Son in a more radical way than Origen had done.[4]

According to Athanasius's understanding of the followers of Arius, the Spirit was a creation of the Son, who was created before time, so the Spirit is twice removed from the Father and is therefore the Father's grandson. But for the most part there seems to have been silence on both sides about the Holy Spirit during the first thirty years of the Arian controversy. If Arius emerges as the champion of an unacceptable subordinationist Son, will he have an acceptable view of the subordinate Spirit? One need not demonize Arius and the much more diverse movement which he inspired. Quite the opposite. One can recognize the authentic religious intentions—for example, safeguarding the transcendence of God and not desiring to go beyond the witness of scripture. However, Arius radicalized the non-ontological economic subordinationism of Origen and other pre-Nicenes, turning it into ontology. He thereby moved the discussion in a decisive way from the history of salvation to metaphysics,

---

[3] Lonergan, *Way to Nicaea*, 67, 126, 41–42. In the 1930s Hal Koch, *Pronoia und Paideusis: Studien über Origenes und sein Verhältnis zum Platonismus* (Berlin: Walter de Gruyter, 1932) 305–21, insisted that in the strict sense Origen was not a metaphysician. Charles Bigg, *The Christian Platonists of Alexandria* (Oxford: Clarendon, 1886) 181.

[4] When exegeting Isaiah 6:3. See Rudolf Lorenz, *Arius judaizans? Untersuchungen zur dogmengeschichtlichen Einordnung des Arius* (Göttingen: Vandenhoeck & Ruprecht, 1980) 166.

from *economia* to *theologia*.[5] If one operates principally within the history of salvation, the tendency—but not an innate necessity—is to move to some kind of unacceptable subordination. What will the move to metaphysics and *theologia* mean for the further history of the subordination of Christ and the Spirit?

At the beginning of the fourth century there was little special interest in the Holy Spirit, and no smoke indicating a controversy in the making. The issue at Nicaea was the subordination of the Son to the Father, and, by implication, of the Spirit to the Son and the Father. If the issue was clear, the solution was not. Lack of an agreed terminology led to a "war of suspicion" even among those whom history would call the orthodox. The key word *homoousios* presented many difficulties, not the least the connotation of materiality, or substance as "stuff." To this was added its previous use by Gnostics already in the second century, and in the third century by Paul of Samosata who earned a condemnation by the Council of Antioch for its use in a trinitarian context. *Homoousios* carried the whiff of heresy. How do you introduce for conciliar use a term condemned by a previous council? Only with difficulty did Nicaea accept it, most likely at the urging of the emperor.[6]

But when the council accepted *homoousios* for inclusion in the creed and added, without elaboration, the short formula ". . . and in the Holy Spirit," the council committed the church to the divinity

---

[5] Athanasius, *Letters to Serapion* 1.10, 15; SC 15.80–81, 109. Hanson, *Search*, 769, contends that this subordinating argument was probably the most frequent. The subordinating argument surfaced also in Gregory of Nazianzus, *Oration* 31.7; SC 250.288. H. B. Swete, *On the Early History of the Doctrine of the Holy Spirit* (Cambridge: Deighton Bell, 1973) 31. Both Rowan Williams, *Arius: Heresy and Tradition* (Grand Rapids: Eerdmans, 2002), and Hanson, seconded by Maurice Wiles, *Archetypal Heresy: Arianism through the Centuries* (Oxford: Clarendon, 1996), call "Arian" and "Arianism" misnomers. Like the earlier Ebionites, the Arians failed because "they were so inflexible, too conservative, not ready to look at new ideas" (Hanson, 873). See also John Thompson, *Modern Trinitarian Perspectives* (New York: Oxford University Press, 1994) 15.

[6] Harry A. Wolfson, *The Philosophy of the Church Fathers* (Cambridge: Harvard, 1964) 337. Lonergan, *The Way to Nicaea*, 90. Hanson, *Search*, 195. Manlio Simonetti, *La crisi ariana nel IV secolo* (Rome: Augustinianum, 1975) 273ff. We are not sure who proposed the term. Ossius of Cordova was the emperor's theologian and was in a position to suggest it. Or it might have been Constantine's own recommendation.

The Tradition of Subordinationism

of the Spirit, though the issue had apparently not been discussed by the Fathers. Nonetheless, Nicaea's inclusion of the Spirit was no innovation. Historically the Spirit had been consistently, though not always, placed on the divine side of the God/creature divide. This is not the same thing as explicitly recognizing the divinity of the Spirit, even when it is evident that a given author did recognize the Spirit as divine. The question was: If scripture had not explicitly said "the Spirit is God," should we go beyond scripture and be more explicit? The battle for the *homoousios* was won for the Son and the Spirit, even though the term is not in scripture, because it represented, as Cardinal Newman noted in a broader context, the sense of scripture as a whole.[7]

Homoousios applied to the Son did not rule out all subordinationism—and by contagion did not rule out subordinating the Spirit. It meant that the Father communicates to the Son all that the Father has and is, the Son receiving the fullness of divine being. The Father initiates, the Son responds, so even with the *homoousios* there is a kind of asymmetry and distinction of functions, which implies an appropriate subordination of the Son. If this is true of the Son, it is equally true—and in the eyes of some, more true—of the Spirit. Having asserted the metaphysical parity of Father and Son (and, by implication, of the Spirit), and that the Son and Spirit are genuinely existent beings, not just operations of the Father, the Council Fathers had to welcome some element of appropriate subordination (relation of origin as in "God from God, Light from Light"), lest they be accused of tritheism.[8]

It is likely the Fathers were concerned that Arius's doctrine cut

---

[7] Basil Studer, *Trinity and Incarnation* (Collegeville: The Liturgical Press, 1993) 108. I take issue with Hanson's contention, *Search*, 739, that "the surprising thing is, not that more attention was not paid to the Holy Spirit, but that the theologians continued to include the Spirit in the framework of their theology." John Henry Newman, *The Arians of the Fourth Century*, 3rd ed. (London: Pickering, 1876) 151–55.

[8] Lonergan, *The Way to Nicaea*, 43, 96. Christopher Stead, *Divine Substance* (Oxford: Clarendon, 1977) 233, says that *homoousios* was not directly intended to make an ontological statement, but only indirectly. Kelly, *Doctrines*, 236–37, suggests that even Athanasius, who puts forward the faith of Nicaea as on a par with "the word of God which remains forever" set down in the Bible, *Letter to the Bishops of Africa* 2; PG 26.1032c, gave *homoousios* a more defined meaning than

off the reestablishment of communion between God and human-kind, a reconciliation only a divine person could effect. Not a messenger, not an angel, but the very God came to save us by sharing divine life through the Son in the Spirit.

HOMOOUSIOS AND THE SUBORDINATION OF THE SPIRIT AFTER NICAEA

The *homoousios* did not restore harmony. Quite the opposite. Indeed, the period after Nicaea is one of the most troubled in the history of the church. The great disturbance was over christology, not pneumatology. The greater part of Greek-speaking churchmen were anti-Arian but also anti-Nicene, because, standing in the tradition of Origen, they thought in terms of three hypostases, and the distinction of persons they saw imperiled by the *homoousios*. But as Jaroslav Pelikan notes, they signed the formula and then went on teaching as they had before. Pelikan also contends that it was not so much the doctrine of Christ as that of the Spirit that brought *homoousios* to a head.[9] But this happened only gradually.

If there was little interest in the Holy Spirit in the first years of the fourth century before Nicaea, there was not much more in the first thirty-five years after. The phrase ". . . and the Holy Spirit" of the creed sparked no protest, gave rise to no immediate wave of theological speculation, prompted no flood of ink. We have no evidence that there is a single treatise on the Spirit in the whole of the first half of the fourth century. Only about 355 did pneumatology come to the fore, and then it was at center stage for only about twenty years. And had *homoousios* been the decisive final word at Nicaea for the christological problematic, as it is often portrayed, it would have been more in evidence when the issue of the Spirit emerged. In fact, neither for the Son nor for the Spirit was *homoousios* the Nicene

the Council of Nicaea intended. Hermann Josef Sieben, *Die Konzilsidee der alten Kirche* (Paderborn: Schöningh, 1979) 57–62, 249–50, 257, 265–67.

[9] In Hanson's view, "The Achievement of Orthodoxy in the Fourth Century A.D.," *The Making of Orthodoxy*, Festschrift for Henry Chadwick, Rowan Williams, ed. (New York: Cambridge University, 1989) 146, "As a contribution to solving the dispute it [the choice of *homoousios*] was a disastrous failure." Pelikan, *The Emergence of the Catholic Tradition (100–600)* (Chicago: University of Chicago, 1971) 203, 211.

banner, or the Nicene battle cry, in the early years after the council.[10]

When the Spirit did emerge as a theological issue, the argument was not carried by transferring the *homoousios* from the Son to the Spirit. *Homoousios* was a hidden, unspoken norm, but rather than the oneness of substance, the emphasis, as in Athanasius, was on the divine operations of the Spirit such as inspiration, being included in the doxologies, the mutual indwelling of the three persons, the presence of the Spirit in liturgical celebration, but most of all, the Spirit fructifying the grace of the incarnation by divinizing the saved.[11] If the Spirit is not divine, how could the Spirit divinize us? If the Spirit were a creature, we would have no share in God. The argument is from effect to cause, and is basically soteriological. The issue is salvation.

The retrieval of *homoousios* after a gap of three decades is the work of Athanasius. He uses it of the Son only once in the authentic three books of *Orations against the Arians* (1.9), written between 339 and 345. About 356 he began defending the term, some thirty years after the close of Nicaea. His initial reservation toward *homoousios* gradually gave way as he began to see it within the creed as the condition of ecclesial reconciliation with those who had difficulty going beyond scripture.[12]

Reconciliation, yes, but not reconciliation at the cost of the faith. Athanasius did not compromise. He was a fortress of strength in the 350s, standing against the world "as the only theologian free of subordinationism" of the Son and the Spirit in any inappropriate form. He was well aware that ultimately the battle was not about a word, but about intention and meaning. We recall again his generous theological vision: "We must not regard as enemies those who

---

[10] Joseph T. Lienhard, "The 'Arian' Controversy: Some Categories Reconsidered," *Theological Studies* 48 (1987) 416. Frances Young, *From Nicaea to Chalcedon* (Philadelphia: Fortress, 1983) 78.

[11] *Letters to Serapion* 4.3; SC 15.178; 1.33; SC 15.143–44; 1.14; SC 15.107; 1.24, 31–32; SC 15.126, 139–43; *Festal Letter* (329) 5; CSCO 151.4; *To Marcellinus on the Interpretation of the Psalms* 28–29; PG 27.40–41; *History of the Arians* 80; PG 25.792; *Tome to the People of Antioch* 3; PG 26:800. Charles Kannengiesser, "Athanasius of Alexandria and the Holy Spirit between Nicaea I and Constantinople I," *Irish Theological Quarterly* 48 (1981) 168–74.

[12] Hanson, *Search*, 202; 418–19. Kelly, *Doctrines*, 246. Hans von Campenhausen, *The Fathers of the Greek Church* (New York: Pantheon, 1959) 74–75.

accept all else that was decreed at Nicaea, but only have reservations about the term *homoousios*. We do not stand in opposition to them as though they were Arian crazed or hostile to the council fathers. Rather we discuss with them as brothers, men who are of the same mind as ourselves and have doubts only about the word."[13]

Athanasius was not alone in maintaining theological tolerance in terminological matters in a climate of great confusion as long as the intent was pure. Gregory of Nazianzus believed that while one could argue about the precise words, what mattered was doctrine. Sometimes the doctrine was orthodox, but the formulation faulty. Especially in the doctrine of the Spirit there were "many" who did not have a "healthy" doctrine, who were honestly stumbling. Of these he says that "a less grave impiety passed as piety." That is, to be slightly in error was common among those who were stumbling in confusion, and were numerous.[14]

When Athanasius did use *homoousios* of the Spirit in 359 or 360, it must have sent a shock through the theological world. "Its application to the Spirit is without precedent." Even so, Athanasius does not flash the word brashly. Only after careful preparation does he dare propose the scandalous term. In a letter now divided into thirty-three sections, *homoousios* surfaces in section twenty-seven, therefore towards the end of the letter. He does not use it again of the Spirit. And he does not use *theos* of the Spirit, but he comes close. He says that the Spirit is "confessed as God" *(theologoumenon)*. When he does use *homoousios,* he is insisting the Spirit is not a creature, and is protesting against an improper subordination to the Word and God. At the same time, he does not want to set the stakes too high for the *tropici,* the adversaries of the divinity of the Spirit. His goal is modest: "It is enough to know that the Spirit is not a creature, nor is he numbered with the things that are made."[15] One might call this equality and divinity by indirection.

---

[13] *On the Synods of Ariminum and Seleucia* 41; PG 26.764–65. E. P. Meijering, *Orthodoxy and Platonism in Athanasius* (Leiden: Brill, 1968) 195. Hanson, *Search,* xix.

[14] *Oration* 21.33; SC 270.182.

[15] *Letters to Serapion* 1.17; SC 15.112; 1.31; SC15.139; 1.27; SC 15.133: Athanasius is arguing that creatures are many. "It is obvious that the Spirit does not belong to the many nor is he an angel. But because he is one, and, still more,

As we have seen, one principle Athanasius enunciated had considerable influence after him, namely, the Spirit is to the Son as the Son is proper to the essence of the Father. This is called the correlative principle. The bishop of Alexandria seems to have a limited purpose—to assert that the Spirit is *homoousios* with the Son as the Son is *homoousios* with the Father. In this way he establishes the identity of essence and equality of the three persons, without which the divine economy fails. But opponents exaggerated the correlative principle, saying that if the Spirit was a son of the Son, then the Spirit is the grandson of the Father. Even if one tolerates the clumsy, not to say dubious formulation "son of the Son," the accusation against Athanasius is valid only if Athanasius's limits are not observed.[16]

All three of the Cappadocians invoke Athanasius's correlative principle. Additionally, they pick up a number of the arguments he proposes in *Letters to Serapion* and in *Against the Arians* to assert the equality and divinity of the Spirit: The one who sanctifies is not of the same nature as the one who is sanctified; the Holy Spirit is holy by the nature of God and not by participation; the three persons are perfectly one and therefore the Spirit cannot be a creature; the divine nature of the Father is given through the Son in the Holy Spirit; the role of the Son and the Spirit in creation; and, finally, the Son as image, reflection, and splendor of the Father.[17]

Though Athanasius is free from subordinationist tendencies, he nonetheless fell partial victim to the way his christology absorbed his soteriology. Like all other writers from the third century on, he had lost the eschatological pneumatology of the New Testament and therefore did not sufficiently relate the Spirit to time. For Athanasius, as for Origen, who erected a Logos imperium and argued with a

because he is proper to the Word, who is one, he is proper to God who is one, and one in essence *(homoousios)* with him." C.R.B. Shapland, *The Letters of Saint Athanasius Concerning the Holy Spirit* (London: Epworth, 1951) 133, n. 7.

[16] *Letters to Serapion* 1.25. John McIntyre, "The Holy Spirit in Greek Patristic Thought," *Scottish Journal of Theology* 7 (1954) 370. Pelikan, *Emergence*, 213. Gregory of Nazianzus refers to the issue in *Oration* 31.8; SC 250.290.

[17] Basil, *On the Holy Spirit* 17.43; SC 17bis.398; *Letters to Serapion* 1.23; SC 15.124; 1.24; SC 15.126–28; 1.2; SC 15.80–82; 1.19–20; SC 15.115–20; *Against the Arians* 3.24, 25; PG 26.373–75; 1.14, 60; PG 26.41c, 137b. Gregory of Nyssa, *Against the Macedonians*, 22, in *Opera*, Werner Jaeger, ed. (Leiden: Brill, 1952–) 3/1.109.

Logos logic, the Spirit remains "an understudy of the Son."[18]

In the pre-Nicene period and for both Nicaea proper and the early post-Nicene years, attention focused on the subordination of the Son to the Father. Even in the years when Athanasius and Basil were writing on the equality and divinity of the Holy Spirit, the argument was carried on in relation to the Son. They used a kind of Logos logic, or the correlative principle, namely, the Spirit is to the Son as the Son is to the Father. This is about equality in a trinitarian dynamic, excluding an inappropriate subordination.

[18] Hanson, *Search*, 751–52. Kilian McDonnell, "Does Origen have a Trinitarian Doctrine of the Holy Spirit?" *Gregorianum* 75/1 (1994) 23–24.

Chapter 14

Basil:
Not Subordination but Communion of Life with the Father and the Son

Impetus for the controversy about the Spirit came from Eunomius, bishop of Cyzicus in the Hellespont, who belonged to the neo-Arian or Anomoian party (Son is relative, is caused, and unlike the Father). This highly skilled dialectician asserts that he is "avoiding the rash opinions of many, but rather keeping the teaching of the saints." While claiming to stand in the central tradition, he writes in his *Apologia* that the Paraclete is third in dignity, order, and nature. In itself this is not, as we have seen, exceptional. But he continues. The Spirit is honored in the third place as "the first creature of the First Born, the greatest of all and the only one such, [but] lacking indeed Godhead and the power of creation."[1]

Numbering the Spirit as the third in a trinitarian order *(taxis)* was common coin, and would have gone unremarked if Eunomius had not deduced that the Spirit was alien to the Godhead. Basil rose to the challenge, looking not only at the naked denial of divinity to the Spirit but also to the rationalism of Eunomius's doctrine. Basil understood Eunomius (and before him Aetius) as holding that God can be adequately known and defined, though it can be doubted that Eunomius's position was this extreme.[2]

---

[1] Basil, *Against Eunomius* 1.25; SC 305.284, 286.

[2] Maurice Wiles, "Eunomius: Hair-splitting Dialectician or Defender of the Accessibility of Salvation?" *The Making of Orthodoxy*, Festschrift for Henry Chadwick, Rowan Williams, ed. (New York: Cambridge University, 1989) 157–72.

Eunomius was no minor figure; almost every theological thinker of his age composed full-scale treatises against him. In 364, while still a priest, Basil wrote *Against Eunomius,* in part a polemic challenging what he perceived as rationalist over-precision, logical overkill, and excessive claims concerning what is known about God. At this early moment in his development, Basil was not of the strict Nicaean party espousing the *homoousios,* but rather of the *homoios* party (of like substance absolutely). Only about 362, thirty-seven years after the conclusion of Nicaea, did Basil move away from a "middle-of-the-road" position toward clearer support of Nicaea and its *homoousios.*[3]

As regards the Second Person of the Trinity, Basil writes that "we confess without blushing our ignorance of the Holy Spirit"—this in the face of how much Basil thought Eunomius claimed to know.[4] Basil was not about to make claims based on "technology," that is, on what he considered logic and dialectics devoid of faith. Rather, he would look to the scriptures and the rule of faith embedded in the liturgy.

THE CASE OF THE SUBORDINATING DOXOLOGY

As we have seen, Basil got into trouble because of one of the two doxologies he used. The first, emphasizing "vertical" relations, raised no eyebrows: "Glory be to the Father through *(dia)* the Son in *(en)* the Holy Spirit." This could be understood as subordinating the Spirit to the Son and to the Father, but not in an ontological sense (inferior in their essential being), which the central tradition saw as unacceptable. Economic subordination (the Son and the Spirit are subordinate to the Father because the Father sends the two on mission) met with the central tradition's approval. In using

---

[3] Apollinarius, Basil, Didymus the Blind, Diodore of Tarsus, Gregory of Nyssa (composed four books against him), Theodore of Mopsuestia, Theodoret of Cyrus, and Sophronius wrote against Eunomius. Slightly later John Chrysostom adds his name to the list. Of these, only Basil's and Gregory's works are extant in full. See *Eunomius: The Extant Works,* Richard P. Vaggione, ed. (Oxford: Clarendon, 1987) xiii. Basil, *Letter* 9.3, in *Lettres,* Yves Courtonne, ed., 3 vols. (Paris: Société d'Édition "Les Belles Lettres," 1957–1966) 1.39. Philip Rousseau, *Basil of Caesarea* (Berkeley: University of California, 1994) 99, 246–48, 253, 276.

[4] *Against Eunomius* 3.6; SC 305.169.

the vertical doxology, Basil was standing not only in the central tradition but at the center of the central tradition.

However, Basil's second doxology, emphasizing "horizontal" relations, gave stronger expression to the equality of the persons: "Glory be to the Father, with *(meta)* the Son, with *(syn)* the Holy Spirit." Eyebrows were raised at this placing of the Spirit on a level with the Father and the Son. The more horizontal form had evidently fallen on ears unaccustomed to it, and Basil was accused of "novelties," the ultimate deviation.[5] Though he contended that both forms of the doxology were traditional, his opponents were not convinced.

From the end of 374 and during most of 375, that is, about four years before his death, Basil wrote *On the Holy Spirit* and a series of pamphlets (*Letters* 223, 224, 226, 244), in response not only to the furor his doxologies elicited, but also to the defection to the Pneumatomachoi of his one-time friend, Eustathius of Sebaste. Eustathius had much of the tradition on his side when he said, "I prefer not to call the Holy Spirit God, but I would not dare call the Spirit a creature." Nicaea's brief ". . . and [we believe] in the Holy Spirit" could be variously interpreted: Was the Spirit a power, divine, semi-divine, or a created being? The tradition had long presupposed the divinity of the Spirit, but was reluctant to go beyond scripture and declare it in explicit terms. Many bishops in Asia Minor were hesitant to follow Basil's lead and place the Spirit on an equal basis with the Father and the Son, but even Basil was afraid that a too explicit affirmation of the divinity of the Spirit would lead some to accuse him of tritheism (three gods)—an accusation the Cappadocians did not entirely escape for all their pains to guard against it.[6] Basil had reason enough to proceed with caution.

Basil recognizes that the frequent designation of the Spirit as "the place of the sanctified" might be understood as diminishing or subordinating the Spirit by confining the unconfined Spirit in a way untrue of Father and Son. Elsewhere he rejects the proposition that

---

[5] *On the Holy Spirit* 1.3; SC 17bis.256–58.

[6] Dörries, *DSS*, 81–90, especially 90. Eustathius, as reported by Socrates, *Ecclesiastical History* 2, 45, 6, in *Sokrates Kirchengeschichte*, Günther C. Hansen, ed. (Berlin: Berlin-Brandenburgische Akademie, 1995) 183. Anthony Meredith, *Gregory of Nyssa* (New York: Routledge, 1999) 35. Henry Chadwick, *The Church in Ancient Society: From Galilee to Gregory the Great* (Oxford: Clarendon, 2001) 337.

the Spirit only supplies creation with "time and place." As John McIntyre phrases it: "The whole Divine economy of salvation is 'brought home' in the Holy Spirit."[7]

Still, this has the taste of instrumentalism, suggesting there is a power in the primary cause not proportionate to the effect, so an instrument is necessary. But in this instance the primary cause, the Father, is completely proportionate to the effect. Instrument also suggests subordination and exteriority, that is, the Spirit is the tool, lesser than the primary cause, which brings about something external to the self of the Spirit. But for Basil, the instrument is not lesser, and is interior to the life and nature the Spirit has in common with Father and Son.

SHY OF TOO EXPLICIT AFFIRMATION OF DIVINITY

Basil, in teaching about our entry into trinitarian life as divinization, is highly disciplined in using a formulation not found in scripture, though some expression was already traditional. For Basil, divinization, "becoming a god" *(theon genesthai)*, is both the way and the goal of the Christian life. "Becoming god" means sharing, having communion in the life of God, like a piece of iron, when taken from the fire, because of its intense heat shares in the nature of fire. Who but God can make like God, or make us to become a god? The equality of the Spirit is the safeguard of the Spirit's role as "the perfecting cause."[8]

However, the controversy concerning the Holy Spirit's divinity did not prompt Basil to give more explicit recognition of the Spirit's divinity. Early in the period of the dispute about the divinity of the Spirit, that is when writing his *Against Eunomius,* Basil is "far more outspoken" in asserting the divinity of the Spirit than he was a decade later, in *On the Holy Spirit*. The earlier treatise introduces the theme of the holiness of the Spirit and the Spirit's sanctifying role, both of which demand the divinity of the Spirit. Anthony Meredith contends that at this early stage Basil says more explicitly than later

---

[7] *On the Holy Spirit* 2.4; SC 17bis.260–62. See also 4.6; SC 17bis.268–70, and Athanasius, *Letters to Serapion* 3.4; SC 15.168. McIntyre, "The Holy Spirit in Greek Patristic Thought," *Scottish Journal of Theology* 7 (1954) 366.

[8] Jules Gross, *La divinisation du chrétien d'après les pères grecs* (Paris: Gabalda, 1938) 239. Basil, *On the Holy Spirit* 9.23; SC 17bis.328; 1.2; SC 17bis.252 ("our destiny is to become like God"); 26.63; SC 17bis.474; 16.38; SC 17bis.378.

that the energies or activities of the Spirit place the Spirit on the same level with the Father and the Son. These energies or activities show "the divine character of the Spirit's nature." The very vocabulary of divinization is stronger in *Against Eunomius* than in *On the Holy Spirit.* One cannot, therefore, easily conclude that over the period of the controversy Basil developed a more emphatic and explicit teaching on the divinity of the Spirit, though he was never in doubt as to its substance. Neither the pleas of friends nor the taunts of opponents could convince him to move beyond the discretion of Nicaea.[9]

Basil's most explicit affirmation of the divinity of the Spirit is that the Spirit "is divine in nature."[10] The closest Basil comes to applying *homoousios* to the Spirit is indirect. He uses *homoousios* of the Son in relation to the Father and then adds, "the Holy Spirit is numbered together with them and worshiped together with them." Basil prefers *koinonia* ("community of the divinity"; *koinonia tes theotetos*) or *oikeiōsin* (kinship) to explain the relation of the Spirit to the Son and the Father. To those who draw false conclusions from the third place order *(taxis)* of the Spirit in the formula "Father, Son, and Holy Spirit," he proposes the equivalency and identity of life of triune communion or *koinonia*. Further, the insistence on triune communion is a guard against tritheism. He also likes to speak of the oneness of God in the *koinonia* of the three persons, but even here he is restrained, though firm. So close is the communion of the three, that if you pull on one in the manner of a chain, you will necessarily draw the others.[11]

[9] *Against Eunomius* 3.3–4; SC 305.154–60; *On the Holy Spirit* 23.54; SC 17bis.444. Anthony Meredith, "The Pneumatology of the Cappadocian Fathers," in *The Cappadocians* (Crestwood, N.Y.: St. Vladimir's, 1995) 198. In a letter to Epiphanius of Salamis, Basil says he does not want to add anything to the Nicene creed "except the doxology addressed to the Holy Spirit, because this point slipped the memory of our Fathers since the debate on this subject had not yet been stirred." *Letter* 258.2; Courtonne, 3.101–02.

[10] *On the Holy Spirit* 23.54; SC 17bis.444. Milton Anastos, "Basil's *Kata Eunomiou*, A Critical Analysis," in *Basil of Caesarea: Christian, Humanist, Ascetic,* Paul J. Fedwick, ed. (Toronto: Pontifical Institute of Mediaeval Studies, 1981) 131. Adolf-Martin Ritter, *Das Konzil von Konstantinopel und sein Symbol* (Göttingen: Vandenhoeck & Ruprecht, 1965) 84, 258–66. Basil, *Letter* 90.2; Courtonne, 1.196.

[11] *On the Holy Spirit* 5.7; 9.23; 10.24; 13.30; 16.38; 18.45–48; 24.55; 25.59;

To those who use the order of the names as a way of improperly subordinating the Spirit to the Son, Basil scornfully replies that God, when giving us the Father, Son, and Holy Spirit, did not number them one, two, three: "He did not make arithmetic a part of revelation . . . [because] inaccessible realities remain beyond numbering." Beware, Basil warns, lest you honor numbering more than the divine nature.[12]

Subnumeration, which Basil uses in an appropriate way, can also be used inappropriately, as when the Spirit is numbered under the Father and Son in such a way that the third in order, the Spirit, is understood as being ontologically subordinate either to the Father, or to the Father and the Son. Scandal and impiety (read heresy) necessarily follow when one numbers in this way, as the Epicurean and Stoic philosophers do, perceiving God "as a thing," as though one were ranking gold and copper coins. Basil appeals to "the apostolic tradition," and to his own baptism as "the beginning of life," as "the first of days." A profound union exists between doxology, profession of faith, and the baptismal invocation, to the point where the liturgical rite of baptism is the "theological starting point" of Basil's pneumatology. "We must be baptized as we have received, and believe as we have been baptized, and worship as we have believed, the Father, the Son, and the Holy Spirit."[13]

26.61; 26.63; 28.70; 30.77; SC 17bis.272, 328, 332, 352, 376, 406–16, 450, 460, 470, 474, 496, 524. In *Letter* 52.2, 4; Courtonne, 1.135–37, Basil speaks of the Son's relation to the Father, twice using *homoousios,* but when speaking of the Spirit's relation to the Son and the Father he does not use *homoousios.* Atanasije Jevtich, "Between the 'Nicaeans' and the 'Easterners': The 'Catholic' Confession of Saint Basil," St. *Vladimir's Theological Quarterly* 24 (1980) 244. John Zizioulas, "The Teaching of the 2nd Ecumenical Council on the Holy Spirit in Historical and Ecumenical Perspective," *CSS,* 1.32–39. *Against Eunomius* 2.12; SC 305.46. *Letter* 38.4; Courtonne, 1.86.

[12] *On the Holy Spirit* 18.44; SC 17bis.402–04.

[13] Ibid. 17.41, 42; SC 17bis.392–98; 10.25–26; SC 17bis.334–36. *Against Eunomius* 2.22 (once); 3.2 (once); 3.5 (four times); SC 305.90, 150, 164. Dörries, *DSS,* 132. Pia Luislampe, *Spiritus vivificans. Grundzüge einer Theologie des Heiligen Geistes nach Basilius von Caesarea* (Münster: Aschendorff, 1981) 122. Benôit Pruche, Note 3 in SC 17bis.339. Rousseau, *Basil,* 99. *Letter* 125.3; Courtonne, 2.33.

Basil's reluctance to use *homoousios* of the Spirit was not a sign of faintheartedness or diplomatic finesse, but of pastoral concern. Shortly after he became bishop he wrote a letter to a group of holy women in which he said that "there are certain persons who never have accepted the word *'homoousios,'* which some others were reluctant to embrace. These might be justly blamed and yet again be considered worthy of pardon. For, to refuse to follow the Fathers [of Nicaea] and to refuse to regard their word as of greater authority than their own opinion is an arrogance deserving of reproach. On the other hand, to hold in suspicion that word which is discredited by others, perhaps, seems to free them somewhat from the charge."[14] In other words, if the Fathers of Nicaea used the word, thus sanitizing it, one should not be obstinate in rejecting it. Basil both chides and forgives. He wants to build "a golden bridge" to the deniers of the Spirit's divinity. If they confess that the Spirit is not a creature and avoid communion with those who say the Spirit is only a creature, that is enough.[15]

Like Athanasius, Basil holds that the issue is not a word but a meaning. As he was shy to apply "of the same substance" *(homoousios)* to the Spirit, so he was shy of even "rendering the same honor" *(homotimos)* to the Spirit, because he evidently considered it too close an equivalent of *homoousios* and therefore liable to shock the weak. In *On the Holy Spirit* he uses the argument of equal honor for equal persons but never actually uses *homotimos* directly of the Spirit, though the doxology itself presupposes that equal honor is given to each person.[16]

Basil does show that he is not stubbornly refusing to use *homotimos*. In 373, three years after he became bishop of Caesarea and from two to three years before he wrote *On the Holy Spirit,* he did use *homotimos* of the Spirit. He was sending his deacon, Sabinus, with a

---

[14] *Letter* 52.1; Courtonne, 1.134.

[15] Ritter, *Das Konzil*, 263. *Letter* 113 and 114; Courtonne, 2.16-19.

[16] Basil uses *homotimos* in *On the Holy Spirit* 5.8, 6.15 (three times), and 17.42, where it is placed in the mouth of an objection. In all these cases it refers to the Son's relation with the Father. In 19.50 it has to do with the Spirit, but in relation to other creatures, not to the Father and the Son. Dörries, *DSS*, 142–43.

Basil: Not Subordination but Communion of Life

letter to the bishops of the West, asking for their help against the
Arians. In summarizing the orthodox trinitarian position, he writes
that the orthodox doctrine is present when "the Son is acknowledged to be consubstantial *(homoousios)* with the Father, and the
Holy Spirit is numbered with them and adored with equal honor
(homotimos)." Unity and equality of praise mean unity and equality
of nature. To go beyond this is to incur the danger of uprooting the
wheat while pulling out the weeds (Matt 13:29-30). This is an
ecclesiological argument based on both the need not to disrupt the
unity of the church unnecessarily and the readiness of the church to
have regard for the good will of the weak.[17]

THE DIVINITY OF THE HOLY SPIRIT
NOT TO BE PUBLICLY PROCLAIMED

Unless one grasps the condition of the churches in the East after
Nicaea, as Basil experienced them, one will be hard pressed to
understand the need for discretion in proclaiming the divinity of
the Spirit. "What storm at sea was ever so ferocious as the one which
disturbs the church. The tempest has moved all of the boundaries
established by the Fathers. All the foundations, every bulwark supporting doctrines have been overthrown. . . . If an enemy does
not first strike us, it is those with whom we work. . . . We find
enemies in each other." "We reserve our most savage warfare for the
members of our own family." In this turmoil everyone with a snatch
of scripture feels competent to hold forth on the deepest mysteries.
"For these reasons I thought it was better for me to keep silent
than to speak."[18]

Gregory of Nazianzus agrees in principle with Basil. "Discussion
of theology is not for everyone, I tell you, not for everyone. It is no
such inexpensive and effortless pursuit. Nor, would I add, is it for
every occasion, or every audience."[19] But when it comes to the
divinity of the Spirit, Gregory, though he understands Basil's
concern, wants to shout it out where Basil wants silence.

This historical context makes understandable Basil's conviction

[17] *Letter* 90.2; 113; Courtonne, 1.196, 2.16–17.
[18] *On the Holy Spirit* 30.77–78; SC 17bis.522–28.
[19] *Oration* 27.3; SC 250.78.

The Other Hand of God

that the divinity of the Spirit belongs to what he calls "dogma," undoubted truths that are not part of the public proclamation. "Kerygma" is no less true, but it is proclaimed to all. "Dogma is one thing, proclamation quite another; the first is observed in silence, the second is publicly proclaimed." The divinity of the Spirit belongs to dogma, not to kerygma, given the circumstances of the 70s of the fourth century as Basil read them. In no way did Basil think he was being overly cautious in restricting the divinity of the Spirit to "dogma." He was not inventing novelties, but proclaiming "the tradition of the Fathers, whose memory has been maintained in unbroken sequence to our day."[20]

Basil asks Amphilochius, Bishop of Iconium, to whom *On the Holy Spirit* is dedicated, to use discretion. Amphilochius was likely present at the liturgical festival when Basil's use of the more horizontal doxology ("Glory be to the Father, with *[meta]* the Son, with *[syn]* the Spirit") elicited protest.[21] Amphilochius, who turned to Basil for counsel on theological matters, was also present at a local council in his see of Iconium in 376 during which the full divinity of the Spirit was defended.

There are unanswered questions. Was the text of *On the Holy Spirit* destined not only for Amphilochius but also for the local council? If it was destined for the council, did Amphilochius feel free to share it with all the attending bishops? In declaring the contents of *On the Holy Spirit* as dogma to be observed in silence, not kerygma for public proclamation, Basil was gently reminding Amphilochius to be circumspect in showing the book to others: "Your calm, well-balanced character is a guaranty against any untimely divulging of what I have said."[22]

Basil's caution in writing about the divinity of the Spirit was not

[20] Basil, *On the Holy Spirit* 27.66; 30.79; SC 17bis.484, 528. The dictum should not be pressed. Dörries, *De Spiritu Sancto* 121–28. Benoît Pruche, "Introduction," SC 17bis.117–26. Jean Gribomont, "Esotérisme et tradition dans la traité du Saint-Esprit de Saint Basile," *Oecumenica: Jahrbuch für ökumenische Forschung* 2 (1967) 43–48. In *Letter* 90.2; Courtonne, 1.196, to the bishops of the West, Basil categorizes the teaching that the Spirit is to "be adored with equal honor" as "kerygma."

[21] *Vita Sancti Basilii* 31.3; PG 29.cxxvd. Pruche, "Introduction," SC 17bis.51.

[22] *On the Holy Spirit* 30.79; SC 17bis.530.

without its problems. The aged Athanasius had to come to his defense against the complaints of three Cappadocian monks, Palladius, John, and Antiochus, who thought Basil wanting in courage. Athanasius counseled the monks to honor Basil's "economy," that is, his silence, recognizing that Basil was weak with the weak in order to win the weak. Gregory of Nazianzus, in his eulogy at Basil's funeral, felt compelled to defend his friend on this point, though Gregory himself was not entirely satisfied with Basil's reticence. While Basil was still alive, Gregory had encouraged him to "clarify" his position because people were saying he "dissimulates." Gregory received not the desired clarification, but a stinging rebuke for listening to theological gossip. Basil felt spied upon and expected better of his friends.[23]

Rather than being flawed, Basil's teaching on the Spirit was the appropriate construction of a temporary, passing formulation in the face of specific historical circumstances, made before the conciliar decision of 381. His contribution was his refusal to be imprisoned in either old or new categories of school theology, or in a controversial word laden with the freight of many battles.[24] He wanted to safeguard the unity of the church while at the same time not placing too great a burden on the backs of the weak, and this without compromising the substance of the faith.

[23] Athanasius, *To Palladius* PG 26.1168d; *To John and Antiochus* PG 26.1168a. Dörries, *DSS*, 25. Gregory of Nazianzus, *Oration* 31.3; SC 250.280; 43.68–69; SC 384.274–82; *Letter* 58, in *Lettres*, Paul Gallay, ed., 3 vols. (Paris: Édition "Les Belles Lettres," 1964) 1.61–63. Basil *Letter* 71; Courtonne, 1.166–68; 119; Courtonne, 2.23–25 (to Eustathius of Sebaste, who seems to have listened to slanders against Basil).

[24] Dörries, *DSS*, 182.

Chapter 15

Gregory of Nazianzus:
The Divine Pedagogy in Stages

Gregory of Nazianzus's ninety-nine poems about himself give us more access to his life than to that of either of the other Cappadocians. Unusually learned but also unusually sensitive and introspective, he was temperamentally ill-at-ease in controversy and unfitted for the fierce theological battles and ecclesiastical turmoil of the second half of the fourth century. Linguistically he was quite happy to use the vocabulary of the schools as long as it was placed in the confessional theology of the central tradition. He was a philosophical rhetorician, not an ontological philosopher like Gregory of Nyssa. He could use ontological categories but preferred logical, grammatical principles. If the tradition is to be trusted, in about 358 he and Basil made excerpts from Origen's writings, producing the *Philocalia* to demonstrate the harmony between faith and reason. Like Basil and Gregory of Nyssa, he was indebted to Origen, "the stone on which we were honed."[1]

Reflecting on why the Spirit was absent from the discussion of the previous years and centuries, Gregory of Nazianzus proposes "an inchoate theory of the development of doctrine." The specific question posed to Gregory is that of the divinity of the Spirit. "What can you say about the Holy Spirit? Where do you get the strange God (the Holy Spirit), [whose divinity] is not in the scriptures?" That the

---

[1] Frederick W. Norris, *Faith Gives Fullness to Reasoning: The Five Theological Orations of Gregory Nazianzen* (Leiden: Brill, 1991) 186, 196, 213. *Philocalia* mentioned by Hesychius in *Svidae Lexicon*, Ada Adler, ed.; 5 vols. (Stuttgart: Teubner, 1933) 3.619.

divinity of the Spirit is not clearly stated in scripture is granted with some embarrassment.[2]

Gregory's opponents said he was proposing "a rival God," "a fraudulently registered God." Basil had been wearied by his own detractors who insisted "time and time again" that his doctrine of the divinity of the Spirit was not in scripture.[3] Both Basil and Gregory say that inference from scripture is necessary. Basil appeals to the unwritten tradition, by which he means the liturgical life of the church, the historic worship practice of the church, an appeal to the *lex orandi, lex credendi* (the law of prayer is the law of belief) which contained the apostolic tradition extending beyond the scriptures even while it was being faithful to what was contained therein.[4] To honor this usage rooted in scripture, but going beyond scripture and controlled by scripture, is also to be apostolic.

GOD'S EARTHQUAKES AT POINTS OF TRANSITION

In answering the charge that scripture is silent on the divinity of the Spirit, Gregory elaborates a doctrine of gradual unfolding, God

[2] Jaroslav Pelikan, *The Melody of Theology: A Philosophical Dictionary* (Cambridge: Harvard, 1988) 128; *The Emergence of the Catholic Tradition (100–600)* (Chicago: University of Chicago, 1971) 211. Gregory, *Oration* 31.1, 21; SC 250.276, 314.

[3] *Oration* 31.26, 3; SC 250.328, 278. Basil, *On the Holy Spirit* 27.68; SC 17bis.490.

[4] I disagree with R.P.C. Hanson's judgment, *Tradition in the Early Church* (Philadelphia: Westminster, 1962) 184, that this is "a disastrously uncritical excursus into history on Basil's part." Basil's perspective is broader, as Jaroslav Pelikan, "The 'Spiritual Sense' of Scripture," in *Basil of Caesarea: Christian, Humanist, Ascetic,* Paul J. Fedwick, ed. (Toronto: Pontifical Institute of Mediaeval Studies, 1981) 359, points out: "The unwritten tradition" and "the secret and mystical tradition" refer specifically to the liturgy as the continuation of the apostolic tradition. Basil's point is valid in principle, though he may not have all the details right. Since the Council of Trent the texts of Basil and Gregory have been much discussed. The bibliography is given in Emmanuel A. de Mendieta, *'Unwritten' and 'Secret' Apostolic Traditions in the Theological Thought of St. Basil of Caesarea* (*Scottish Journal of Theology Occasional Papers,* 13) (Edinburgh: Oliver and Boyd, 1965). Pelikan is sharply critical of de Mendieta. Basil's text in *On the Holy Spirit* 27.66 belongs to the history of the famous *partim . . . partim* and *et . . . et* formulations at Trent. Peter Canisius had used a Latin text rendering the flexible *ta men . . . ta de* of Basil as *partim . . . partim,* supporting a two-source theory. Yves Congar, *Tradition and Traditions* (New York: Macmillan, 1967) 48, 411–12.

luring believers from stage to stage. After acknowledging that there were glimpses of the divinity of the Spirit in the New Testament, Gregory goes boldly to the period after Jesus has departed. God "persuaded" the tradition of the divinity of the Spirit through the "addition" of clarity by progressive revelation, "in gradual states proportionate to their capacity," extending beyond the scriptures to "a later stage," that includes Gregory's own period of history. He speaks of "the progress of the doctrine of God," by which he means a gradual unfolding in history.[5]

The transition from the worshiping of idols to the Law, from the Law to the gospel, and from the gospel to the period after the departure of Jesus for the Father—each of these represents a new stage in the unfolding history, comparable to an earthquake, a new ordering of divine pedagogy. In the Old Testament there was a clear manifestation of the Father but a less definite showing of the Son. "The New [Testament] made the Son manifest and gave us a glimpse of the Spirit's Godhead." Only a glimpse, not full-bodied revelation. If the Son is fully revealed in the New Testament period, the Spirit is also experienced there. But Gregory then sees the "fullest revelation of the Spirit outside of the scriptures as a necessary and fulfilling inference from what had gone before" in the scriptures.[6]

Gregory's argument that the post-biblical tradition unfolds in a fuller manner what was present in the biblical witness does not make that development extra-biblical in his mind. The tradition is also biblical because it is one with the reality present in the biblical witness. "At the present time the Spirit resides amongst us, giving us a clearer manifestation of himself than before."[7] Inference from scripture is not only allowed, but necessary.

THE PEDAGOGIC DANGER OF EXCEEDING WHAT IS PROPER TO EACH STAGE

Gregory thinks it would have been "dangerous" for the Son to be openly preached during the Old Testament period, while the Godhead of the Father was still not fully acknowledged. Recognizing

---

[5] Gregory, *Oration* 31.26–27; SC 250.326–30. Gregory also appealed to the liturgy of baptism: *Oration* 40.43; SC 250.63.

[6] *Oration* 31.26; SC 250.326. Norris, *Faith Gives Fullness To Reasoning*, 206.

[7] *Oration* 31.26; SC 250.326.

that he is using daring language, Gregory contends that it would also have been dangerous during the New Testament period to be too preoccupied with the proclamation of the Spirit before the Son had been fully established or received. Strong meat should not be given to weak stomachs; too much light must not be given to feeble eyes. To do so would put at risk what did lie within their powers to receive. Such is not God's plan of education. "God meant it to be by piecemeal additions, 'ascents,' as David called them, by progress and advance from glory to glory." When God's progressive plan is observed, then "the light of the Trinity should shine with more clarity." Gregory assures us that in this developing history we are "lured into the gospel by partial changes." This progressive illumination Gregory calls "the order of theology," that is, the contemplation of God *(theologia)* is expressed in successive stages of God's design in history *(oikonomia).*[8]

In laying out God's progressive educative process with such clarity, Gregory thinks he may be breaking new ground, though he is not certain of this. But of this much he is certain: The Lord said that after he has departed for the Father, the Spirit dwelling within will teach "everything" (John 14:26; 16:13). One of "the things" to be taught after the Lord has gone to the Father "I take to be," says Gregory, "the Godhead of the Spirit," which will be clearer "when the knowledge is timely, capable of being received."[9]

Though the ancient church learned its theology from the reading of the unfolding economy of salvation, Gregory has added a new dimension. Theology itself changes because it submits itself to the evolving history. History changes; theology changes. Before the gospel, believers lived (if one were to speak in crude, simplistic terms) as though there were only one God. At the proclamation of the good news, everything took place as though there was only God and the Son who is fully God. But after the departure of Jesus we know God, the Son, who is fully God, and the Spirit, also fully God. And this developmental process has a pedagogic purpose.[10]

[8] Ibid.

[9] *Oration,* 31.27; SC 250.328–30.

[10] Auguste Luneau, *L'histoire du salut chez les pères de l'église: la doctrine des âges du monde* (Paris: Beauchesne, 1964) 155–59. See also SC 250.326 n. 2.

Gregory's ideal in demonstrating the equality of the Spirit is to "keep within the limits of orthodoxy, maintaining a balance between extremes." But where the boundaries were, which authors had found the balance and which not, were all unclear—pneumatology has "something specially difficult about it." He is well aware that no one has an absolute icon of God, but only faint and tremulous resemblances or analogies. He, like Basil, uses logic, but he rails against logic-choppers and syllogistic athletes in the area of the Unknowable One who is manifest in history.[11]

No one was exempt from the dilemma. Gregory admitted that even the best faltered.[12] He was likely aware that orthodox economic trinitarian formulation could be used to promote inappropriate doctrinal subordination (as in the case of Marcellus of Ancyra, who accepted the *homoousios* but had the Father absorbing the Son and the Spirit), and also aware that a deficient or unbalanced formulation could exist with balanced intent.

The equality he sought was determined by a trinitarian dynamic. "Do not give a false dignity to the Father at the expense of the Only-Begotten . . . and to the Son at the expense of the Spirit." In other words, do not think that the Father alone is divine. Do not think that the Son and the Spirit are ontologically less than the Father. Do not think that what is ascribed to the Son is taken away from the Father, or what is ascribed to the Spirit is taken away from the Son. This is not to abandon the dynamic of triune life, where the kingdom is ultimately handed over to the Father, but to respect the full personhood of each. Nor is it to retreat from the rightful

---

[11] *Oration* 20.5; SC 270.68; 31.2; 27.3; 31.8; SC 250.276, 76–78, 290. Basil, *On the Holy Spirit* 3.5; 6.13; SC 17bis.266, 288. Basil opts for "the simplicity and spontaneity of the faith." Gregory contends that those who pry into the difference between "begetting" and "proceeding" will go mad. "Thus God escapes your syllogistic toils and shows himself stronger than your exclusive alternatives." Dörries, *DSS*, 48, calls these technical logicians "verbal magicians" or "verbal acrobats." In honoring the apophatic approach, the Cappadocians were careful not to give positive content to the words "Father, Son and Holy Spirit." Zizioulas, "The Teaching of the 2nd Ecumenical Council on the Holy Spirit in Historical and Ecumenical Perspective," *CSS*, 1.44 n. 44. Norris, *Faith Gives Fullness to Reasoning*, 210.

[12] *Oration* 21.33; SC 270.182.

christological focus of pneumatology, but to check the move to christomonism. The Spirit is not "a rival God."[13]

Gregory's coinage, *theosis* (divinization), is a bold stroke. As George Florovsky notes, *theosis* "may be a hard word, but is the only adequate phrase to denote that intimacy of fellowship with God." More than any other theologian, Gregory is insistent and consistent in using it. It has been calculated that Gregory uses the verb form *(theoō)* twenty-one times and the noun form *(theosis)* ten times.[14] Gregory never sought to support it on scriptural grounds; it was a biblical concept, not a biblical term.

Both at the beginning and the end of his oration on the Spirit, Gregory invokes a soteriological principle embedded in the liturgical life of the church. He argues first from the role of the Spirit in Jesus' own baptism in the Jordan, then to the fact that the Spirit divinizes in our baptism, and finally to the divinity of the Spirit. "The Spirit testifies to the divinity, because the Spirit hastens toward the One [Jesus at the Jordan] to whom the Spirit is like." "Were the Spirit not to be worshiped, how could he deify me through baptism? If he is to be worshiped, why not adored? And if adored, how can he fail to be God?" This concatenation of baptismal divinization with the incontestable divinity of the Spirit constitutes "a truly golden chain of salvation," revealed in scripture and made clear in post-biblical times through the indwelling Spirit. The goal of salvation is not just personal happiness, but sharing in the rhythm of divine life, in becoming divine, while remaining integrally human. The experience of the church testifies to this. But if the Spirit is a creature and less than God, then we may be "banished from the Trinity," or in the words written in his last years, banished from "my Trinity."[15]

[13] *Oration* 31.12, 26; SC 250.298–300, 328. In *Oration* 30.5; SC 250.234, Gregory accuses Eunomius of viewing the Son as "a bandit, an enemy of God."

[14] Florovsky, "The Lamb of God," *Scottish Journal of Theology* 4 (1951) 19, quoted in Winslow, *The Dynamics of Salvation: A Study in Gregory of Nazianzus* (Cambridge, Mass.: Philadelphia Patristic Foundation, 1979) 181. Anthony Meredith, *The Cappadocians* (Crestwood, N.Y.: St. Vladimir's, 1995) 48.

[15] *Oration* 31.12, 27–28; 39.16; SC 250.300, 328–32; SC 358.184. It goes without saying that divinization has to do with transformation, not an escape from humanity. The currency of divinization in Roman Catholic thought today is seen in its frequent occurrence in the *Catechism of the Catholic Church* (Washington, D.C.: United States Catholic Conference, 1994). The very first sentence (7) announces

The formalizing of the biblical category into the non-biblical term *theosis* excludes an inappropriate subordination of the Spirit in the eternal Trinity, that is, it excludes an ontological subordination of the Spirit to the Father and the Son. But the category of *theosis* retains a biblical non-ontological subordination in the history of the economy of salvation, as in the Father sending the Son and the Spirit.

what becomes a unitive theme: "God, infinitely perfect and blessed in himself, in a plan of sheer goodness, freely created man to make him share in his own blessed life." I am indebted to my late confrère, Godfrey Diekmann, O.S.B., for this insight. Gregory, *De Vita Sua: Einleitung, Text, Übersetzung, Kommentar*, Christoph Jungck, ed. (Heidelberg: Winter, 1974) 144, line 1852 (see also 148, line 1948): "My Trinity, for you alone I care."

Chapter 16

The Council of Constantinople, 381:
The Triumph of Discretion

The debate over the divinity of the Spirit reaches a climax at the Council of Constantinople (381), and traces of that debate are embedded in the creed bearing the council's name. The history of the Nicene-Constantinopolitan Creed is long and complicated, and has been ably told by Hermann Dörries, N. Q. King, Adolf-Martin Ritter, J.N.D. Kelly, and R.P.C. Hanson, to whom these pages are indebted.[1]

In the year 379 Gratian, emperor in the West, called Theodosius from behind the plow in Spain to be emperor in the East, when Theodosius was only thirty-two. Shortly thereafter, Theodosius became ill in Thessalonika and asked for baptism, contrary to the imperial custom, established by Constantine and Constantius II, of postponing baptism until just before death. At the end of February 380 Theodosius I imposed the Nicene formula of faith as a dogmatic rule, hoping to bring unity and peace to the empire. This decree anticipated the results of the council by confessing Father, Son, and Holy Spirit as one deity. Heretics were excluded from worshiping in churches and from gathering within the walls of any town. The correct Nicene doctrine was explained, but explicit faith in the divinity of the Spirit was not required.[2]

---

[1] Dörries, *DSS*, 163–76. King, *The Emperor Theodosius and the Establishment of Christianity* (Philadelphia: Westminster, 1960) 17–49. Ritter, *Das Konzil von Konstantinopel und seine Symbol* (Göttingen: Vandenhoeck & Ruprecht, 1965). Kelly, *Creeds*, 296–365; Hanson, *The Search for the Christian Doctrine of God* (Edinburgh: T. & T. Clark, 1988) 805–75.

[2] Latin text in King, *The Emperor Theodosius*, 34, n. 1.

After his solemn entry into Constantinople, either in late 380 or early 381, Theodosius published a decree of convocation for a synod of bishops of the Eastern Empire. One hundred fifty bishops gathered in the capital in May 381 and deliberated until the end of July. Theodosius did not attend the sessions, leaving the leadership to Meletius of Antioch, the highly controversial bishop of one of the most important Christian communities, who brought with him seventy-one bishops from areas known to be friendly to him.[3] Unfortunately, neither official acts or minutes nor any ordered account of the council survived. We know of its decisions mostly from a council which met in the same city a year later.

FERMENT AND CONFLICT

Before the council of 381 began, Gregory of Nazianzus was elected bishop of Constantinople, and it appears that the Council Fathers confirmed the appointment. When the first president of the council, Meletius of Antioch, died during the sessions, Gregory was elected to succeed him. Gregory wanted to put the notorious schism in Antioch to rest by electing Paulinus as the next bishop of that city to succeed Meletius, but the council opposed his wishes and elected Flavian.

Gregory, always sensitive, was angered both by this election and by the Egyptian delegation of bishops (they arrived late) who questioned the validity of his translation from his episcopal see in Asia Minor to Constantinople, something forbidden by canon 15 of Nicaea, but repeatedly violated. Gregory knew that the challenge was a political move, as the Nicene canon was obsolete almost from the moment it was promulgated if non-observance is any standard. But Gregory, not well suited to the stresses of public office, followed a pattern of inability to cope on the public stage and retreated from obligations he had assumed. He resigned, and after a face-saving dignified farewell address, departed. Years later, in retirement, he wrote a bitter attack on the council and especially on its formulation of the creed.[4]

---

[3] A look at a map of sees represented at Constantinople 381 makes it clear how decisively it was an eastern council. If the lists are correct, only three sees on the European side of the Bosphorus were present: Constantinople, Anchalus in Thrace, and Marcianopolis in Moesia. See King, *Emperor Theodosius*, 98.

[4] Norman Tanner, *Decrees of the Ecumenical Councils*, 2 vols. (Georgetown: Georgetown University, 1990) 1.13. Hanson, *Search*, 808, especially n. 79. Ritter,

The heat of discussion in the council was reflected on the streets and in the shops of Constantinople. Gregory of Nyssa relates: "Hardly anyone is without an opinion. In the narrow lanes, at the crossroads, in the forums, among peddlers of garments, tellers at the banks, and those who sell you fruit, if you ask for change, the man launches into a theological discussion about begotten (Son) and unbegotten (Father); if you enquire about the price of bread, the answer is given that the Father is greater and the Son subordinate; if you remark that the bath is nice, the man pronounces that the Son is from non-existence."[5]

We have no knowledge of the sequence of the few facts in our possession. We do know that Theodosius wanted the council to unify the Eastern Empire, and we know that he would have been able to call on the authority of Basil, now dead about two years, and Athanasius, eight years gone, both firm believers in the divinity of the Spirit, but who were, as we have seen, discreet in their affirmations. Theodosius probably thought discretion could be an instrument of unity. Like Theodosius himself, both Basil and Athanasius wanted to bring along those who did not want to go beyond the clear words of scripture. Theodosius wanted the council to affirm the Nicene faith and give the conservative Macedonians a text they could sign. Around 379 the Macedonian party had organized itself into a real faction, with Eustathius of Sebaste, the one-time ascetic friend of Basil, among its leaders. The Macedonians would not be docile lambs at the council. They would want their say in the formulation of any creed, invoking both tradition and the silence of scripture.

THE ELUSIVE CREED

What precisely did the council do in the matter of the creed? There has been a long dispute over whether the council ever issued a formal creed. The accepted standard position, best formulated by Kelly, is that between the Council of Constantinople in 381 and the Council

---

Das Konzil, 104–11. Hans von Campenhausen, *The Fathers of the Greek Church* (New York: Pantheon, 1955) 95. Gregory of Nazianzus, *De Vita Sua: Einleitung, Text, Übersetzung, Kommentar*, Christoph Jungck, ed. (Heildelberg: Winter, 1994) 1506–18.

[5] Gregory of Nyssa, *On the Deity of the Son and the Holy Spirit*, in *Opera*, Werner Jaeger, ed.; 11 vols. (Leiden: Brill, 1952–1996) 10/2:121.

of Chalcedon in 451 there is no trace of the creed. Chalcedon cites and names the creed as that of 318 Fathers at Nicaea and the 150 Fathers at Constantinople. The wording of the first two articles of the Nicene-Constantinopolitan Creed differs markedly from the Nicene Creed. A statistical lexigraphical comparison of the creeds shows that the later cannot be a modified form of the earlier.[6] The creed we call the Nicene-Constantinopolitan was very likely in existence and in liturgical use in the 370s as a baptismal creed before the council took it up. Though the creed adopted by the Council of Constantinople is not the creed of Nicaea, it is Nicene in character.

Since Kelly published, R.P.C. Hanson has demonstrated small but significant indications that the council in 381 did produce its own creed. The archdeacon of Constantinople stood up at the Council of Chalcedon and read a text taken supposedly from the archives of Constantinople. Further, we have a text called the *Third Macedonian Dialogue* that likely predates Chalcedon by several years. In this dialogue a Macedonian berates an orthodox believer: "Have you not added to the creed of Nicaea?" The Orthodox responds: "Yes, but nothing that contradicts it." To which the Macedonian answers: "Still, you have added [to it]."[7]

Further evidence is the *Confession* of St. Patrick, containing the words, "And he poured upon us richly the Holy Spirit, gift and pledge of immortality, who makes those who believe and obey to be sons of God and co-heirs of Christ, whom we confess and adore one God in the Trinity of holy name." The last phrase came more likely from the creed of Constantinople ("who with the Father and the Son is worshiped and glorified") than from any other source. Hanson believes it unlikely that Patrick could have learned of the creed of Constantinople after Chalcedon.[8]

A final piece of evidence comes from Gregory of Nazianzus himself. Toward the end of his life he wrote an autobiographical poem

[6] Kelly, *Creeds*, 296–331.

[7] PG 28.1202–49, esp. at 1204. Hanson, *Search*, 813, calls it the *Second Macedonian Dialogue*, but the Migne text he refers to calls it the *Third Macedonian Dialogue*.

[8] Hanson, "Witness from St. Patrick to the Creed of 381," *Analecta Bollandiana* 101 (1983) 297–99 (see extended note in *St. Patrick, confession et lettre à Coroticus*, SC 249.75, n. 4); *Search*, 814.

in which he berates the Fathers of the council: "What a situation that was! The sweet and pure stream of the old faith, which brought together into one the venerable nature of the Trinity, whose school Nicaea once was. This I witnessed being wretchedly muddied by the foul tributaries of waverers, whose opinions are those which Authority favored. . . . Whoever they were, they came together, under coercion and reluctantly, but still they came together, any who still had some trace of free speech left, those whose ignorance was their assistant in doing wrong, trapped by the ambiguity of the doctrines."[9] A little later Gregory describes the late arrival of the delegation from Egypt, which set about attacking the legitimacy of his translation from one see to another.

All of this would suggest, not prove, that the creed was crafted while Gregory was still president of the council, though he lost the battle in the council over the wording of the creed. Hanson believes that in the texts from *De Vita Sua* just quoted, Gregory indicates that the wording was dictated by the will of the emperor ("whose opinions are those which Authority favors") and that the wording of the creed was decided before the arrival of the Egyptians and the Macedonians.[10] Gregory was bitterly opposed to any indirection, any diplomatic strategy, any comfortable accommodation in formulating the text about the divinity of the Spirit. He found the final text of the creed much too responsive to the wishes of the Macedonians.

The conclusion to all this evidence, admittedly scattered and made up of historical scraps, is that the council did put together its own creed, using some pre-existing text as its basis, one that was in broad terms like that of Nicaea.

The emperor's hope to have a text all could sign was dashed. Nothing could succeed in bringing together the majority, who wanted to defend the divinity of the Spirit, and the Macedonians (while they were still part of the proceedings), who rejected the divinity, even though among the Macedonians there were shades of opinion. They would not accept the formulation which so clearly implied the divinity of the Spirit. The majority were willing to sign a

[9] Gregory of Nazianzus, *De Vita Sua*, Jungck, 1703–08; 1750–58.
[10] Hanson, *Search*, 815. Ritter, *Das Konzil*, 78–85, believes the text was formulated after the Macedonians arrived.

text which introduced no philosophical categories, no words taken from the schools, did not use the word "God" or *"homoousios"* of the Spirit, but remained with the biblical vocabulary, and was, however indirectly, a profession of the divinity of the Spirit. Clearly out-voted, and having reached an impasse, the Macedonian bishops walked out of the council. According to Socrates, their leaders wrote to the churches under their charge that they "were under no circumstances to agree to the creed of Nicaea."[11] In other words, they were to have no communion with the Nicenes, who won the day at Constantinople.

WE STAND IN THE CONTINUITY OF DOCTRINE

The 150 Fathers at the Council of Constantinople were clearly reluctant to go beyond the text of Nicaea, but they found themselves in a new situation, principally the explicit denial of the divinity of the Spirit by the Macedonians. The first canon of the Council of Constantinople shows how determinedly they wanted to stand with the Council of Nicaea: "The profession of faith of the holy Fathers who gathered in Nicaea in Bithynia is not to be abrogated, but is to remain in force." Shortly after the council ended, Gregory of Nazianzus responded to a letter from Cledonius asking for "a concise definition and rule of our faith": "We for our part have never esteemed, and never can esteem, any doctrine preferable to the faith of the holy fathers who assembled at Nicaea to destroy the Arian heresy. We adhere with God's help, and shall adhere, to this faith, supplementing the gaps which they left concerning the Holy Spirit because this question had not then been raised."[12]

The continuity with the Council of Nicaea, which the Council of Constantinople insisted upon, is again stated as a principle at Chalcedon: "We have proclaimed to all the creed of the 318 [Fathers

[11] Socrates, *Ecclesiastical History* 2.45; PG 67.360b.
[12] Tanner, *Decrees*, 1.31. *Letter* 102; PG 37.193. This letter, together with *Letter* 101, was excluded from the critical edition of his correspondence, *Saint Grégoire de Nazianze: Lettres*, Paul Gallay, ed., 2 vols. (Paris: Société d'Édition 'Les Belles Lettres,' 1964–1967) (see 2. Avant-propos), because it does not belong to the manuscript tradition of the letters of Gregory of Nazianzus but to his discourses. Neither could I find it in the SC edition of the Discourses. Therefore I give the PG reference.

gathered at Nicaea]; and we have made our own those Fathers who accepted this agreed statement of religion—the 150 who later met in the great Constantinople and themselves set their seal to the same creed." It was not a question of the creed of Nicaea being placed on the same level with that of Constantinople. As Kelly points out, the Fathers at Chalcedon believed the creed of Nicaea had more weight. They wanted to say that nothing was lacking at Nicaea, yet Constantinople had added scriptural testimonies to Nicaea's all-too-brief third article: "We decree that pre-eminence belongs to the exposition of the right and spotless creed of the 318 saintly and blessed Fathers who were assembled at Nicaea when Constantine of pious memory was emperor: and that those decrees also remain in force which were issued in Constantinople by the 150 holy fathers in order to destroy the heresies then rife and to confirm this same catholic and apostolic creed."[13]

THE COMPOSITION OF THE TEXT

It will be recalled that the third article of the Nicene Creed was terse: "[and we believe] in the Holy Spirit." The expansion in the Nicene-Constantinopolitan Creed reads, "the Lord and Giver of life, who proceeds from the Father, Who is worshiped and glorified together with the Father and the Son, Who spoke through the prophets: and in one holy, catholic, and apostolic Church. We confess one baptism for the remission of sins. We look forward to the resurrection of the dead and the life of the world to come. Amen."

What of significance for pneumatology was added to the creed of Nicaea? In a general negative sense, the creed of Constantinople wanted to reprobate those who opposed the orthodox pneumatology, which the council identified in its first canon when it named the principal heretics: Arians, Semi-Arians (Pneumatomachoi), Sabellians, and Apollinarians. Positively, the council wanted to hand on the faith of Nicaea with the addition of the expanded third article. The formulation makes it clear that the third article did not have the character of an "autonomous" declaration, that is, the Fathers did not want to present a pneumatology apart from its trinitarian context. Indeed, they did want to make a contribution to the much-discussed *fighters of the spirit*

[13] Tanner, *Decrees*, 1.83–84. Kelly, *Creeds*, 330–31.

question of the inner-trinitarian relation of the Spirit.[14]

All in all there were twelve changes, whose contents indicate that the Fathers were guided by the doctrine of the Nicene Creed, but the creed they worked from was not that text. In the second article, after "became incarnate" they added "by the Holy Spirit and the Virgin Mary." Very likely this phrase was added to combat Apollinarianism, which denied the integrity of Christ's manhood. They contended that the incarnate Son did not possess a human soul or mind. The phrase "by the Holy Spirit and the Virgin Mary" was a specification of what "incarnate" meant.[15]

Staying with scripture might have seemed safe, but did not solve all problems. The Council Fathers mistakenly thought that John 15:26 ("who comes from the Father") was a statement about the eternal procession of the Third Person of the Trinity from the Father, and quoted the verse in that sense, that is, it was about the inner life of God, not God as manifested in history. Most modern exegetes, though not all, would agree with Raymond Brown: "The writer [of the Fourth Gospel] is not speculating about the interior life of God; he is concerned with the disciples in the world."[16] The inclusion of John 15:26, as it was then understood, would certainly be an affront to the Pneumatomachoi, who thought the derivation

[14] Tanner, *Decrees*, 1.31. Ritter, *Das Konzil*, 295.

[15] Hanson, *Search*, 817. But Kelly, *Creeds*, 336–37, thinks that there is nothing specifically anti-Apollinarian about the phrase "by the Holy Spirit and the Virgin Mary." He believes it was retained by the Fathers of Constantinople simply because it was found in the text of the creed they were using as their basic text.

[16] *The Gospel According to John XIII–XXI* (Garden City: Doubleday, 1970) 689. Brown adds that the one who sends the Paraclete, the Father or Jesus, "is not really significant at the theological level, for in Johannine thought the Father and Jesus are one." See also Rudolf Schnackenburg, *The Gospel According to St. John*, 3 vols. (New York: Crossroad, 1982) 3.118: "Most of the church Fathers and several twentieth-century Catholic exegetes interpret this 'proceeding from the Father' in an internally trinitarian sense as a proceeding of the third divine Person of the Trinity from the Father (in case of the Greek Fathers) and the Son (in the case of the Latin Fathers: *filioque*). Although this interpretation is in itself possible and is consistent as a dogmatic idea, it did not come within the Johannine vision." In a similar sense see Francis J. Moloney, *The Gospel of John* (Collegeville: The Liturgical Press, 1998) 434. Marie-Joseph Lagrange, *Évangile selon saint Jean*, 2nd ed. (Paris: Lecoffre, 1925) 413, admits that the text does not refer to the eternal *spiratio*, but to temporal mission. Nonetheless he believes that there is an

of the Spirit from the Father derogatory to the Son. They believed that the Spirit was derived directly from the Son.[17] In any event, both orthodox and Pneumatomachoi were mistaken on the meaning of the text in John 15:26.

The text of the creed is a tissue of biblical phrases. The use of "Lord" for the Spirit is biblical (2 Cor 3:17), though, as Kelly remarks, "Lord" was too widely used in the Hellenistic world to be decisive by itself as proclaiming the divinity of the Spirit. The creed speaks of the Spirit as "the Spirit of life" (Rom 8:2), and more specifically as "the Giver of life" (John 6:63 and 2 Cor 3:6). The phrase, "who comes from the Father" (John 15:26), has only a change of the preposition from *para* to *ek,* a change supported by Paul's language when he writes of "the Spirit that is from God" (1 Cor 2:12). "Who spoke through the prophets" was not an original credal element but had a long history, going back to the primitive proclamation as found in 2 Peter 1:21: "No prophecy ever came by human will, but men and women moved by the Holy Spirit spoke from God."[18]

The words that most decisively declare the council's intent are these: "Who with the Father and the Son is together worshiped and glorified." The phrase is an almost verbatim citation from Athanasius, but the council is even more discreet than the great theologian. Athanasius wrote, "He, therefore, is not a creature, but is one with the Son as the Son is one with the Father, who is glorified with the Father and the Son, who is confessed as God with the Word, who is active in the works which the Father works through the Son. Is not the one who calls him a creature guilty of a direct impiety against the Son himself?"[19] The one who is worshiped and glorified with the Father and the Son is evidently divine. But the council did not use technical, non-biblical words, such as *homoousios,* nor did it directly assert that the Spirit is "Confessed as God," as Athanasius had done.[20]

allusion to the eternal procession, because mission follows and manifests procession. Though Lagrange's theological reasoning is correct, few exegetes would attribute even an allusion to the eternal procession.

[17] Ritter, *Das Konzil,* 300.

[18] Kelly, *Creeds,* 341–42.

[19] Athanasius, *Letters to Serapion* 1.31; SC 15.139.

[20] Ibid.

THE ECCLESIOLOGICAL STRUCTURE OF FAITH

The ecclesiology of the Nicene-Constantinopolitan Creed is found
not in the second article, devoted to the Son, but in the expansion
of the third article, allocated to the Spirit: "[We believe] in one,
holy, catholic and apostolic church. We confess one baptism for the
remission of sins. We look forward to the resurrection of the dead
and the life of the world to come." But it would be a mistake to
think that the christological focus should now be replaced by a
pneumatological one. The creed has a trinitarian logic, so that the
Son is not added to the mystery of the Father, the Spirit is not
added to the mystery of the Son. Or put differently, one does not
leave the mystery of the Father when one moves on to the mystery
of the Son, and likewise one does not leave the mystery of the Son
when one moves on to the mystery of the Spirit. Ecclesiology is
structured according to a trinitarian mode, characterized by a concentration which is both christological and pneumatological, the
one informing the other.

There has been a concerted effort over the centuries, whether in
relation to the Nicene-Constantinopolitan Creed or the Apostles
Creed, to distinguish between "believing" in the Father, Son, and
Spirit, and "believing" in the church, or "believing" the church.
The church is not, cannot be, the object of faith in the way God is.
The distinction between believing in God and believing in the
church, as Henri du Lubac said, is not a matter of nuance, but of an
abyss. Augustine is confident that right belief in God, orthodoxy, is
found in the church, but the church is not properly an object of
faith: "The church is holy and catholic because her faith in God is
right. So, we have not invited you to believe in the church as we
must believe in God, but understand well what we have told you
and tell you again: you who are now within the holy, catholic
church, believe in God."[21]

WHO WON?

The short answer is, discretion won. Not only could the fathers call
upon Athanasius, but also upon Basil, who would have been happy

---

[21] De Lubac, *The Christian Faith* (San Francisco: Ignatius, 1986) 174. Pseudo-
Maximus of Turin, *Tractatus* 2: *De Baptismo*; PL 101.776c.

with the outcome of the council. The tone of Constantinople is not belligerent. The council had not used the operative word *homoousios* of the Spirit, and did not apply "God" to the Spirit. Even with these omissions, those who opposed the divinity of the Spirit could not have signed the creed. If the Spirit is co-worshiped and co-glorified with the Father and the Son, the logic is clear. And even if one wanted to argue that the creed of Constantinople itself is not without ambiguity, the *tomos* of the synod of Constantinople of the next year, 382, makes it evident that the earlier synod had intended to establish the full divinity of the Spirit, the Spirit's consubstantiality with the Father and the Son, without saying so expressly. Also significant, it established the Spirit's existence as a separate person *(hypostasis)*.[22]

At the conclusion of the council the Fathers sent a letter to Theodosius requesting that the decisions of the council be given the force of law.[23] The creed effected a theological peace, bringing the trinitarian controversy to an end, but, in the hands of Theodosius, the creed was also the assurance of civil peace in the Eastern Empire.

---

[22] Dörries, *DSS*, 174, is surely correct in saying that Basil would have formulated the text of the creed differently, but that the general character of the creed is Basilian. Hanson, *Search*, 818, also believes the creed "summarizes very nicely the doctrine of Basil of Caesarea."

[23] Sozomen, *Ecclesiastical History* 7.9; PG 67.1436–40.

Chapter 17

Experience of the Spirit in the New Testament and Early Church

Religious experience is conventionally understood to mean special elevations of an individual believer, but there is also experience of what Pseudo-Dionysius called "the theological tradition," meaning the scriptures and the liturgy in the total life of the church. In addition to individual and liturgical experience, there is the broader ecclesial experience, the experience of the church in its historical theological development and on-going life. Faith is not an act of the naked intellect, or a leap into a great unknown void, or an absolute risk; it is based on experience.[1]

   Biblical scholars underscore the significance of experience for Christian understanding of the Spirit. C. K. Barrett: "No more certain statement can be made about the Christians of the first generation than this: they believed themselves to be living under the immediate government of the Spirit of God." Eduard Schweizer: "Long before the Spirit was a theme of doctrine, He was a fact in the experience of the community. . . . If the new creation was already present, the Spirit could not be merely a preliminary sign of what was still to come, a mere exception. The Spirit had to represent the new existence as such." Franz J. Schierse: "[It is] the biblical conviction that the Holy Spirit represents the presence and reality of the salvation event in a way that can be experienced with the

---

[1] Pseudo-Dionysius, *Letter* 9; PG 3.1105. Klaus Koch, *The Prophets: The Assyrian Period* (Philadelphia: Fortress, 1983) 123.

senses."[2] But care should be taken not to interpret the biblical texts in a rigorous systematic way. To say that the Spirit was a fact of experience in the early Christian community is not the same as to say that *in principle* the Spirit falls under experience, a position which could not be defended. The first statement is historical; the second is theological.

PAUL ON EXPERIENCE

In Paul, experience of the Spirit does not seem to carry the sense of the individualistic or subjectivistic. Only rarely does Paul speak of the Spirit in individual terms; rather, it is shared in the conversion-initiation process, to which Paul could recall his converts (2 Cor 1:21-22; Gal 3:2-5). Indeed, the common experience of the Spirit constitutes the one and sufficient term in Paul's definition of belonging to Christ (Rom 8:9). The wondrous unity of communion and fellowship is a creation of the Spirit, "for in one Spirit we were all baptized into one body" (1 Cor 12:13). "Experience of the Spirit is not merely one aspect of the new life of the believing community; it is the principle of it."[3]

In his earliest letter, Paul wants the Thessalonians to recall the experience of conversion-initiation when the gospel came "not in word only, but also in power and in the Holy Spirit and with full conviction" (1 Thess 1:5). Power, Spirit, and full conviction are almost synonymous. The Spirit, the manifestation *par excellence* of power (Rom 15:13, 19; 1 Cor 2:4, 5), is a matter of experience— power set at the interior, forming the person, and "experienced as really operative."[4]

Paul asks the Galatians, whom he calls "the people of the Spirit" (6:1), to recall the initial experience of the Spirit on the occasion of

---

[2] Barrett, *The Holy Spirit and the Gospel Tradition* (London: SPCK, 1947) 1. Schweizer, *The Theological Dictionary of the New Testament*, 6.396, 424. Schierse, "Die neutestamentliche Trinitätsoffenbarung," *MS*, 2.112.

[3] D. F. Büchsel, *Der Geist Gottes im Neuen Testament* (Gütersloh: Bertelsmann, 1926) 442, 443. C. H. Dodd, *The Apostolic Preaching and its Developments* (New York: Harper & Row, 1964) 59. G.W.H. Lampe, *God as Spirit* (New York: Oxford University Press, 1977) 73.

[4] Traugott Holtz, *Der Erste Brief an die Thessalonicher* (Einsiedeln: Benziger, 1986) 47. Ingo Hermann, *Kyrios und Pneuma* (Munich: Kösel, 1961) 57.

the proclamation (Gal 3:2-5). So evident was the experience of the Spirit that Paul does not raise it as an issue. Rather, the issue is: What did the experience mean? Did they have the experience "in vain?" The Galatians received salvation through faith in Christ occasioned by the preaching of the gospel and the experience of the Spirit, but they will not attain salvation if they fall away from the power that made salvation accessible to them. Paul therefore appeals to the experience of the Spirit to demonstrate their justification by faith alone.[5]

Paul points, at least implicitly, to the initial experience of the Spirit "in our hearts" (2 Cor 1:21-22) as the down payment, the remainder being paid in full when the person of faith enters completely into the mode of existence determined solely by the Spirit. Already experienced here, the Spirit makes us capable of the resurrection.[6] The Spirit is "the pledge of our inheritance" (Eph 1:14).

The Spirit as the ink in which the letter of Christ is written, not on parchment but on human hearts (2 Cor 3:3, 6), is the new spirit and the new heart promised by Ezekiel (11:19; 36:25). The Spirit is "an experiential givenness characterizing the New Covenant," not just specially elect individuals.[7] Without this new spirit and new heart in the community, will the pagans ever again exclaim "God is really among you?" (1 Cor 14:25). In Philippians 2:1 Paul again appeals to the conscious experience of communion in the Spirit as the starting point of unity.

The experience of the Spirit is essentially christological because the Spirit is essentially the Spirit of Christ (Rom 8:9; Gal 4:6; Phil 1:19). Those who are led by the Spirit have the Spirit of Jesus' sonship, and they cry "Abba! Father!" (Rom 8:15; Gal 4:6). As

[5] David J. Lull, *The Spirit in Galatia: Paul's Interpretation of Pneuma as Divine Power* (Chico, Calif.: Scholars Press, 1980) 42. Hans Dieter Betz, "In Defense of the Spirit: Paul's Letter to the Galatians as a Document of Early Christian Apologetics," in *Aspects of Religious Propaganda in Judaism and Early Christianity*, Elisabeth Schüssler-Fiorenza, ed. (Notre Dame: Notre Dame University, 1976) 109–11; "The Literary Composition and Function of Paul's Letter to the Galatians," *New Testament Studies* 21 (1974–75) 370. Otto Kuss, *Der Römerbrief* (Regensburg: Pustet, 1963–78) 551.

[6] James D. G. Dunn, *Jesus and the Spirit* (Philadelphia: Westminster, 1975) 311.

[7] Jürgen Becker, *Die Briefe an die Galater* (Göttingen: Vandenhoeck & Ruprecht, 1976) 30, 31.

Ernst Käsemann says, in this call "the congregation is uttering an ecstatic cry in response to the message of salvation." The Spirit bears witness to our spirit that we are indeed adopted children of God. "The cry 'Abba' is beyond all human capabilities, and is only possible within the new relationship with God" given by the Son in the Spirit. That cry expresses an experiential participation in the most intimate relationship of Jesus' life, his relationship to the Father, a consuming and defining communion. Believers are "joint heirs with Christ" (Rom 8:17; Gal 4:7) of the Father's glory. The Spirit is the miraculous power of the heavenly world that breaks through into the earthly sphere to fashion totally new creatures and lead them to the Father's glory, and in no way cancels the sharing in the cross (Rom 8:17) that is also part of our inheritance. But the suffering "builds up to eschatological glory."[8]

Integral to faith, and not apart from it, the experience of the Spirit is a fact in the life of the communities Paul pastored. James D. G. Dunn contends that Spirit is "essentially an experiential concept" for Paul. Not only in Galatia, but also in Corinth and Rome, "the Spirit is acknowledged as a primary datum of Christian experience."[9]

JOHN ON EXPERIENCE

The frequency of such terms as "loving," "knowing," "believing," "seeing," "touching" betrays the reality of religious experience in the Johannine community.[10] The experiential lurks in Jesus' words to Nicodemus, "No one can enter the kingdom of God without being born of water and Spirit" (John 3:5); to the Samaritan woman concerning "living water" and the water becoming "a spring of water gushing up to eternal life" (4:10-14); to the disciples, "It is the Spirit that gives life. . . . The words that I have spoken to you are spirit and life" (6:63); during the festival of Tabernacles, "Let anyone who is thirsty come to me, and let the one who believes in me drink. As the scripture has said 'Out of the believer's heart shall

---

[8] *Romans* (London: SCM, 1980) 228. Joachim Jeremias, *The Prayers of Jesus* (Naperville, Ill.: Allenson, 1967) 65. Joseph Fitzmyer, *Romans* (New York: Doubleday, 1993) 502.

[9] *Jesus and the Spirit*, 201. Lull, *Spirit in Galatia*, 40.

[10] Dunn, *Unity and Diversity in the New Testament*, 2nd ed. (Philadelphia: Trinity, 1990) 198.

flow rivers of living water'" (7:37-39)—and John interprets the water as the Spirit. To this list one can add Jesus' words to Philip concerning the Spirit of truth, "You know him, because he abides with you, and he will be in you" (14:17).

In the Johannine community, as it interpreted the teaching of the Fourth Gospel, the experiential seems implicit: "You have been anointed by the Holy One, and all of you have knowledge," with the anointing abiding in them (1 John 2:20, 27); the knowledge of the Son abides in the believers "because he has given us of his Spirit" (4:13), and finally, the Spirit is "the one that testifies, for the Spirit is the truth" (5:6).[11]

Like Paul, the Johannine circle ascribes to the Spirit a strong christological accent. Jesus is the bearer of the Spirit (John 1:32-33), but Christ gives the Spirit (1 John 3:24; 4:13). However, he does not give the Spirit during his public life, "for as yet there was no Spirit, because Jesus was not yet glorified" (John 7:39). The Spirit, who is life and power, is given only after the resurrection (John 20:22), when the disciples "will draw water from the wells of salvation" (Isa 12:3), the well, in John's mind, being the glorified Christ. And when the Paraclete as Spirit comes it reveals the true reality of Jesus (John 14:26; 16:13), and, in fact, is "the personal presence of Jesus in the Christian while Jesus is with the Father."[12]

Christological safeguards are indeed in place but, as Rudolf Schnackenburg notes, "there can be no doubt that for the Johannine community the Spirit was an experienced reality. Here it is not a case of special manifestations of the Spirit (the charisms of 1 Cor 12:7-11). . . . Rather it must mean a 'regular' inner experience of the Spirit, a conscious awareness of its presence. Paul witnesses to the same reality, but in a different way in Galatians 4:6 and Romans 8:14-16. The modern critical reserve concerning such an experience of the Spirit should not obscure the fact that early Christianity was convinced of it. On the contrary the witness of Paul, as of Johannine

[11] 1 John does not mention the Spirit with any frequency and passes over in silence the many roles given to the Spirit in the Fourth Gospel. Raymond E. Brown, *The Community of the Beloved Disciple* (New York: Paulist, 1979) 140.

[12] John L. McKenzie, "Spirit," *Dictionary of the Bible* (New York: Macmillan, 1965) 844. Brown, *The Gospel According to John XIII–XXI* (Garden City: Doubleday, 1970) 1139.

Christianity, poses a question to us. In this matter have we not become blind and poor?" The Johannine community forges strong links between the Spirit and the awareness of the Spirit's presence and effects. "Nowhere in the other New Testament texts is the post-Easter experience of the Spirit so stressed. It is raised to a principle of pneumatology."[13]

THEOLOGY OF THE CROSS AND THEOLOGY OF RESURRECTION

Nonetheless, experience is not the whole fire, just the spark. The gospel suffers a basic perversion if all is reduced to the experience of the Spirit. What about the experience of the cross, the power of the cross, and the critical function of the cross? Paul struggled with the enthusiasts of his day to keep the communion between Spirit and cross.

The famous appeal of Paul to the Galatians' experience of the Spirit, treated above, is set in the sequence of (1) hearing Jesus Christ publicly exhibited as crucified, (2) believing the gospel, (3) witnessing the miracles. The proclamation of the crucified Christ effected the Galatians' first experience of the Spirit.[14] The sole authenticating mark of those who claim the possession of the Spirit is the confession that Jesus is Lord (1 Cor 12:3), that is, the crucified and risen Savior. The purpose of the crucifixion is the imparting of the Spirit in faith (Gal 3:13-14). The Spirit as creator of the new life of faith has its origin in the death on the cross.

In Romans 8 Paul, writing in a broad trinitarian mode, begins with the ideas of the enthusiasts and the experiences of the Spirit they have in worship, and then breaks with them when they conclude that they are thereby safe from worldly threats, confronting them with the theology of the cross. No one gets to live on the mountain top. We live in the valleys, often in the desert. The Spirit the Romans experience is the Spirit who imposes on them tempta-

---

[13] Schnackenburg, "Die johanneische Gemeinde und ihre Geisterfahrung," *Die Kirche des Anfangs: Festschrift für Heinz Schürmann* (Leipzig: Benno, 1977). Schnackenburg, Josef Ernst, and Joachim Wanke, eds. (Freiburg im Breisgau: Herder, 1978) 286. Felix Porsch, *Pneuma und Wort: ein exegetischer Beitrag zur Pneumatologie des Johannesevangeliums* (Frankfurt am Main: Knecht, 1974) 405.

[14] Lull, *Spirit in Galatia*, 53.

tion, struggle, and pain. Where the crucified Christ is present in the Spirit there is no escaping the cross.[15] If the Spirit is power (Rom 15:13; 1 Cor 2:4), so is the cross (1 Cor 1:17). The Spirit turns us away from the allure of resting in the exaltation and turns us back to the cross as the place of salvation, the source of the gospel's power. The cross identifies and defines God.

EXPERIENCE AND THE SPIRIT IN ORIGEN

While there is certainly evidence of the experience of the Spirit in the period between the New Testament and the beginning of the third century, it is Origen who, with great range and systematic intent, first gives extensive attention to the Spirit. Origen complained of those who "entertained low and unworthy views of his [the Spirit's] deity."[16]

Origen's typical "experiential" formulations have to do with the Logos, but he also relates experience to pneumatology. For Origen, the Spirit is the "voiceless cry" in our hearts saying "Abba! Father!"; "a bodiless voice" that forms the words in an illumined mind. To think that the Spirit does not speak in this way is to depart from the faith of the church. Origen was the first to develop the doctrine of the spiritual senses, divine faculties of perception, charisms of the Spirit, involving hearing, sight, touch, smell, and taste.[17]

Origen's view of experience is also embodied in his use of erotic models for knowing God. When Adam joins himself sexually to Eve the text says, "Now the man knew his wife Eve" (Gen 4:1). As men and women become one body in sexual intercourse and therefore

---

[15] Käsemann, *Romans*, 229.

[16] *On First Principles*, 2, 7, 3; SC 252.332.

[17] Origen speaks of visitations of the Logos which he experienced: "God is my witness that I have often perceived the Bridegroom drawing near me and being most intensely present with me; then suddenly he has withdrawn and I could not find him though I sought to do so. I long, therefore, for him to come again and sometimes he does so. Then, when he has appeared and I lay hold of him, he slips away once more; and, when he has so slipped away, my search for him begins anew." *Homilies on the Song of Songs* 1.7; SC 37.75; see also *On John* 6.52; SC 157.336. Frédéric Bertrand, *Mystique de Jésus chez Origène* (Paris: Aubier, 1951). *Homilies on Exodus* 5.4; SC 16.143. *Homilies on Genesis* 3.2; SC 7bis.116–18. *Origen, Spirit and Fire*, Hans Urs von Balthasar, ed. (Washington: Catholic University of America, 1984) 218–57.

"know" each other, so whoever is united to the Lord is one Spirit
with him (1 Cor 6:16-17), and therefore "knows" God. For Origen
this knowing is still the knowledge of faith but it is not the knowledge of faith alone. "There is a great difference between knowledge
which is added to faith and faith alone." Knowledge gives faith its
perfection.[18] Implicit in this sexual model of knowing God is
Origen's view of religious experience.

Whoever is one Spirit with the Lord, and knows the Lord, can
speak the word of the Lord and hand on the Spirit. Not only Jesus
hands on the Spirit when proclaiming, but "everyone who speaks
God's word in his name actually hands on the Spirit of God to those
who listen . . . while you are speaking the fire of the Holy Spirit
will inflame the hearts of your hearers immediately and make them
warm." Though Origen believes that "every rational creature without distinction receives a share in the Holy Spirit," he limits "the
special coming of the Spirit" (with the emphasis on "special") to the
worthy—the saints, those who are "already turning to better things
and walking in the ways of Jesus Christ."[19]

HILARY OF POITIERS: "INTENSE JOY"; GREGORY OF NYSSA: "EROTIC PASSION"

Commenting on the baptism of Christ, Hilary of Poitiers says that
here the Lord "fully realized the mysteries of human salvation," indeed, here "the order of the heavenly hidden mystery is expressed,"
that is, the plan of salvation. In detail Hilary outlines the economy:
"Through the testimony of the vision [of the dove] and the voice
[of the Father] we learn . . . that according to what is fully realized
in Christ, the Spirit . . . rushes down upon us *(in nos involare)*
so that we might bathe in the anointing of heavenly glory. . . .
For the truth has prefigured in the very reality of the facts, and the
image of the mystery *(sacramenti imaginem)* has thus been prefigured for us."[20] The Spirit that rushes down upon Christ in the

[18] *On John* 19.4, 21–25; 19.3, 20; SC 290.58–60, 56; 10.37, 241; SC 157.526.
[19] *Commentary on Romans* 6.13; PG 14:1100; *On First Principles*, 2, 7, 2; 1, 3, 5;
SC 252.328, 152–54. On Origen's concept of the worthy see Kilian McDonnell,
"Does Origen Have a Trinitarian Doctrine of the Holy Spirit?" *Gregorianum* 75/1
(1994) 19–23.
[20] *On Matthew* 2.5; SC 254.110.

Jordan is the order and image for the Spirit rushing down in Christian baptism and life.

Late in life, in his *Commentary on the Psalms,* Hilary returns to the Spirit rushing down in the mystery of his own baptism as an adult. "We who have been reborn through the sacrament of baptism experience intense joy *(maximum gaudium)* when we feel within us the first stirrings *(initia sentimus)* of the Holy Spirit. We begin to have insight into the mysteries of faith, we are able to prophesy and to speak with wisdom. We become steadfast in hope and receive gifts of healing." Hilary employs the Latin word *sentire,* meaning to perceive with the senses. In commenting on Psalm 118, he indicates that such an experience of the Spirit is not a rarity. "Among us there is no one who, from time to time, does not feel the gift of the grace of the Spirit *(donum spiritalis gratiae sentiat)*." The liturgical rite of baptism is a transforming event for Hilary personally, but essentially the graces and charisms given during baptism are gifts of the church *(ecclesiae munera)* for the upbuilding of the community. In a lapidary formula Hilary sums up the particular importance of the Spirit, ending on a note of experience: The Spirit is "infinity in the eternal, revelation in the image, experience in the gift" *(infinitas in aeterno, species in imagine, usus in munere).*"[21]

Gregory of Nyssa says that together with the Father and the Son, the Spirit brings about "every grace, power, guidance, life, comfort, the change to immortality, the passage to liberty, and every good that exists and descends on us." Gregory understands the experience of the Spirit as leading in the Son to the perfection of life, the Father. Gregory takes up the erotic imagery, used by Origen, as the experiential model of union with God. "In order to have us understand its profoundest doctrine, the scriptures use as a symbol that which is the most violent of all pleasures, I mean erotic passion. . . . [When we exercise discipline] our mind may seethe with passion for the Spirit alone, and be warmed by that fire which the Lord came to cast upon the earth (Luke 12:49)." The fire cast on the earth, through either the eschatological conflagration, or the fire of purification (Lev 13:52; Num 31:23) or of discernment (Jer 23:29), or of judgment (Gen 19:24), was widely identified in antiquity with the Spirit.

[21] *Commentary on the Psalms* 64.15; CSEL 22.246; 118.12, 4; SC 347.76. *On the Trinity* 2.1; CCh 62.38.

Gregory is not, however, speaking about an experience measured by the senses: "If a person pays attention to the senses and is drawn by pleasure in the body, he will live his life without tasting the divine joy, since the good can be overshadowed by what is inferior. For those who desire God, a good not shadowed over by anything awaits them; they realize that what enters the senses must be avoided."[22]

JEROME THE GREEK: "AS A PREGNANT WOMAN EXPERIENCES THE MOVEMENT OF THE FETUS"

Jerome the Greek, a shadowy fourth-century figure also known as Jerome of Jerusalem, composed a dialogue in which a Christian is asked, "How do you know you are a Christian?" and he answers, "because I believe in Christ." A second question follows: "How do you know you are baptized?" The questioner explains that perhaps his parents were secret pagans and did not baptize their child. To this the Christian replies, "I know from the effect [of baptism]. Whoever in baptism receives the Holy Spirit in the inward parts, in the most secret places of the heart, knows by the movements, motions, the strong impulses, exaltations, operations, and, as I call it, a kind of dance of the grace of the Spirit—such a one most certainly knows in the inward heart that one is baptized. No unbaptized person on earth experiences this kind of grace or effects, even if observing all the commandments of God and performing works of justice. This happens only to those who have been regenerated by water and the Spirit, accept the grace of the Spirit in their inward parts, and keep it pure and untarnished. As a pregnant woman

[22] The burden of Gregory's argument, *To Ablabius That There are not Three Gods*, PG 45.125, is the unity of the divine operation, the unity of the divine trinitarian movement: "Every operation of God which enters into creation takes its departure from the Father, passes through the Son, and reaches its term in the Holy Spirit." See Gaston Isaye, "L'unité de l'opération divine dans les écrits trinitaires de Saint Grégoire de Nysse," *Recherches de science religieuse* 27 (1937) 421–39. Martien Parmentier, "St. Gregory of Nyssa's Doctrine of the Holy Spirit," *Ekklesiastikos Pharos* 60 (1978) 725. *Commentary on the Song of Songs*, 1, 10, in *Opera*, Werner Jaeger, ed. (Leiden: Brill, 1952–) 6.27, 314. Joseph A. Fitzmyer, *The Gospel According to Luke X–XXIV* (Garden City: Doubleday, 1985) 996. Cornelius à Lapide, *Commentaria in Scripturam Sacram* (Paris: Vivès, 1866) 16.181, mentions Athanasius, Cyril of Alexandria, Jerome, Augustine, Gregory the Great.

experiences the movement of the fetus within her, so these [Christians] know that the Spirit of God dwells in them from that most interior grace, joy, and exaltation in their hearts. All of this they receive in baptism." Jerome expands on the image. Just as "a pregnant woman knows accurately that she has conceived, not just from words, but from discernible facts and the motions of the fetus, so also a Christian ought to know and have certain knowledge from the heart that one has been baptized," and that the Spirit dwells within.[23]

Jerome singles out the liturgical celebration of the Eucharist and of baptism as moments when "the experience and fiery breath of the Spirit" witness that the Christians have indeed been baptized. Further, it is not those who simply go through the motions of becoming Christians who experience the Spirit, because many evil persons come into the church. But "we feel within us with our deepest senses the evidence—the gift, the charism, and the treasure—bestowed in baptism."[24]

Jerome is not erecting a second, experiential way, alongside and in addition to faith and baptism, for validating Christian authenticity. He recognizes the objective instruments of faith, namely, "the gospels, prophets, apostles and the doctors teach us the word of God by hearing." He is reacting against an excessive intellectualizing of the faith. The evidence is also interior and is experienced especially during liturgical celebration. "God teaches what it is to be a Christian, not [only] by words, but by actions interior to the soul."[25]

SYMEON THE NEW THEOLOGIAN: YOU CANNOT POSSESS THE SPIRIT UNAWARES

It has been said that if one does not know Symeon, the New Theologian (949–1022), one cannot understand the development of the mystical teaching of the East. While arguably "the most christological of the Greek Fathers," Symeon reinforced the teaching that the

[23] *Comment Useful to Some Christian*; PG 40.861. Pierre Batiffol, "Jérome de Jérusalem d'après un document inédit," *Revue des questions historiques* 39 (1886) 248–55.

[24] *Comment*, PG 40.864–65.

[25] Ibid. Jerome teaches that married prophets and prophetesses, who have a normal sexual life, have the same experience of the Spirit as others: "For the Holy Spirit neither flees from nor abominates" the marriage bond.

grace of the Spirit is conscious in principle—and he upped its voltage.[26] He rebukes those who teach others without themselves having experience, and even holds that tradition of theology is not possible unless it has its origin in the experience of the Spirit. Symeon belongs to that broad school which assumes that the human person is neither all intellect nor all will, but has a psychological awareness that grasps the whole interior reality, including grace. For those who belong to this school, grace means both the supernatural reality and the awareness of that reality.

Symeon may be dependent on Jerome the Greek when he uses the same image of a pregnant woman. Taking his departure from Galatians 4:19 ("I am in the pain of childbirth until Christ is formed in you"), Symeon asks the question "In what part of our body is Christ formed?" He answers: "You did not suspect that Christ is formed in you bodily? Do not think that, for [Christ] takes form incorporeally and in a manner fitting for God. However, in the same way as the woman clearly knows that she is pregnant, that the child moves in her womb, and she would not be able to be ignorant that she carries the child, so likewise the one who has Christ formed within knows it from [Christ's] movements, that is to say, from the illuminations, and is conscious of [Christ's] formation within." In basing himself on Galatians, Symeon guards against accusations of a conception purely sensualist in nature. He belongs to what Hausherr calls "a school of sentiment or consciousness of the supernatural."[27]

Symeon took over from his spiritual master, Symeon the Elder, the teaching that mystical experience is the ultimate sign of holiness. He teaches that in a faith experience, under the impulse of the Spirit, one can truly see the essence of God, not just that which is around God. He warns against becoming a confessor or spiritual father before one has experienced the Spirit: "Do not try to be a

---

[26] *Vie de Syméon le Nouveau Théologien*, Irénée Hausherr and Gabriel Horn, eds. (Rome: Pontifical Oriental Institute, 1928) xii. Basil Krivocheine, *St. Symeon the New Theologian: Life-Spirituality-Doctrine* (Crestwood, N.Y.: St. Vladimir's, 1986) 393. George A. Maloney, *Russian Hesychasm: The Spirituality of Nil Sorskij* (The Hague: Morton, 1973) 188.

[27] *Ethics* 10.872–85; SC 129.322. Hausherr, "Les grands courants de la spiritualité orientale," *Orientalia Christiana Periodica* 1 (1935) 126.

mediator on behalf of others until you have yourself been filled with the Holy Spirit, until you have come to know and to win the friendship of the King of all with conscious awareness in your soul."[28]

Symeon stands as a true representative of Byzantine spirituality, emphasizing the numinous transcendence of the God who is beyond all understanding, the knowability of God in this life through direct personal experience, the union with God as the vision of divine radiance.[29] What shocked his adversaries and posterity was his view that the person who does not feel grace does not have it.

Do not say, It is impossible to receive the Holy Spirit. . . .

Do not say, It is possible to be saved without him.

Do not say, then, that one can possess him without knowing it.

Do not say, God does not appear to men.

Do not say, Men do not see the divine light [God]. . . .

On the contrary, [it is] altogether possible for those who so wish.[30]

Untiringly Symeon returns to this theme. "Do not go on to say in your heart that all of us who have been baptized in Christ . . . without feeling anything, that we are sons of the day and sons of the light." There are "those who say that they have the Spirit of God in an unconscious fashion and imagine they possessed [the Spirit] since baptism. They are persuaded that they undoubtedly have the treasure, but without recognizing the weight [of the treasure] in them. They admit that they have felt absolutely nothing at baptism, and suppose that it is in an unconscious and insensible manner that the gift of God indwells them since then [the time of baptism], and [they suppose] that [the Spirit] subsists in them even until now. And this is not all. They affirm that they have never had the sensation in contemplation and revelation and received this only from faith and

[28] *Ethics* 9.29, 44; SC 129.220–22. *Letter* 1.10; Karl Holl, *Enthusiasmus und Bussgewalt beim griechischen Mönchtum: Eine Studie zu Symeon dem neuen Theologen* (Leipzig: Hinrisch, 1898) 119.

[29] Kallistos Ware, "The Eastern Tradition from the Tenth to the Twentieth Century," *The Study of Spirituality*, Cheslyn Jones et al., eds. (New York: Oxford University Press, 1986) 236–37.

[30] *Hymn* 27.125–32; SC 174.288.

reason, but not from experience." Symeon warns that if the possession of the Spirit is unconscious now, so it also will be in eternity:
"We will not contemplate the light of God [not have the vision of
God]. On the contrary, we shall remain dead and insensible—then
just as now." He says the Spirit itself gives the answer to those who
say one can put on the garment of Christ unconsciously. Can one
put on a garment without experiencing it?[31] Understandable is the
fear of the official Greek church that Symeon was promoting a
direct line to the Holy Spirit away from liturgical life and that he
was caught up in preoccupations with mystical ascensions. Attempts
were made to sanitize his teachings.

It would be a mistake to read Symeon as proposing an easy road
to holiness through experience. For him there was no other way to
holiness than through the crucifixion and a voluntary death to the
world. Symeon is an unsystematic writer, and he does at times allow
for a real, hidden, yet unconscious activity of the Spirit, but the
whole momentum of his spirituality goes beyond the unconscious to
the conscious perceptible possession of the Spirit. Like Jerome the
Greek, Symeon protests that this grace is available to all, not just to
holy persons in the past or celibates in the present. Contemplation
with experience is for everyone.[32]

[31] *Ethics* 10.165; 5.1–2; 10:501–03; 5.21, 70; SC 129.270, 78–80, 501–17, 80, 84.
[32] *Theological Chapters Gnostic and Practical*, 76; SC 51.104. *Catechesis*
26.60–67; see Ware, "Eastern Tradition," 238. Maloney, *Russian Hesychasm*, 105.

Chapter 18

Experience of the Spirit in Medieval Monasticism

The dialectic between experience and speculation is built into Christian identity—beginning, as we have seen, in the New Testament itself. The twelfth century offers a particularly clear demonstration of this interplay, in the contrast between theology as pursued in the schools—abstract, metaphysical, determined by speculative grammar—and monastic theology, ordered by biblical and historical categories. This theology of the cloister, like the whole of the monastic program, has as its purpose "to seek God." Though Bonaventure and Thomas Aquinas in the thirteenth century will give a significant role to religious experience in their theologies, it was precisely the greater role the monastics gave to experience that distinguished them from the masters in the schools.[1]

The rationally oriented *quaestio* (question) is the literary form of the schools; the spiritually determined *collatio* (conference) is the genre of the monastic theologians. The *collatio* is not interested in secondary causes, as is the *quaestio,* but refers all to God, the primary cause. Not in the philosophy of the masters, says Rupert of Deutz (ca. 1075–ca. 1129), but in the scriptures one finds the pearl of great price, the wisdom of the incarnate Son. "I am not lacking in the secrets [of Christ's wisdom] which are given only to friends. By experience I know by use that the living fountain of the continually flowing waters of Christ is better than the pools of water and cisterns of men [read 'philosophy']." Commenting on the knowledge required

[1] Jean Leclercq, *The Love of Learning and the Desire for God: A Study of Monastic Culture*, 3rd ed. (New York: Fordham University, 1982) 85, 212.

to understand the words addressed to the church at Pergamum in the Apocalypse, "Let anyone who has an ear listen to what the Spirit is saying to the churches" (Rev 2:17), Rupert writes: "This knowledge does not come from an outer, as if foreign, document, it comes from an inner and personal experience. Those who are puffed up with learning, let them increase their knowledge—or at least what they think is knowledge—as much as they will, as much as they can, they will never acquire that particular comprehension."[2]

The tradition seems to have picked up the biblical conviction that the Spirit is essentially experiential. Those who were at pains to retain this aspect of the New Testament witness were often reacting against a formalized religious observance, rite without a soul, arid liturgical celebrations without fire. Some fell into enthusiasm, that is, an unhealthy isolation of religious experience to the detriment of liturgy, discipline, assiduous prayer, and ecclesial life. Two who balanced pneumatology, experience, and the common life were William of St. Thierry and Bernard of Clairvaux.

WILLIAM OF ST. THIERRY: "SO THAT I MAY KNOW BY EXPERIENCE"

William, a Benedictine who became an abbot at age thirty-four, and Bernard, the Cistercian abbot, were close friends—meeting for the first time about 1121—the former struggling for years with a desire to become a Cistercian monk, only to be restrained by Bernard. Finally, in 1135, at age fifty, and apparently without consulting Bernard, William became a simple monk at the Cistercian abbey of Signy.

William's trinitarian accent is present in the very first of his writings, *On Contemplating God*. Odo Brooke contends that William "evolved a theology of the Trinity which is essentially mystical, and a mystical theology which is essentially trinitarian." Like Augustine, William made Romans 5:5 ("God's love has been poured into our hearts through the Holy Spirit that has been given to us") central to his trinitarian doctrine. In his more formal trinitarian tract, *The Enigma of Faith,* William sees the Trinity less as a question of logic

---

[2] Marie-Dominique Chenu, *La théologie au douzième siècle* (Paris: Vrin, 1966) 343, 345. Rupert, *On the Apocalypse* 2.1; PG 169.881.

for the schools and more as the known and unknowable, indispensable source of life for Christians. "The knowledge of God is trinitarian, or there is no knowledge."[3] His argument follows the sequence of Trinity, christology, pneumatology, love, knowledge, experience, all informed with a circular trinitarian dynamic.

William holds that because of our participation in the circular inner-trinitarian life, the Spirit becomes for us what the Spirit is in relation to the Father and the Son, a participation in the intersubjective life of the Spirit who is not simply one with the Father and the Son but is their very oneness. When William speaks of the unity *of* the Spirit, he means the unity which *is* the Holy Spirit *(unitas, id est spiritus)*. The Holy Spirit ought to be properly called this name as the one who is not the Spirit of one of them, but the one in whom the very community of the Father and Son is manifested.[4]

William's anthropology is also trinitarian. Behind the dictum "Know yourself!" in William's thought is the *imago trinitatis*. "Be entirely present to yourself, and use all of your faculties to know yourself and know whose image you are, so that you can discern and understand what you are, and what you can do in the one in whose image you are." But we can never fully know the mystery of our own being made in the trinitarian image. Through grace and contemplation the image of the Trinity *(imago trinitatis)* should attain the likeness of the Trinity *(similitudo trinitatis)*, pointing to the transformative character of contemplation. For William *contemplatio* is a synonym for *experientia*. He speaks of ecstasy *(extasis)*, and calls it an embrace, that is the Holy Spirit, who is the communion of the Father and the Son.[5]

[3] William, *On Contemplating God* 16.11; SC 61bis.94–109. Brooke, *Studies in Monastic Theology* (Kalamazoo: Cistercian, 1980) 8. Ferdinand Cavallera, "La doctrine de saint Augustin sur l'Esprit Saint à propos du De trinitate," *Recherches de théologie ancienne et médiévale* 2 (1930) 365–87; 3 (1931) 5–19, holds that Romans 5:5 "is the true center of [Augustine's] spirit doctrine, the point from which everything emanates, and to which everything returns." Paul Verdeyen, *La théologie mystique de Guillaume de Saint-Thierry* (Paris: FAC, 1990) 87, 273.

[4] Bernard McGinn, *The Growth of Mysticism* (New York: Crossroad, 1996) 272. Robert Thomas, "William of St. Thierry: Our Life in the Trinity," *Monastic Studies* 3 (1965) 159–64. William, *The Mirror of the Faith* 110; SC 301.180.

[5] *On the Song of Songs* 66, 83, 132; SC 82.166, 220, 282; *On the Nature and Dignity of Love* 2; PL 184.382.

William's trinitarian mysticism is essentially "Spirito-centric." In a theme William shares with Basil of Caesarea, the Spirit leads us to the "place of God" *(locus Dei),* to be taken not geographically but functionally, as locating "the unity of the Father and the Son, the consubstantiality of the Trinity," which is the Spirit. Having the Spirit means the locality of God is within us: "You have found God in yourself." This is an experience of what it means to be a child of God, "a sense of life from the Spirit of life." We breathe in the Spirit and then the Spirit truly breathes in us: "I draw in the breath of my love, I open my mouth in your direction, I breathe in the Spirit." Love, when free, draws us and makes us like to God. "Whoever lives by the Spirit of life experiences you."[6]

"SUPERABUNDANT AND PALPABLE"— ## THE NATURE OF EXPERIENCE

For William, union with God means being taken up into the whole trinitarian dynamic, conformed to the trinitarian image and likeness, being drawn to the immutable Word, true love through connaturality, breathing the Spirit. Experience is a result, an effect of union, and is, for all its importance, ancillary. In chronological terms, experience will be simultaneous with all the instrumentalities of union and love. When love invades, bringing with it an "abundance of grace to the point of a positive and palpable experience of something of God, suddenly, in a new way, something comes within the grasp of the sense of enlightened love which exceeds the reach of any bodily sense, the consideration of reason, and all understanding, except the understanding of enlightened love."[7]

When the bride says, "Show me, O you whom my soul loves, where you feed, where you have your couch in the midday," William responds, "Speak within my heart, tell me what I long to ask, and let me feel it in myself by the sensing of a most sure experience

[6] David N. Bell, *The Image and Likeness: The Augustinian Spirituality of William of St. Thierry* (Kalamazoo: Cistercian, 1984) 253. Basil, *On the Holy Spirit* 26.62; SC 17bis.470–72. William, *The Prayer of Dom William*; SC 61bis.124–26; *Song of Songs* 5.67; Preface; SC 82.168, 70; *The Mirror of Faith* 7.75; SC 301.144; *On Contemplating God* 12; SC 61bis.114.
[7] *Song of Songs* 94; SC 82.218.

(ut sentiam in memetipsa, per sensum certissimae experientiae). Breathe upon me so that I may know experimentally *(ut sciam per experimentum)* through awareness of delight in you." In his *Meditations* William asks, "Is love one thing, and the feeling of love another?" He answers, "The capacity to love is a natural endowment, but to love God exceeds nature," and "the feeling of love is a manifestation of grace," referring to the work of the Spirit. "Our love toward God is the Holy Spirit."[8]

MEMORY AND DESIRE

Experiences are brief. In the first of his works William says that when he opens his mouth to breathe in the Spirit, "sometimes, you do put something in my mouth. . . . When I receive it, then I want to grasp it, and think about it, and assess its flavor; but forthwith it is gone." Or he will say that one can enjoy the possession of the experience "for a short instant." At the voice of the beloved the bride "makes haste to see and lay hold of him, suddenly he who has appeared disappears. . . . She who is his love loses the confidence of friendship."[9]

William is speaking the language of memory, delight in recalling real experienced events of varying levels, by no means all ecstatic. He himself remembers the times at prayer when the soul's efforts to experience God brought forth only "sweat of the brow" *(in grave sudore vultus)*, and the soul was "compelled to return to the house of her poverty," that is, to return to itself without experiencing God. The pursuit of God is divided between grief and joy: "grief for the absence of the Bridegroom and joy at his presence."[10] The experience of God's absence, God's indifference, is essential to any quest for God.

William's sustained, elevated, intense rhetoric is less the expression of a sustained experience, and more the rhetoric of desire, the vernacular of hunger. As William reads the *Song of Songs*—the drama of God luring, enticing, laying snares, peeking through the lattices,

[8] Ibid., 55; 99; SC 82.148, 150, 226; *Meditations* 12.29; SC 324.210; *On Romans* 3; CCCM 86.66.

[9] *On Contemplating God* 12; SC 61bis.114. Augustine has a similar expression in *Confessions* 10, 40, 65; CCh 27.191. Song of Songs 155, 166; SC 82.330, 346.

[10] *The Prayer of Dom William*; SC 61bis.122; Song of Songs 32; SC 82.114.

hiding behind the wall, leading into the treasure room, conducting into the banquet hall—he finds himself in the theater of promise. The pledge of experience of high elevation is fulfilled proleptically in this life, perhaps; surely, in full reality, in the next. If memory looks back at fleeting experience, promise grasps at an enduring future.

LOVE-KNOWLEDGE (*AMOR-INTELLECTUS*)

The concreteness of experience does not stop with sensing God, but demands a kind of transformation into what is sensed, God. On this William is quite specific: "Every sense experience changes the one experiencing it in some way into that which is sensed, otherwise there is no sensation *(alioquin non est sensus)*."[11] Experience launches one on a transformative trajectory ending in the perfect likeness to the archetype, the Trinity.

Experience is basic to the process of knowing, but experience is at the lowest end of the theological spectrum. William refers to the highest end of that spectrum, saying that it is by "the Spirit of life, that is the Holy Spirit" that one experiences and knows anything of God.[12] The Spirit is the primary, the ultimate carrier of love, knowledge, and experience of God precisely because the Spirit is the mutual substantial love of the Father and Son. Through the Spirit we participate in that circle of love which is trinitarian communion.

Not all love of God is knowledge in the sense of "loving itself is knowing," but only that enlightened love grounded in the unity of the Holy Spirit, in *unitas spiritus*. At this level the believer "is in God by grace, what God is by nature." The Spirit is both the reciprocal love of Father and the Son and their mutual knowledge. Those who have attained the *unitas spiritus* have this knowing love and this loving knowing in an entirely new, divine mode *(modo quodam novo)*, a higher Spirit-loving and Spirit-knowing.[13] Divinization is possible because the Holy Spirit is the subsisting love of Father and Son. And since the Spirit is the substantial will, the *unitas spiritus* effects a participation in the will of God, so that the will of the believer does not will apart from that sharing.

[11] *On the Nature of Body and Soul* 1; PL 180.705c–706a.
[12] *The Mirror of Faith* 10:96; SC 301.168.
[13] *Song of Songs* 94; SC 82.218.

Johannes Schuck characterizes Bernard's theology as *credo ut experiar* (I believe that I might experience) rather than *credo ut intelligam* (I believe that I might understand). The expression fits Bernard's reflection on the Bridegroom-Word seeking the bride-soul/church: "What they do not know from experience, let them believe so that one day, by virtue of their faith, they may reap the harvest of experience. . . . We must add that the soul which knows this by experience has fuller and more blessed knowledge."[14] Bernard's notion of experience is broad, embedded in desire, delight, love, awe, wonder, anticipation.

And it is specifically monastic. In speaking of experience, Bernard presupposes the reading and praying of the scriptures in private, in the monastic choir, and in the celebration of the mysteries. This hearing and reading is specifically contemplative, directed to tasting, to the heart, to experience. One does not move from reading to prayer; reading or listening to the Word with the ear of the heart is already prayer. "What one hears from without, one feels within" *(quae foris audit, intus sentit)*. Of St. Paul's words concerning the incomprehensible ways of God (Rom 11:33) Bernard says: "If you are holy, you understand and you know; if you are not holy, be holy, and you will understand by experience."[15]

SEARCHING IN EXPERIENCE

How does this experience come about? By the Holy Spirit who alone knows the depths of God and alone knows what is in the interior of the believer. The monk is to walk in the Spirit and have the Spirit as a moderator so that "your interior experience corresponds to what

[14] Schuck, *Das Hohe Lied des Hl. Bernhard von Clairvaux: Dokumente zur mittelalterlichen Christus- und Brautmystik* (Paderborn: Schöningh, 1926) 11. Bernard, *Song of Songs* 84:7, in *S. Bernardi Opera*, 8 vols. in 9, Jean Leclercq, C. H. Talbot, H. M. Rochais, eds. (Rome: Editiones Cisterciensis, 1957–1977) 2.306.24–26; *On Consideration* 5.30; 3.492.10–11. In what I say about Bernard I am drawing on my article, "Spirit and Experience in Bernard of Clairvaux," *Theological Studies* 58 (1997) 3–18.

[15] *Song of Songs* 37.3; *On Consideration* 5.30; Leclercq/Talbot 2.11.2; 3.492.10–11.

I speak exteriorly." The Spirit, not the eloquence of the speaker, elicits the experience. Therefore Bernard recommends that those who hear or read his words should "search in experience" *(experientiam magis require)* rather than in what he is saying. When Bernard is going to expound the text "Let him kiss me with the kiss of his mouth," he gives a programmatic principle: "Today the text we are going to study is the book of our own experience *(in libro experientiae).* . . . You must turn your attention inward."[16]

The event Bernard is referring to is a composite of biblical experience and one's own experience, or even a composite of others' experience and one's own. He is well aware that many of the monks have not had a transforming experience; but the penitent sinner also advances by degrees and is not devoid of experience. On occasion he will appeal to his own experience, and also to the experience of others. Some who hear him expound the Word may have had more experience than he. In fact, he invites his audience to authenticate the message he brings against their own experience.[17]

Experience is a kind of authority. "Listen to the one with experience!" "Believe the one with experience." The appeal is even to "daily experience." While the scriptures he is expounding are both the source and means of experience, the scriptures themselves are subject to experience. "Only the anointing [of the Spirit] teaches this kind of canticle," says Bernard of the scriptural *Song of Songs;* "beyond that only experience learns. Let those with experience recognize this, and those without experience burn with desire so that they will not so much know as experience."[18] Bernard sees the

---

[16] *Song of Songs* 21.4; 3.1; *On Conversion* 13.25; Leclercq/Talbot 1.124.20–25; 1.14.7; 4.99.17. In *On the Ascension* 6.2; Leclercq/Talbot 5.151.21–22, he repeats the phrase "in the book of one's own experience."

[17] Ulrich Köpf, "Die Rolle der Erfahrung im religiösen Leben nach dem Heiligen Bernhard," *Analecta Cisterciensia* 46 (1990) 319. *Song of Songs* 51.3; 38.2; 22.4, 39.3; Leclercq/Talbot 2.85.21–22; 2.15.20-23; 1.130.14; 2.19.27–28. See Köpf, "Erfahrung als Voraussetzung bei Bernhard und seinen Hören," in his *Religiöse Erfahrung in der Theologie Bernhards von Clairvaux* (Tübingen: Mohr [Siebeck], 1980) 23–26.

[18] Köpf, "Die Rolle der Erfahrung," 314. *Song of Songs* 31.1; 29.3; 1.11; 1.7.28–30; *Letter* 106.2; Leclercq/Talbot 1.14.16; 1.204.16–19; 7.266.23. Brian Stock, *The Implications of Literacy: Written Language and Models of Interpretation in the Eleventh and Twelfth Centuries* (Princeton: Princeton University, 1983) 414.

scriptures, hearers, readers, and himself as bound together by experience of the same Spirit operative in each—coinherence is a contemplative principle of understanding.

The link between the Spirit, experience, and the scriptures indicates that Bernard's references to experience do not refer primarily to isolated individual moments of spiritual elevation, though these do occur, and he does mention them. He is speaking of experience in a broader context in which the monk is aware that he is caught up in the drama and rhythm of God's economy, participating in the mysteries of salvation proclaimed in the scriptures, celebrated in the liturgy. Experience does not exist either outside of, or apart from, the monastic and ecclesial culture created by scripture, liturgy, and communal life.[19]

THREE STAGES OF EXPERIENCE

Bernard lays out three stages of experience: We are far from God (the experience of sin); we are caught up in a movement of redemption (the experience of our insertion into Christ); and the principle of this insertion is the Holy Spirit (the experience of the Spirit).[20]

Experience begins at the start of a pilgrimage, with the sense of our own misery and sin, the struggle with the law of sin within us. As a monk, Bernard took sin with great seriousness. The discord between the law of sin and the law of the Spirit—he quotes Galatians 5:17 no fewer than twenty-three times—takes place in the body "as a splendid residence," in the soul as "a magnificent and agreeable dwelling place." No denigration of humanity here. Still, daily we have the experience of alienation from God.[21] There is no need for an exterior teacher in the matter of alienation because all "are

[19] Claude Bodard, "La bible, expression d'une expérience religieuse chez s. Bernard," in *Saint Bernard théologien: actes du Congrès de Dijon, 15–19 septembre, 1953* (Rome: 1953) 40.

[20] Ibid., 26.

[21] *On Conversion* 17.30; *Song of Songs* 81.7–10; 82.6–7; *Praise of the New Knighthood* 11.24; Leclercq/Talbot 4.106.11–16; 2.288–91; 2.296–97; 3.233.21–23. Raffaele Fassetta, "Le rôle de l'Esprit-Saint," *Analecta Cisterciencia* 46 (1990) 353. Bernard also quotes Wisdom 9:15 ("A perishable body weighs down the soul") to the same purpose twenty-seven times. See also *On the Vigil of Christmas* 2.3; Leclercq/Talbot 4.206.9–14. *On the Dedication of a Church* 2.1; Leclercq/Talbot 5.375–76. Bodard, "La bible," *Saint Bernard théologien*, 26–30.

taught by their own proper experience."

In Bernard, this experience of the rupture of our relation with God is not seen in isolation from the restoration of the form or image of God. "The Holy Spirit wishes to trace the road we ought to follow, and imprint in us the form we ought to have."[22] In other words, Bernard is not ultimately preoccupied with sin, but with the triumph over sin we have in the Spirit through Christ. The measure of our misery is not law, but the holiness of God.

Beyond this experience of sin we have the experience of Christ, of being inserted into the mystery of Christ, who is for us a new principle of life by reason of his death and resurrection. Experience at this christological level is two-fold: according to the flesh, and according to the Spirit. According to the flesh: Bernard's medieval devotion to the humanity of Christ is at play here, with the special accent on the sanctification of the humanity by the Holy Spirit. According to the Spirit: we know that we have the sense of Christ because the Spirit gives testimony to our spirit that we are children of God (Rom 8:16).[23]

In true trinitarian fashion, interior to the experience of Christ is the experience of the Spirit, and the experience of the Spirit is through the experience of Christ. This is a matter of reciprocity and coinherence of the Spirit in Christ and Christ in the Spirit. This trinitarian expression is seen in Bernard's exegesis of "the kiss of the mouth" *(osculum de ore),* which he clearly distinguishes from "the kiss of the kiss" *(osculum de osculo).* The first is the kiss that is the trinitarian love between the Father and the Son, namely, the Holy Spirit, and by participation it is extended to the bride, who is both the church and the individual believer. The risen Christ gives the kiss to the church when he breathes on the disciples "Receive the Holy Spirit" (John 20:22). This participated kiss is called "the kiss of the kiss." One and the same plenitude of the Spirit is in God and in the church. This theme is expressed in the phrase "one spirit with him" from 1 Corinthians 6:17, a verse Bernard cites fifty-four times, more frequently than any other verse

---

[22] *On the Ascension* 3.4; Leclercq/Talbot 5.133.18.
[23] *Praise of the New Knighthood* 11.23–24, 29; Leclercq/Talbot 3.232–34, 236. Fassetta, "Le rôle," 354.

in the Bible.[24]

Only the Spirit can reveal the mystery of the kiss. Since the kiss is also revelation, only those who have experienced it can grasp it. "If marriage according to the flesh constitutes two in one body, why should not a spiritual union be even more efficacious in joining two in one Spirit?" Another favorite text, cited forty times, is 2 Corinthians 3:18 ("seeing the glory of the Lord . . . being transformed into the same image from one degree of glory to another; for this comes from the Lord, the Spirit").[25]

Bernard has a deep ecclesial commitment, confirmed in his identification of the bride as the church in the doxological formulations at the close of many of his lectures. He moves back and forth from the bride as the soul to the church as the bride. His writings show the Spirit acting in a twofold direction: by the infusion *(infusio)* of the graces necessary for spiritual growth, and the effusion *(effusio)* of these very graces from the recipient on to the neighbor. As Galatians 4:19 suggests, whoever is espoused to the Word becomes a mother, like the church, so that the infusion of the Spirit becomes effusion in forming Christ in others.[26] Bernard's most striking expression concerns friendship in relation to the Spirit. "I call the Spirit of truth as my witness of the desire which I feel in myself, in the bowels of Jesus Christ, the Spirit by which this love is poured forth in our hearts."[27] No privatized inwardness here, but the effusion of the Spirit to others. The spousal relationship with church (and believers) is not formed at the incarnation, but when the risen Christ breathes the kiss, the Spirit, on the infant church, imparting the

[24] *Song of Songs* 8.8; 8.1 and 4; 8.2; *Sermons on Diverse Topics* 89; Leclercq/Talbot 1.41.4–5; 1.36.221–24; 1.38.13–14; 1.37.8; 6/1.335–36. Bernard will also say, Song of Songs 2.23; Leclercq/Talbot 1.9–10, that the Word is the one who does the kissing and the assumed humanity is the one receiving the kiss. This kiss unites the two natures in one person, the mediator between God and humankind. This kiss happens only once. The kiss the Word passes on to the humanity is the Holy Spirit. Fassetta, "Le role," 384, n. 193.

[25] *Song of Songs* 7.8; 8.6; 3.1; 83.6; Leclercq/Talbot 1.36.3–6; 1.39.18; 1.14.10–13; 2.302.18–19. Fassetta, "Le rôle," 379.

[26] Ibid., 358–87, especially 358. *Song of Songs* 18.6; Leclercq/Talbot 1.107.

[27] *Letter* 368.1; Leclercq/Talbot 8.327.

gifts of the Spirit.

EXPERIENCE IS DECEPTIVE, FAITH IS NOT

For Bernard, experience adds to faith but faith transcends experience. Experience never stands outside of faith, as though it were absolute. When Bernard says, "We speak of divine things, which can only be known from experience," he is speaking within the faith context. If through the monastic discipline of community life, if through personal conquest, the right environment for experience is constructed, this is a secondary achievement. The experience itself is a given within the context of faith—and the church. Experience is never at the initiative or disposal of a believer. God gives or God does not give. "By the light he [the Spirit] gives us, by a sure experience day after day, we are convinced that our desires and groanings come from him and go to God." One should be sure that one is acting under the promptings of the Spirit, and not follow "one's own erratic feelings" (sequamur sensum deviantes). Experience can deceive, or be interpreted falsely, because it is produced in us invisibly.[28]

The woman at the tomb sees the risen Christ but does not recognize him because she does not believe the promise Jesus had given before his death that he would rise. She wants to see. But Bernard remonstrates: "So why strain with your eyes? Prepare rather to hear [the word of faith]." She is not consoled by the earlier promise, "because she valued experience above faith." Then, in an emphatic expression, Bernard says, "But experience is fallacious" (aut experimentum fallax). Please, Bernard admonishes, recognize the narrow boundaries of sense knowledge: "What you may learn from the senses [of sight or touch] is of limited value." The risen Christ invites the woman at the grave to move "to the more certain knowledge of faith, to what the senses do not know, to what experience does not find."[29]

[28] Song of Songs 84.7; 41.3; 59.6; 17.1; On Grace and Free Will 47; Leclercq/Talbot 2.306–07; 2.30.15; 59.6; 2.30.15; 2.139.5–9; 1.98.13; 3.199.26–28; Letter 228; PL 182.398a. Bernard Bonowitz, "The Role of Experience in the Spiritual Life," Analecta Cisterciensia 46 (1990) 324–25, rightly criticizes Ulrich Köpf's contention that the experience of God cannot in any way be prepared for by the subject. Bodard, "La bible," 44–45.

[29] Song of Songs 28.7–9; Leclercq/Talbot 1.196.22–198.4.

Then, in a play on the fallaciousness of experience, he writes, "Faith cannot deceive" *(fides nescia falli)*. "Faith does not know the poverty of the senses, it transcends . . . the bounds of experience." If the scriptures norm experience, so does faith: "Therefore judge by faith, and not by your experience, because faith is true, but experience is fallacious" *(sed et experimentum fallax)*.[30] The conclusion: What is not of faith is fallacious.

Bernard sets "experience is fallacious" alongside "faith is not fallacious." This striking parallelism should not make one forget that for Bernard experience is almost always positive. Faith and experience are not enemies. In the first place both are radically rooted in the life of the spouse, the church, giving both a kind of texture. Faith gives birth to experience; faith norms experience. But experience gives another dimension of actuality and firmness to faith. Experience is another way of knowing. What is given to experience is not taken away from faith, because true experience exists only in faith. In the spacious meaning Bernard gives to experience, it constitutes the broad highway of commerce between God who takes the initiative to touch and the person who reaches out with desire.

For William and for Bernard there is no choice but to be essentially positive toward experience, in spite of the pitfalls and land mines along the way. Unless God is to be displaced into some transcendental beyond history, there is a need to experience God somewhere within the room where one experiences oneself. Religious experience cannot be replaced by texts, theological demonstration, authority, papal documents, or anything else.[31] Otherwise one asks whether faith is not dangerously intellectualized. Without some dimension of experience, is faith even viable?

---

[30] Ibid., 28.9; *On Quadragesima* 5.5; Leclercq/Talbot 1.198.6–8; 4.374.20–21. McGinn, *Growth of Mysticism*, 185.

[31] Michael J. Buckley, *At the Origins of Modern Atheism* (New Haven: Yale University, 1987) 360–62.

Conclusions
and
Reflections

Conclusions and Reflections

Chapter 19

The Role of Pneumatology in an Integral Theology

A THEOLOGY OF THE HOLY SPIRIT

The student of pneumatology is like someone who has a fistful of jewels but is not sure how they relate to one another. How does one pull together various strands of pneumatology when the Spirit is by definition anonymous? If the Spirit lacks a name—and, therefore, revelation is ambiguous—how can the theologian be clear? How does one gather, if not into a systematic whole, at least into a semblance of rational order, the divine Person who cannot be grasped, who is without designation of a relationship (like Father and Son have), who evokes no countenance or even discernible distinctive features; who has the solidity of breath or wind; who is invisible, infiltrating imperceptibly; who can be addressed only indirectly; who never speaks of self; whose image is not in another person; who works in secret; who blows at will; who represents interrupted-ness; who also represents the trans-historical or meta-historical even when manifested in history? And to make an end to the list: the Son proceeds from the Father by generation, the Spirit by spiration. That there is a difference between generation and spiration all assert; but no one can say precisely what that difference is.

The difficulty is announced over and over again. Hilary of Poitiers: "Concerning the Holy Spirit we should neither be silent nor should we speak. But we cannot remain silent because of those who do not know him"; Pavel Florensky: "It is quite evident that the holy fathers know something from their own experience; but what is even clearer is that this knowledge is so deeply hidden away, so 'unaccountable,' so unspeakable, that they lack the power to clothe it in precise language"; Wolfhart Pannenberg: "There is almost no other subject in modern theology so difficult to deal with as the doctrine of the Holy Spirit"; Helmut Thielicke: "The hermeneutics of the Holy Spirit means that the truth intended cannot possibly fall under the general categories which are the epistemological conditions for the general definition of truth."[1]

The frustration of which Pannenberg and Thielicke speak is echoed in the relief Yves Congar expressed when he came to the end of his three-volume work, saying that it had been "a long and thankless study." So many problems arose for Henrikus Berkhof when he accepted an invitation to give lectures on the Holy Spirit that he almost canceled the series.[2]

THE SPIRIT AS PRINCIPLE OF IDENTITY FOR CHRIST AND THE CHURCH

In spite of the intractable character of the Spirit, an attempt needs to be made to give some order. But where does one start? The choice is dictated by revelation, but revelation can be read in different ways. The beginning of proclamation of the good news in the synoptic gospels is the baptism of Jesus in the Jordan (Matt 3:13-17; Mark 1:9-11; Luke 3:21-22), a key to understanding all that follows. In the Jordan event Jesus is revealed as "the beloved Son" when the Holy Spirit descends upon him, the anointed Messiah (Isa 11:2) and Servant of Yahweh (Isa 41:1). Condescension in the baptism in the Jordan corresponds to exaltation in the passion accounts (Phil 2:5-10). The revelation of the identity of Jesus through the descent of the Spirit and the voice of the Father occurs as Jesus comes up from the water. "Here we stand in proximity to the proclamation of the Easter event." Paul is likely using an old kerygmatic formula when

---

[1] Hilary: *On the Trinity* 2.29; CCSL 62.64. Florensky, "On the Holy Spirit," *Ultimate Questions*, Alexander Schmemann, ed. (New York: Holt, Rinehart and Winston, 1965) 141. Pannenberg, "The Working of the Spirit in Creation and in the People of God," *Spirit, Faith and Church*, Pannenberg, Avery Dulles, and Carl E. Braaten, eds. (Philadelphia: Westminster, 1969) 13. Thielicke, *The Evangelical Faith*, 3 vols. (Grand Rapids: Eerdmans, 1974) 1.202.

[2] Congar, *I Believe in the Holy Spirit*, 3.272; Berkhof, *The Doctrine of the Holy Spirit* (Atlanta: John Knox, 1964) 9.

he writes that Jesus Christ "was declared to be the Son of God with power according to the spirit of holiness by the resurrection from the dead" (Rom 1:4; see Acts 13:33). So the synoptic accounts of the baptism of Jesus anticipate the Easter proclamation.[3] The infancy narrative (Matt 1:18-20; Luke 1:35) and the baptism in the Jordan point to the Spirit as a principle of identity.

There is a broader pattern in which the Spirit functions as the principle of identity within the New Testament. In the pre-gospel period, christological thought was dominated by the decisive and awe-inspiring event of the resurrection. Christological awareness developed backwards (Rom 1:4), from resurrection to the beginning of public ministry (Luke 4:14-22), then further to the baptism of Jesus (Matt 3:16-17), and finally to the conception of the infancy narrative (Matt 1:18, 20). At every stage of this reverse chronological development, the Spirit identifies who Jesus is. This is a primary datum in the relation of christology to pneumatology, the precondition for the Son's breathing the Spirit on the disciples (John 20:22) and baptizing the church in the Holy Spirit (Acts 1:5; 2:1-13).[4]

The New Testament accounts take their cue from the Old Testament, where the spirit was constitutive of the identity of Yahwism and Israel. It is also clear that New Testament pneumatology and christology have common roots. Yves Congar wrote that "the health of pneumatology is in Christology."[5] But according to the biblical tradition, it was the Father who sent the Son (Gal 4:4; John 3:17) and the Spirit (Gal 4:6; John 14:16) on mission. One could transpose Congar's "the health of pneumatology is in Christology" into "the health of pneumatology is in Trinity," a reformulation with which Congar would agree. In the Jordan event the Trinity tells us who Jesus is. The controls for both christology and pneumatology are in Trinity.

As we saw in chapter 9, John Zizioulas correctly lays out two New Testament models for the relationship between christology and pneumatology: a pneumatology which is dependent on christology and a christology which is dependent on pneumatology. The

---

[3] Franz J. Schierse, "Die neutestamentliche Trinitätsoffenbarung," *MS*, 2.101.

[4] Raymond E. Brown, *The Birth of the Messiah* (Garden City: Doubleday, 1977) 29–32.

[5] "Actualité de la pneumatologie," *CSS*, 1.25.

disappearance of the New Testament synthesis of these two models manifests itself in a fissure at the base of the church, and Zizioulas is convinced that the ecumenical problems between East and West will not be solved until there is an awareness of their roots at the level of pneumatology.[6] The issue is not to choose between the two models—pneumatology dependent on christology, christology dependent on pneumatology—but, while maintaining balance, to give the emphasis the church needs at a given moment in history.

If we line up the biblical evidence, the balance might seem to tip slightly in favor of christology dependent on pneumatology: Christ at his birth (Matt 1:20; Luke 1:35), entrance into public ministry (Luke 4:1-19), resurrection (Rom 8:11; 1 Cor 6:14). The Spirit identifies and is constitutive of the church (Acts 1:5; 2:1-13; 1 Cor 12:1-13). However, Paul calls Christ the Lord of the Spirit and says the Spirit stands under the Lordship of Christ (Rom 8:9-11): pneumatology dependent on christology. At this moment in history I choose a christology dependent on pneumatology as an antidote to the imbalance arising from the dominance in the West of pneumatology dependent on christology.

THE WHOLE OF THE ECONOMY
GIVEN OVER TO THE SPIRIT?

When Irenaeus says that "the Spirit manifests the Word, and therefore the prophets announced the Son of God, but the Word articulates the Spirit, and therefore it is Himself (the Son) who gives their message to the prophets and takes up man and brings him to the Father," he incorporates both the synoptic preference for a christology dependent on pneumatology, and pneumatology dependent on christology found in John, Paul, and Acts. But Irenaeus goes further: "It is the Spirit who spoke through the prophets . . . nor does any other of the prophets speak in his own name, for it is not a man who utters the prophecy; but the Spirit of God, taking form and shape in the likeness of the person concerned [here it is David], who spoke in the prophets; sometimes he spoke on the part of Christ, sometimes

---

[6] "Implications ecclésiologiques de deux types de pneumatologie," *Communio Sanctorum: Mélanges offerts à Jean Jacques von Allmen* (Geneva: Labor et Fides, 1982) 145–46.

on that of the Father." Here we have a universalizing of the work of the Spirit in the economy, an important aspect of early Christian pneumatology. Irenaeus continues, speaking of Christ: "For he is named Christ [Anointed] because through him the Father anointed and arrayed all things, according to his coming as man, because he was anointed by the Spirit of God his Father, as he also says speaking of himself through Isaiah: 'The Spirit of the Lord is upon me. . . .'"[7] The whole economy is given over to the Spirit in the way that all God's self-giving comes to us through Christ in the Spirit, and the only way we can go to God is through Christ in the Spirit.

The dictum that the whole of the economy is given over to the Spirit is not a systematic deduction, but, as Otto Kuss remarks in a different context, a biblical insight. Irenaeus must have perceived it in the sacred text: "For those who are bearers of the Spirit of God are led to the Word, that is, to the Son; but the Son takes them and presents them to the Father, and the Father confers incorruptibility. So without the Spirit there is no seeing the Word of God, and without the Son there is no approaching the Father; for the Son is the knowledge of the Father, and the knowledge of the Son is through the Holy Spirit. But the Son, according to the Father's good pleasure, administers the Spirit in a charismatic mode as the Father wills, to those to whom He will." Elsewhere Irenaeus speaks of "the totality of the economy of God . . . received in the Church, which we guard with care . . . under the action of the Holy Spirit. . . . Such is the task which God has confided to his church; he has placed in her the universal operation of the Spirit." This universalizing of the work of the Spirit is not set over against the work of Christ, but operates at the interior of that work.[8] Deep calls unto deep.

Athanasius speaks in much the same vein, but sees the Spirit as the mediation of the Word: "There is nothing which is not originated

---

[7] Irenaeus, *The Demonstration of the Apostolic Preaching* 5; 49; 53; SC 406.90, 156, 160.

[8] Otto Kuss, *Der Römerbrief* (Regensburg: Pustet, 1963–78) 540–65. Irenaeus, *Demonstration* 7; SC 406.92. See Paul Galtier, *Le Saint Esprit en nous d'après les pères grecs* (Rome: Gregorian University, 1946) 42. Irenaeus, *Against Heresies* 3.24.1; SC 211.474, sees the church as the privileged locus of the Spirit: "Where the church is, there also is the Spirit of God; where the Spirit is, there is the church and all grace."

and actuated through the Word in the Spirit."[9] The work of the Spirit as the mediation of Christ is not less expansive, not less universal, than the work of the Word.

The giving over of the whole economy to the Spirit seen in Irenaeus and Athanasius appears in a different image in Gregory of Nyssa. He depicts the body of Christ as entirely anointed with oil/Spirit, so that anyone who wants to touch Christ must first touch the oil/Spirit: "On all sides the Holy Spirit is met by those who by faith approach the Son."[10]

This habit of seeing the whole economy given over to the Spirit as the very mediation of Christ, which one meets in ancient writers and in modern authors such as Mühlen, Kilmartin, Kasper, Rahner, Barth, and Nissiotis, raises the question of the mission of the Spirit.

THE TWO HANDS OF THE FATHER

In a crude way Irenaeus was dealing with the issue of mediator and mediation when he wrote that "it was not the angels who made and formed us . . . as though he (God) did not have his own hands . . . for he always had before him the Word and the Wisdom, the Son and the Spirit." God did not need angels when God made the world and modeled human beings for whose sake the world was created: God has created the world with "his two hands, the Son and the Spirit, the Word and the Wisdom."[11] Irenaeus is here reflecting the biblical doctrine of the two missions. The Father sends the Son and the Spirit, as mentioned in Galatians 4:4-6 ("God sent his Son . . . God has sent the Spirit of his Son"). John, too, speaks of a double mission (7:37-39; 14:26; 15:26; 20:21-22).

These biblical texts have been fashioned in systematic theology into the teaching on divine missions, which includes two characteristics: (1) that the person sent proceeds from the person sending (e.g., the Son proceeds from the Father), and (2) that a new effect is produced. The visible mission of the Son from the Father terminated in the incarnation, the new effect (Matt 1:20; Luke 1:35). In the case of the Spirit, the "visibility" is of a different order, namely, in signs: the

[9] *Letters to Serapion* 1.31; SC 15.139.

[10] *Against the Macedonians* 16, in *Opera*, Werner Jaeger, ed. (Leiden: Brill, 1952–) 3/1.103.

[11] *Against Heresies* 4.20.1; SC 100.624–26; also 4.7.4; SC 100.464.

descent of the dove and the tongues of fire at Pentecost (Acts 2), indicating the presence and action of the Spirit. Invisible missions, categorized under "grace" in Western theology, are more complex, having to do with the divine interior communication, as when Jesus says "We will come to him, and will make our abode with him" (John 14:23; 1 John 1:1-4).

One hesitates to number the missions as first and second, though there may be temporal factors. To say that the mission of the Spirit is second might imply a quasi-ontological subordinationism, as though both the person of the Spirit and the mission of the Spirit were of a second order—still exalted, still divine, but of a lower dignity, a junior-grade person with a junior-grade mission. "We have to understand that according to the Scriptures, the work of the Paraclete, the Spirit of Truth, is as important as that of Christ. Without this work, nothing can exist in history, neither the reality of the Incarnation and the reconciliation in Christ, nor personal commitment to him in his community of faith. Everything degenerates into easy generalization and docetic abstractions."[12] If the mission of the Spirit is less important than the mission of the Son, then the whole doctrine of the Trinity collapses. As the Spirit is constitutive of the identity of Jesus and is the principle of identification, so the Spirit (from whom the Son is not absent) is constitutive of the identity of the church.

PENTECOST

It has been traditional to say that Pentecost is the birthday of the church. But in what sense? Is Pentecost simply the occasion on which the church emerges? Or is the Holy Spirit, as communion/ *koinonia* (2 Cor 13:13), constitutive of the church, making a group of believers to be communion, those who come together to confess Jesus and celebrate the mysteries? Does the Holy Spirit on the day of Pentecost animate and vivify an already existing body which, in the first instance, had been erected in christological terms? Despite some denials this latter perspective seems to be operative in paragraph 4 of the Second Vatican Council's Constitution on the Church *(Lumen gentium):* "When the work which the Father gave the Son

---

[12] Nikos Nissiotis, "Pneumatological Christology as a Presupposition of Ecclesiology," *Oecumenica: Jahrbuch für ökumenische Forschung* 2 (1967) 239.

to do on earth (cf. John 17:4) was accomplished, the Holy Spirit was sent on the day of Pentecost in order that he might continually sanctify the Church, and that, consequently, those who believe might have access through Christ in one Spirit to the Father (cf. Eph 2:18)."[13] If the Spirit is added in a second moment, that is already too late, in two senses. First, it gives the impression that the Spirit was not operative before the day of Pentecost, in the people of Israel and in the person and ministry of Jesus. Second, it adds the Spirit to an already existing body constituted in the first moment by Christ and only in a second moment vivified by the Spirit.

There seems to be recognition of this defect in *Lumen gentium,* which was issued at the end of 1964, because the Decree on the Missionary Activity of the Church *(Ad gentes divinitus),* issued at the end of 1965, inserted "a correction" in paragraph 4: "Without doubt, the Holy Spirit was at work in the world before Christ was glorified." This enabled the document on missions to see parallels between the way Jesus is constituted and identified ("Christ was conceived in the Virgin Mary with the coming of the Holy Spirit"), the manner in which the Spirit is constitutive of Jesus' ministry ("Christ . . . was moved to begin his ministry by the descent of the same Holy Spirit"), and the way the church was "manifested" *(manifestata)* on the day of Pentecost. In all three instances, the Spirit has a constitutive, identifying function.[14]

HOW ARE THE MISSIONS OF THE SON AND THE SPIRIT RELATED?

To insist on the equality of the Spirit and of the Spirit's mission, it is neither necessary nor advisable to postulate a distinct "economy of the Spirit," as does Vladimir Lossky.[15] There is one economy from the Father constituted by the missions of the Son and the Spirit, each of the missions being present and active at the interior of the other.

---

[13] *Vatican Council II: The Conciliar and Post Conciliar Documents*, rev. ed., Austin Flannery, ed. (Northport, N.Y.: Costello, 1987) 351–52.

[14] Ibid., 816.

[15] *The Mystical Theology of the Eastern Church* (Crestwood, N.Y.: St. Vladimir's, 1976) 156–73.

One place of entry into the trinitarian economy and into salvation history is christology, or, more specifically, the mission of the Son. One can speak of "a second place" of entry which is "the historical and salvific experience" of the Spirit, the other "hand" by which the Father reaches into history, which defines the mission of the Spirit. But "first" and "second" are problematic because the "second" is often interpreted in the unacceptable sense of a consequent pneumatology, demonstrated by the difference between the texts of *Lumen gentium* and *Ad gentes divinitus*. Though visible mission of the Son in the incarnation and the "visible" mission of the Spirit in the events of Pentecost do occur in a temporal sequence, the "invisible" mission of the Spirit is simultaneous with the visible mission of the Son in the incarnation.[16] The equality of the person and mission of the Spirit is not—cannot be—a subtraction from the person and mission of the Son. What is "given" to the Spirit is not taken away from the Son.

It is a given in trinitarian theology that each of the three divine persons communicates the divine personhood to us freely, gratuitously, in a proper personal particularity and diversity unrepeated in the other two persons.[17] The threefoldness of this self-communication is not to be understood as a merely verbally distinct communication, as though what was communicated was absolutely and in every respect the same, but because of our weak understanding is named with different words by a purely external literary device. In salvation history the distinction of this self-communication is "real." Within the historical order—that is, within salvation history—the self-communication of the triune God takes place through a double sending, corresponding to the mission of the Word and the Spirit. The character of this twofold sending is determined by the specificity of the manner of origin (procession), which manner is constitutive of the Word and the Spirit, who are more than verbally distinct.

While insisting on the "real" distinction between the two missions of the Word and Spirit, there is danger of conceiving of them as two foci at the ends of an ellipse, thus:

[16] Here I depart from the tradition in relating the "invisible" mission of the Spirit also to the incarnation.

[17] Karl Rahner, *The Trinity* (New York: Seabury, 1974) 34–35.

Such a conception, although not necessarily heretical, would be dangerous and might lead to a kind of economic tritheism. The relation of the double mission of Word and Spirit has been expressed in the formula "from the Father through Christ (Word) in the Spirit." In this conception, the two distinct invisible missions ("We will come and will make our abode with him" John 14:23) are coextensive. And if one retains the circle as a means of demonstrating the theological conception, the two missions are visualized as two circles of equal size and equal "depth," which only appear to be superimposed on one another to the point where they seem to be one, but are in reality unmixed and without confusion, forming one geometrical reality (if that is not a violation of geometric laws), in a way reflective of the unity and diversity proper to God.

But alongside the distinction of missions is a radical relating of the one to the other. The Father sends the Spirit in the name of the Son (John 14:26), and the Son sends the Spirit from the Father (John 15:26). The source of both is the Father. Luke also has this mutuality of Spirit and Son (Luke 24:49; Acts 2:33). In a different perspective, Paul reaches the point where the mutuality expressed in "Lord" and Spirit" makes the names almost interchangeable (Rom 12:5, 11; 1 Cor 6:11; 2 Cor 3:17, 18). Paul did not resolve this mutuality into complete identification; while remaining distinct, the Spirit becomes the mode of the risen Lord's existence.[18]

A further caution: The mission of the Son is operative and effective only in the mission of the Spirit ("through Christ in the Spirit"). This seems to be what Paul is saying in Romans 15:18-19: "For I will not venture to speak of anything except what Christ has accomplished through me to win obedience from the Gentiles, by word and deed, by the power of signs and wonders, by the power of the

---

[18] Eduard Schweizer, "pneuma," *The Theological Dictionary of the New Testament* 6.419; Raymond E. Brown, *The Gospel According to John XIII–XXI* (Garden City: Doubleday, 1970) 1139.

Spirit of God." Though one can say that Christ works through the Spirit, this cannot be turned around. The Spirit does not work through Christ.[19] In some respects Christ and the Spirit are interchangeable, but not in all.

If both missions go out from the Father, both lead back to the Father. Building on the biblical witness (Rom 8:15-17; Gal 4:6; Eph 2:18; 1 Cor 15:24), the early authors developed the theology of the movement from the Father through Christ in the Spirit to the church and world, and back by the same movement to God. In the fourth century, liturgical formulas varied but a pattern emerged: "From the Father, through Christ his Son, in the Spirit, to the Father, blessed Trinity, one God."[20]

[19] Sigisbert Regli, "Firmsakrament und christliche Erfahrung," *MS*, 5.325.
[20] Cyprian Vagaggini, *Theological Dimensions of the Liturgy* (Collegeville: The Liturgical Press, 1976) 116. Josef Jungmann, *The Place of Christ in Liturgical Prayer* (Staten Island, N.Y.: Alba House, 1965) 172–212.

Conclusions and Reflections

Chapter 20

The Continuing Quest
for a Theology of the Holy Spirit

The linking of pneumatology and christology is, according to Ernst Käsemann, "a decisive feature and perhaps even an original insight of Pauline theology," something evidenced in the manner in which Paul interprets the formulae "in Christ" and "in the Spirit." "Being in the Spirit" and "being in Christ" mutually interpret each other. Käsemann suggests that perhaps Paul initially used, changed, sharpened (and possibly tamed?) "in the Spirit," which he took over from the enthusiasts, with "in Christ." Even if this is so, the reciprocity in the two formulae is "derived from pneumatology and understood in the light of it."[1] Incorporation "in Christ" is specifically the work of the Spirit, "for by one Spirit were all baptized into one body" (1 Cor 12:13), which body is Christ/church. "In Christ" is extended by "in the Spirit" and vice versa.

[1] *Commentary on Romans* (London: SCM, 1980) 221–22. One is somewhat at a loss when Käsemann later declares. "Both in terms of history-of-religions development and in terms of the theological center it is completely misleading to interpret being in Christ in the light of being in the Spirit. The very opposite is both true and necessary if Christ is not to be merely one interchangeable power among others and the church is not to be a mere band of enthusiasts who glory in the integration into the supernatural world." Ibid. The contradiction is resolved if, as seems to be the mind of Käsemann, the poles between Christ and the Spirit are resolved in favor of the Spirit. Then the Spirit would be the unique center. In which case the reciprocity between Christ and the Spirit would have been diluted, if not

"In Christ" means being incorporated into the body of Christ by baptism, although baptism need not be mentioned in each instance (Rom 8:1; 2 Cor 5:15; Gal 2:17). Since the church into which one is incorporated by baptism is, by virtue of the Spirit, the eschatological community, to be "in Christ" has both ecclesiological and eschatological meanings. "If anyone is in Christ, there is a new creation" (2 Cor 5:17), a clear eschatological reference. Further, since one becomes a member of Christ by the reception of the Spirit at baptism (1 Cor 12:13; 2 Cor 1:22), "being in the Spirit" is also an ecclesiological formula. In sum: since "in Christ" is interchangeable with "in the Spirit," "being in the Spirit" indicates the eschatological meaning of "being in Christ," or "in Christ" expands the ecclesiological content of "in the Spirit," and "in the Spirit" expands the eschatological content of "in Christ."[2]

In Paul "the Spirit determines the Christian life as a whole . . . 'being in the Spirit' becomes the proclamation of 'being in Christ' both as the crucified and the resurrected one." When Paul writes that "anyone who does not have the Spirit of Christ does not belong to him" (Rom 8:9), he is giving a moral exhortation and at the same time pronouncing "one of the most important sayings" in his theology.[3] In fact, the Spirit is the sphere in which the Christian lives through union with Christ. One can be even more daring: The distinctive character of the Christian is possessing the Spirit. One can say this in a bold, unadorned way only if the Spirit is understood as standing under the Lord, Jesus Christ, who is present. The Spirit is and remains the Spirit of Christ (Rom 8:9; Gal 4:6; Phil 1:19). The difficulty of unraveling the mutuality between "in Christ" and "in the Spirit" keeps one from a simplistic interpretation of how the Christian is united to Christ.[4]

abolished. Also operative here is Käsemann's great aversion to the enthusiasts. Nevertheless, Käsemann is quite right in saying that "the primacy of christology even over the church is retained." Ibid. The church is the body of Christ, not the body of the Spirit.

[2] Rudolf Bultmann, *Theology of the New Testament*, 2 vols. (New York: Scribner, 1951) 1.311, 136, 224.

[3] Ibid., 136, 224.

[4] Joseph Fitzmyer, *Romans* (New York: Doubleday, 1993) 481–83.

In Johannine theology, also, there is no lofty revelation of the Spirit-Paraclete independent of Christ's identity. The revelation of the Paraclete is "an application of the revelation of Jesus." The Spirit who begets and the Spirit who is communicated in baptism comes from above, from the Father, but there is no act or manifestation of the Spirit which is not through Christ.[5]

TO EXALT THE SPIRIT IS
TO DIMINISH THE CROSS?

To insist that the person and mission of the Spirit are as important as the person and mission of the Son might be interpreted as diminishing the saving work of Christ on the cross. Instead of preaching Jesus Christ and him crucified, are we now to preach Pentecost as the central content of the gospel? Further, one might read into the insistence on the equality of the persons and missions an assumption that there are two economies, one for the Son, another for the Spirit. A distinct economy of the Spirit, a parallel economy to that of Christ, would seem to diminish the significance of the cross. But while there are two missions from the Father, that of the Son and that of the Spirit, there is only one economy. The cross points forward to the imparting of the Spirit as to a goal.

That the person and mission of the Spirit is of weight and dignity equal to that of the person and mission of the Son within the one economy is seldom denied explicitly, but often implicitly. The denial constitutes a theological attitude—one of many attitudes not easily identifiable at first glance but betrayed in a theological presentation that is not truly and rigorously trinitarian in maintaining the equality of the persons and missions, each mission operative at the interior of the other. In the broad central tradition, the significance of the person and mission of the Son is rarely impoverished, but we cannot say this of the Spirit, because pneumatology has not been integrated in an organic way into the whole theological process. And redress for the pneumatological deficit is not effected by sprinkling references to the Holy Spirit in what we write and say.

[5] C. K. Barrett, *The Gospel According to St. John* (London: SPCK, 1955) 390. Raymond E. Brown, *The Gospel According to John I–XII* (Garden City: Doubleday, 1966) 162.

Though the Spirit is not a threat to the cross of Christ, does insisting on the Spirit as the universal mediation constitute a de facto
displacement of Christ? The suggestion has even been made that
pneumatology should be exalted in pneumatological revenge for
past subservience to christological domination—a kind of pneumatological affirmative action.[6]

Such a shift would be a major theological distortion. Even if the
sixth-century Cyrus of Edessa was right in calling Paul "the trumpet
of the Spirit," the center of the good news in Paul is Jesus Christ
crucified and risen from the dead. Even if one thinks that the Holy
Spirit is "the forgotten God," or is convinced that pneumatology is
too thin, too casual, too truncated, too dominated by christology,
neither the New Testament nor the theological tradition makes the
Holy Spirit the central content of the gospel, the dominant theme
of proclamation, or the principal topic of theological reflection. And
this is as it should be. Heribert Mühlen is right—every dogmatic tract
is basically about Jesus of Nazareth.[7] But it is the Spirit that makes
theological speech about Jesus the Christ possible. Because the Spirit
is the touch of God—that universal mediation where God touches the
church, humankind, and the world, so that at no point does God
touch us outside of the Spirit—the Spirit cannot be another objectified
center or body of teaching in addition to, or over against, Christ.

Whether we think of God reaching out through Christ to touch us,
or of our reaching out to touch the Christ who is the Way to God,
the Spirit, as Gregory of Nyssa tells us, is the universal oil/media-
tion that covers the body of Christ, and to touch Christ one must
first touch the Spirit. But we need care in choosing our words.
The Spirit is not mediator, but the very mediation of the mediator,
Jesus Christ. The universal mediation of the Spirit makes it possible

[6] G. J. Sirks, "The Cinderella of Theology: The Doctrine of the Holy Spirit,"
Harvard Theological Review 50 (1957) 88.

[7] Cyrus, *Explanation of the Passion* 3.8, in *Six Explanations of the Liturgical
Feasts by Cyrus of Edessa: An East Syrian Theologian of the Mid-Sixth Century*,
CSCO 356.66. John Reumann, *Righteousness in the New Testament* (Philadelphia:
Fortress, 1982) 116. Mühlen, "Das Christusereignis als Tat des Heiligen Geistes,"
MS, 3/2.513–14.

for Christ to be the center of the gospel.

The apostles proclaimed Jesus Christ and him crucified. The Spirit and Christ both occupy the center, each according to a proper function, even while the doctrine of Christ remains the content object of theological proclamation and reflection.

NO TRACT APART

If the Spirit is that universal horizon where God and creation meet, if the Spirit as mediation is as universal as the work of Christ the mediator, and if the Spirit is not a junior grade person, but equal with the Father and the Son, then surely the Spirit must be given "equal time." Not so. The norm is not whether a theology gives equal time to the Spirit, or even whether pneumatology is addressed in a special section, but whether the Holy Spirit permeates the whole, in the same way that "being in Christ" is always and everywhere permeated with "being in the Spirit." That the mission of the Spirit is equal to the mission of the Son must be evident, as an interpretative perspective, in the whole of theology. A systematic theology may well dedicate a long, separate chapter—a "tract apart"—to the Spirit and still be woefully inadequate. What is necessary is an integral theology controlled by trinitarian norms and a trinitarian movement: God reaches through the Son in the Spirit to reconcile and transform, leading the church and the world in the Spirit through the Son back to the Father.

Whether a "tract apart" is theologically suspect depends on methodology, not material content. Pneumatology is apart in the bad sense when "in the Spirit" is not the interpretative core of "in Christ," and when the two are not related in mutuality and reciprocity at the center of each other as a part of the movement to the Father. Basil's *On the Holy Spirit,* Athanasius's *Letters to Serapion,* Louis Bouyer's *Le Consolateur*—all are separate books on the Holy Spirit, but none is theologically disqualified as a "tract apart."

This radical interconnectedness of "in the Spirit" and "in Christ," or "in the Spirit through Christ," is clear from the way the early writers approached specific trinitarian topics, avoiding any "tract apart" approach. *On the Trinity,* by Hilary of Poitiers is really about christology and soteriology. Hilary, like Augustine, did christology in a trinitarian mode. Neither was under any compulsion to give the Holy Spirit a separate tract or equal time. Athanasius's four *Letters to Serapion* are a defense of the divinity of the Spirit, but the argument is essentially, even aggressively, trinitarian—if you hold the Spirit to be a creature, you tear asunder the Trinity. Athanasius developed no pneumatology apart from christology and soteriology, not as a tactic but as a demand of his trinitarian hermeneutic. Gregory of Nyssa's *On the Holy Spirit to Eustathius* is for good reason also called *On the Trinity to Eustathius.*

In the twentieth century, Sigurd M. Daecke criticized Karl Barth for not having arrived at a formal, explicit treatment of pneumatology after having written thirteen volumes of his *Church Dogmatics.*[8] But the critique is misplaced. Barth should be judged not on whether he devoted a volume or a specific section to the Holy Spirit, but on whether pneumatology permeates the whole work.

Barth is one of the great trinitarian theologians of the twentieth century, and pneumatology was a major systematic concern. For Barth, the sole possibility of a human being's hearing and believing the word of God is rooted in faith, which is effected by the Spirit alone. Whatever its defects, Barth's pneumatology "is at its core a search for a theologically legitimate principle of mediation at the center of Christian dogmatics—at the point where the transition is made between Christ and the Christian. Only the Holy Spirit, the divine mediator, can validly serve this function." This search for a principle of mediation makes it possible for Barth to become "more and more a pneumatocentric theologian," without abandoning his christocentrism. "The very possibility of human nature's being adopted into unity with the Son of God is the Holy Ghost."[9] In the last year of his life Barth published a critical evaluation of Friedrich Schleiermacher, with whom he had a long-standing love-hate relationship. In this essay Barth projects "the possibility of a theology of the third article, a theology where the Holy Spirit would dominate and be decisive. Everything that one believes, reflects, and says about God the Father and God the Son in understanding the first

[8] "Neue Konjunktur für den Geist," *Evangelische Kommentare* 9 (1975) 520.
[9] Philip Rosato, *The Spirit as Lord: The Pneumatology of Karl Barth* (Edinburgh: T. & T. Clark, 1981) 21, 43. Barth, *Church Dogmatics* (Edinburgh: T. & T. Clark, 1936) 1/2.199.

and second articles would be demonstrated and clarified basically through God the Holy Spirit, the *vinculum pacis* between the Father and the Son. The work of God on behalf of creatures for, in, and with humanity would be made clear in a teleology which excludes all chance. I give only indications of what I occasionally dream of regarding the future of theology."[10] Barth clearly understands that the Spirit as the universal horizon.

But one senses that Barth feared someone would produce a tract apart in the methodological sense, or an overblown pneumatology in which the Spirit would be a theological center over against the centrality of Christ. Even in the act of dreaming of a theology in which Father and Son and all creation would be understood in the light of the Holy Spirit, Barth had misgivings concerning those who might rush his suggestion to completion: "I give a warning! If I am to be spared the accusation of sheer insanity, then only very spiritually and intellectually competent people, a truly 'knowledgeable Theban' will be of use in designing and developing a theology of the third article."[11]

"No tract apart" is not an absolute prohibition—but an essential caution. Richard McBrien cannot be criticized for omitting a separate section on the Holy Spirit in his two-volume *Catholicism*. Maurice Wiles properly raises the question whether a frontal, direct attempt to elaborate a nuanced pneumatology is the best way to take care of a historic deficiency.[12]

THE SPIRIT AS THE KINGDOM

The issue of no tract apart, no contextless adoration of the Spirit, no equal time is seen in the way the tradition handled a variant reading of the Lord's Prayer. Instead of "Your kingdom come" of Luke 11:2, the variant reads "May the Holy Spirit come upon us and cleanse us." Though the variant in Luke is found in the heretic Marcion in the second century, it was picked up by Evagrius in the fourth century and Maximus in the fifth. Gregory of Nyssa thought it worthy

[10] *Schleiermacher-Auswahl mit einem Nachwort von Karl Barth*, Heinz Bolli, ed. (Munich: Siebenstern-Taschenbuch, 1968) 311.

[11] Ibid., 312.

[12] McBrien, 2 vols. (Minneapolis: Winston, 1980) 1.369–70. Wiles, "The Holy Spirit in Christian Theology," *Explorations in Theology* 4 (London: SCM, 1979) 67.

of comment as long as it was given a specifically trinitarian interpretation, related to the trinitarian dynamic.[13] In the way that mediation is related to mediator, the Spirit is the very kingdom itself as related to the king. Through the mediation one touches the mediator, through the kingdom one arrives at the king; the Spirit is the kingdom which is as extensive as the power of the king. To equate the kingdom with the Spirit is not a slighting of the Father and the Son.

THE POLITICAL SPIRIT?

The formulation of the doctrine of the Spirit has been dominated either by ecclesiology (inspiration, infallibility) or by the interior life (grace). But what about the secular order, programs of social transformation, public service, politics? In pneumatology this aspect is underdeveloped. But the tradition Jesus inherited gave the Spirit of God a considerable role in the elders (Num 11:25-29)—judicial/political; judges (Judg 3:10; 11:29; 13:25)—military; some prophets (1 Sam 10:10; 19:23; Ezek 2:12, 22; Neh 9:30; Zech 7:12)—both prophetic and political; some kings (1 Sam 11:36; 16:13-14)—political, especially the messianic king (Isa 42:1). The Spirit has a public face. Nor was the Spirit limited to Israel, as one sees in the Persian king Cyrus (Isa 48:16) and in Balaam, the non-Israelite diviner (Num 22–24).

Jesus himself appropriated this public Spirit at the beginning of his ministry (Isa 61:1-11; Luke 4:18-19) when he characterized his messianic mission to the poor, captives, and oppressed. However, as we have seen, there is a consensus among exegetes that there is little about the Spirit in the synoptic gospels (in contrast to the Fourth Gospel and Paul), since Jesus himself seldom spoke of the Spirit. But care must be taken in interpreting this, as other considerations, such as the messianic secret, enter. Though some of the Spirit-sayings of Jesus in the synoptics have been questioned, the one in which Jesus promises the Spirit to those facing persecution by human tribunals, by "rulers and authorities" (Luke 12:11-12) both religious and political, seems so well attested that it is hardly

---

[13] Gregory of Nyssa, *On the Lord's Prayer* 3; PG 44.1157c–1161a. See Reinhart Staats, "The Nicene-Constantinople Creed as a Foundation for Church Unity: Protestant Thoughts on Its Centenary, 1981," *Irish Theological Quarterly* 48 (1981) 224, n. 36.

possible to doubt its authenticity. Precisely in the sociopolitical arena, tradition hands down Jesus' assurance that the Spirit will speak in the believer brought to judicial judgment and troubled by the prospect of mounting a convincing defense. Although the disciples are condemned by human tribunals, the Paraclete in the Fourth Gospel will offer the real meaning of the events, and the judges will take their place among judged and condemned (John 16:7-15).[14]

The role of the Spirit is also cosmic. Because believers have received the Spirit, they are children of God, putting them in a unique relationship to Christ, the unique Son of the unique Father. In Romans 8:15-16 the prayer of the Spirit in us crying "Abba! Father!" is precisely a cry of children to their Father, lifting up the whole of the created order which shares in Adam's ruin. Echoing Yahweh's promise to Noah of the covenant to be made "between me and you and every living creature" (Gen 9:12-13), Paul affirms solidarity of the nonhuman world with the human world in the redemption Christ has wrought. Therefore the cosmos groans as if in labor to share in our liberty and freedom as those who live the life of the Spirit, making us God's children. The Spirit praying in us asks God to free the whole of creation from temptation and decay in favor of a mode of being that belongs to God alone, lived in the Spirit that made believers into sons and daughters. Paul does not consider the body as something separate from the rest of creation. At the triumph of redeemed humanity, the cosmos will not stand aside, as though it were scaffolding and could now be discarded. Like the body itself, the universe, of which the body is a part, will be transformed, and in its own way glorified.[15] The issue is cosmic redemption in solidarity with human redemption. In the Spirit there is no creationless redemption. Salvation is for the whole of the created order.

[14] Barrett, *The Holy Spirit in the Gospel Tradition* (London: SPCK, 1947) 130. Stanislaus Lyonnet, "The Paraclete," in Ignace de la Potterie and Lyonnet, *The Christian Lives by the Spirit*, (Staten Island: Alba, 1971) 74–75. Michael Welker, *God as Spirit* (Minneapolis: Fortress, 1994), is strong on the socio-political aspect of pneumatology.

[15] Fitzmyer, *Romans*, 506. Käsemann, *Commentary on Romans*, 237. Ignace de la Potterie, "Perfection of the Christian 'Led by the Spirit' and Action in the World According to St. Paul," *Christian Lives by the Spirit*, 236–37.

Conclusions and Reflections

Chapter 21

Toward a Theology in the Holy Spirit

If Jesus Christ is the material content of all theological reflection, is there any sense, beyond what has already been indicated, in which the Holy Spirit is the object of theological inquiry? Or is "object" the correct term?

We find help for answering this question in Gabriel Marcel's reflections on mystery. "A problem is something which I meet, which I find complete before me, but which I can therefore lay siege to and reduce. But a mystery is something in which I myself am involved, and it can therefore only be thought of as 'a sphere where the distinction between what is in me and what is before me loses its meaning and its initial validity.' A genuine problem is subject to an appropriate technique by the exercise of which it is defined; whereas a mystery, by definition, transcends every conceivable technique."[1] Marcel warns against the temptation to treat a mystery as an object. As a kind of presence, mystery is in principle beyond the possibility of being grasped or laid hold of. To face mystery and to acknowledge its true nature can be done only from the inside.

The Holy Spirit cannot be objectified and viewed from a distance because, though distinct, the Spirit is not separable from the very faith processes by which an attempt is made to "define" who the Spirit is. The Spirit can never become an object of theological reflection in the sense that the sacrament of baptism can, because the Spirit is the universal comprehensive horizon within which any and all theological reflection is possible.

---

[1] *The Mystery of Being* (London: Harvill, 1950) 211.

The scholastics discussed a similar issue in their epistemology. They said that the formal principle of understanding does not allow itself to be adequately reflected upon because this reflection is nothing else but itself.[2] A person trying to reflect on reflection itself is moving in a circle, because to think about thinking is already doubling. One is already using thinking in attempting to discover what the object of thinking is. In much the same way we must use the Spirit to understand the Spirit. The Spirit cannot be objectified.

In Erich Schaeder's "coinherence," the object and the subject dwell within each other. This is why for Schaeder all talk about the nonobjectivity of God is rooted in pneumatology. The Spirit known (object) is discovered by the Spirit knowing (subject). The Spirit is not properly a separate theological object to be analyzed on the model of christology or ecclesiology. In the Spirit every theological statement is made and becomes intelligible. "The Spirit searches everything, even the depths of God. . . . No one comprehends what is truly God's except the Spirit of God" (1 Cor 2:10-11). Pneumatology is to theology what epistemology is to philosophy.[3]

That the Spirit operates at the interior of every statement about the Spirit is not simply a Christian insight. Martin Buber, working out his I-Thou relationship, said that "the Spirit is not the *I,* but the between *I* and *Thou.* It is not like the blood that circulates in you, but like the air in which you breathe."[4]

Within this same Hebrew conception of the *ruach* as the ground of all life, Wolfhart Pannenberg theologizes about the Holy Spirit. The divine Father and the Son, transcendent and distinct from the believer, have an object-like character, facing the subjectivity of the

[2] Heribert Mühlen, "Das Christusereignis als Tat des Heiligen Geistes," *MS* 3/2.513–14.

[3] Schaeder, *Das Geistproblem der Theologie* (Leipzig: Deichert, 1924), as quoted in Hans-Jürgen Goertz, *Geist und Wirklichkeit: Ein Studie zur Pneumatologie Erich Schaeders* (Göttingen: Vandenhoeck & Ruprecht, 1980) 29–30. Mühlen, "Soziale Geisterfahrung als Antwort auf eine einseitige Gotteslehre," in Claus Heitmann and Heribert Mühlen, eds., *Erfahrung und Theologie des Heiligen Geistes* (Munich: Kösel, 1974) 154. See also Otto Dilschneider, "Geist und Kirche," in Claus Heitmann and Fidelis Schmelzer, eds., *Im Horizont des Geistes* (Paderborn: Schöningh, 1971) 9–19. Klauspeter Blaser, *Verstoss zur Pneumatologie* (Zurich: Theologischer Verlag, 1977) 20–21.

[4] *I and Thou* (Edinburgh: T. & T. Clark, 1937) 39.

believer. The transcendent Father and Son, as it were, "spring over" to embrace the subjectivity of the believer. In the knowledge of God there is something which faces us, transcendent to us—"objective." When we know other terrestrial objects, a house or a mountain, our knowledge "repeats" the object. But when we know the transcendent God, the Holy Spirit suspends and absorbs this repetition. The Spirit of God within us knows in a different manner from our knowing house or mountain. It is a knowledge of God facing the human, but known by the Spirit within the human: the objective becomes nonobjective.[5]

THE HOLY SPIRIT IN THE RULES OF FAITH

Whether those who composed the earliest credal formulas had grappled in any formal way with the "nonobjectivity" of the Spirit is doubtful, but it is likely they dealt with it in some oblique way. Some early "rules of faith" *(regulae fidei)* mention the Spirit. The rules of faith made their claim to be based on the tradition of Galatians 6:15-16: "For neither circumcision nor uncircumcision is anything; but a new creation is everything! As for those who will follow this rule—peace be upon them, and mercy, and upon the Israel of God." Conforming to Paul's rule and following the Spirit are the same thing—"If we live by the Spirit, let us also be guided by the Spirit" (Gal 5:25).[6]

Rules of faith were formulated to give a clear statement of the essentials of the Christian faith, to guide interpretation of scripture, and to distinguish the orthodox tradition from the traditions to which the heretics appealed. The rules were often inspired by the rite of baptism, and therefore had a broad trinitarian character. Such a formula is found, for example, in Irenaeus: "We have received baptism for the remission of sins in the name of God the Father

---

[5] *Jesus: God and Man* (Philadelphia: Westminster, 1968) 175, n. 146. For a critique of Pannenberg's view of the objective becoming nonobjective, see William J. Hill, *The Three-Personed God: The Trinity as a Mystery of Salvation* (Washington, D.C.: Catholic University, 1982) 163: "All knowledge, including knowledge of God, is objective in some sense. But the knowledge of God, due to its unique content, mediates a suspension and absorption of its own objectivity, whereby it tends, not to indefiniteness, but to the nonobjectivity of God."

[6] Hans-Dieter Betz, *Galatians* (Philadelphia: Fortress, 1979) 321.

and in the name of Jesus Christ, the Son of God, incarnated, dead, and risen, and in the Holy Spirit."[7]

However, many rules of faith do not allude to the Spirit. Irenaeus offers an example of this type too: "The rule of faith is that there is one all-powerful God, who created all things through his Word, one God, maker of heaven and earth, announced by the law and the prophets, and one Christ, Son of God, given for us."[8] No mention of the Spirit.

The absence of the Holy Spirit does not mean that faith in the Spirit was a matter of individual choice or that the faith would be essentially complete minus the Spirit. Binitarian rules of faith were not meant to be complete expositions of the faith. They are short statements, easy to remember, which could be given when the first proclamation of the faith was given to pagans or Jews, as Irenaeus clearly stated.[9]

A rule of faith included the Holy Spirit only when one had already embraced the faith and been accepted into the community by baptism—and now the time had come to explain why the Father had missioned the Son, and what the Son did and continues to do. Thus are explained baptism and the trinitarian economy, "summed up in the giving of the Spirit *(donatio Spiritus)*." When injected into theological debates, the Spirit was invoked as the "source of the demonstration of the truth, the conserver of the tradition, the one who guarantees the rule of faith because the Spirit is the teaching subject, not the object taught."[10]

THE HOLY SPIRIT AS A WAY OF KNOWING

Pneumatology is the divine point of entry into the world and church as God reaches out to history—God's descent. In our ascent to

---

[7] *Demonstration of the Apostolic Preaching* 3; SC 62.32.

[8] *Against Heresies* 3.1.2; SC 211.24; see also 1.22.1; SC 263.308–10.

[9] Ibid., 3.12.13; SC 211.236, 238.

[10] Joseph Moingt, *Théologie trinitaire de Tertullien*, 4 vols. (Paris: Aubier, 1966–69) 1.79. See also Irenaeus, *Against Heresies* 3.6.1; SC 211.64–68; 3.21.4; SC 211.408–14. Hans-Jochen Jaschke, *Der Heiligen Geist im Bekenntnis der Kirche* (Münster: Aschendorff, 1976) 43. Care should be taken not to reduce to a simple identification a baptismal creed on the one hand and a rule of faith (*regula fidei*) and a rule of truth (*regula veritatis*) on the other, even while recognizing that the

God, the Spirit is the portal to the christological and trinitarian mystery. Within this "place" of meeting—the very mediation of the mediator, the termination point of God's descent, and the point of departure for our ascent—we know in the Spirit.

Here Karl Barth gives some idea of the dimensions of the problem. To make the Trinity integral to the theological task, we have to avoid appending the tract on the Trinity or giving the Trinity an extrinsic treatment that leaves the essential structure and movement of theology untouched. Karl Rahner referred to this when he said that theology is often presented in such a way that were the Trinity simply dropped, nothing would have really changed.[11]

Barth placed the Trinity in the prolegomena to his *Church Dogmatics,* covering 194 pages of the whole of 1/1. This positioning of trinitarian doctrine was dictated by Barth's conviction that while there is an objectifying of the being of God, it is not to be understood as God's becoming intelligible as an object in the way a human subject is available as an object to be known. The God of scripture who encounters a human person in the objectivity of the divine One "is not identical with a human subject who knows Him, so also He is not one object in the series of other objects" of human knowing. The knowledge of God is "an utterly unique occurrence in the range of all knowledge." Barth concludes, "Certainly we have God as an object; but not in the same way as we have other objects." Objectivity of this kind differs from other objectivities of human knowing because the separating out from the range of all knowledge takes place in God, something seen more clearly in Barth's doctrine of revelation.[12]

For Barth, revelation is not something God gives to humankind; God is not in every respect something other than the revelation given. When Barth says that God is Revealer (Father), Revelation (Son), and Revealedness (Holy Spirit), he is saying that the Trinity

terminology is somewhat fluid; see F. J. Badcock, "Le credo primitif d'Afrique," *Revue Bénédictin* 45 (1933) 9.

[11] "Remarks on the Dogmatic Treatise 'De trinitate,'" *Theological Investigations,* 23 vols. (New York: Crossroad, 1966–1992) 4.79.

[12] *Church Dogmatics* (Edinburgh: T. & T. Clark, 1936) 2/1.14, 15, 21. Eberhard Jüngel, "God's Being-As-Object," in his *The Doctrine of the Trinity: God's Being Is in Becoming* (Grand Rapids: Eerdmans, 1976) 42–60.

belongs to the very structure of revelation.[13] In this sense, God is not someone who reveals; God as Trinity is revelation.

Barth's teaching on the Trinity is highly christological, but it also has a pronounced pneumatological character. For Barth, the role of the Spirit in uniting the Son of God to the humanity of Jesus is paralleled by the role of the Spirit in mediating the revelation, God's Word, to humankind. The Spirit is the sole source of a relationship with God and the sole hope of salvation. "The indwelling of the Spirit in us, the self-inaugurated motion of the Spirit toward us, by which men are related to God, and which is their death and life, is necessary for the establishing of our relation to God. There is no other means of union, and this one is sufficient."[14]

The Christian's relationship to Jesus Christ comes about through the Spirit, present to the believer, saying "yes" to the Word. This yes "is the mystery of faith, the mystery of knowledge of the Word of God, but also the mystery of willing obedience, well-pleasing to God. All of it exists for man 'in the Holy Spirit,' to wit, faith, knowledge, obedience." The Spirit is the sole possibility of any knowledge of the Father and the Son. In Barth, pneumatology fulfills a mediating function.[15]

While rejecting neither historical knowledge nor critical reflection, Barth contends that the task of theology is the same as that of preaching. The preached biblical message is grasped "by the reason of the *Spirit* that is *identical* with its content, and that in faith." Theological exegesis of this kind was not accepted by either the critical or the conservative theologians, but it did spark a rethinking of New Testament hermeneutics. The situation was not greatly helped by Karl Girgensohn of Griefswal, who proposes that historical exegesis be supplemented by a higher "pneumatic exegesis" directed by the Spirit, or by Helmut Thielicke, who stands in this

[13] *Church Dogmatics* 1/1.417.

[14] Barth, *The Epistle to the Romans* (Oxford: University Press, 1933) 291. See also Philip Rosato, *The Spirit as Lord: The Pneumatology of Karl Barth* (Edinburgh: T. & T. Clark, 1981) 47, 68–69, 72, 77–78.

[15] *Church Dogmatics* 1/1.518–19. There are long sections in *Church Dogmatics* 1/2 on "The Holy Spirit the Subjective Reality of Revelation," 203–42, and "The Holy Spirit the Subjective Possibility of Revelation," 242–79. See also Rosato, "The Act of the Spirit: Barth's Mediating Principle," *Spirit as Lord*, 17–21.

same general tradition of pneumatic exegesis but with a justified realism. This two-tiered approach—theological scholarship and faith knowing—met with even less approval than Barth's suggestion, on the grounds that the Spirit could not be critically verified or made the presupposition to scientific method.[16]

If these solutions are not acceptable, still they point to a dimension of exegetical and theological hermeneutics with which we need to reckon. By reason of faith, the Spirit opens to every believer, and therefore to the theologian, that horizon where the Spirit operates in a unique way, within which revelation is mediated and appropriated. We can push further and ask: Can theology, as today's reflection on the enduring faith, be moved, carried along, and animated by the Spirit who is that expansive point of contact where God's knowing touches human knowing as faith understanding? It would be difficult to separate theology from a personal and communitarian confession of faith, simply because this profession, if it partakes of the full character of faith in the sense of the New Testament, is elicited by the Holy Spirit (1 Cor 12:3).[17]

Basil the Great faced the same problem Barth addressed. As we have seen, in elaborating a theology of the Spirit, Basil complained about those who make only "technology" in place of theology, meaning those who attach excessive importance to philosophical subtleties. The bishop of Caesarea spoke of the knowledge of God attained in the Holy Spirit in terms similar to those Barth uses, but similar also to Marcel's vocabulary of mystery as something we find complete before us, but where the distinction between what is in me and what is before me loses its initial validity. After having stressed the necessity of discipline and asceticism, Basil goes on to demonstrate that the

[16] Barth, *Theologische Fragen und Antworten, Gesammelte Vorträge* (Zollikon: Evangelischer Verlag, 1957) 3.10. On Girgensohn: Werner Georg Kümmel, *The New Testament: The History of the Investigation of Its Problems*, 2nd ed. (Nashville: Abingdon, 1969) 371. Thielicke, *The Evangelical Faith*, 3 vols. (Grand Rapids: Eerdmans, 1974) 1.202: "The hermeneutics of the Holy Spirit means that the truth intended cannot possibly fall under the general categories which are the epistemological conditions for the usual definition of truth. We are thus confronted again by the familiar phenomenon in theology that when the terms are transferred to theology they undergo a sharp modification of sense. Linguistically we still have the same word 'truth,' but it now denotes something very different."

[17] Adolf Darlap, "Der Begriff der Heilsgeschichte," *MS*, 1.37.

knowledge of God is knowledge of and in the Spirit, knowledge from within: "If we are illumined by divine power, and fix our eyes on the beauty of the image (Son) of the invisible God, and through the image are led up to the indescribable beauty of its source (Father), it is because we have been inseparably joined to the Spirit of knowledge. He gives those who love the vision of truth the power which enables them to see the image, and this power is himself. He does not reveal it to them from outside sources, but leads them to knowledge personally. 'No one knows the Father except the Son,' and 'no one can say "Jesus is Lord" except in the Holy Spirit.' Notice that it does not say *through* the Spirit, but *in* the Spirit. . . . He reveals the glory of the Only-Begotten in himself, and he gives the true worshipers the knowledge of God in himself. The way to divine knowledge ascends from one Spirit through the one Son to the one Father."[18]

Knowledge of this kind is from within, a theology in the Spirit, and is not attainable by merely exterior means, even by study. If one does not know God in the Spirit, one does not know God at all. For Basil, as for Barth, the Spirit is the point of entry into the christological and trinitarian mystery, the universal touch, the universal mediation.

KNOWING AND THE SPIRIT IN SYRIAC OPTICS

In the Syriac linguistic tradition (that is, non-Greek and non-Latin), Philoxenus of Mabbug (c. 440–523) presents a similar position on the pneumatological roots of the knowledge of God, conditioned by an ancient theory of optics in which sight occurs when the external light of the sun meets the interior light already in the eye. Without the likeness of these two forms of light, no sight is possible.[19]

Philoxenus holds that the Holy Spirit dwells in the believer and is

[18] *On the Holy Spirit* 9.23; 18.47; SC 17bis.288, 412. Dörries, *DSS*, 48 translates "technology" as "verbal prestidigitation" or "verbal acrobatics." See also Basil, *Letter* 90.2, in *Lettres*, Yves Courtonne, ed., 3 vols. (Paris: Société d'Édition "Les Belles Lettres," 1957–1966) 1.196. J. M. Hornus, "La divinité du Saint-Esprit comme condition du salut personnel selon Basile," *Verbum Caro* 23 (1969) 33. Theodoret of Cyrrhus (5th c.), *Résumé of Heretical Fables* 4.3; PG 83:420b, referring to the rationalist Eunomius, wrote of those who make fables by doing "technology" instead of theology.

[19] Roberta C. Chesnut, *Three Monophysite Christologies* (Oxford: University Press, 1976) 95.

that very interior light which links the believer with the exterior light of God and spiritual realities. Because of the likeness of the interior light (Spirit) in the believer and the exterior light (God), knowledge of God is possible. The Spirit gives proportionality. Without the Holy Spirit the believer is like a blind person in the presence of a table; the table which should be seen is not seen, because what is in the eye to make it operate correctly is absent. The table remains present, but unseen. In like manner, without the Holy Spirit one cannot see the God who is present.[20] In this sense God is object, but only because God is seen with the seeing proper to God. For Philoxenus there is no access, no contact, no sight of divine realities, no knowledge of God apart from the Spirit.

THE SPIRIT GIVES PROPORTIONALITY

If one moves back from Philoxenus to the New Testament, one discovers in the Johannine materials the conviction that the possession of the Spirit "becomes a way of knowing" (1 John 3:24; 4:13), leaving no doubt that the presence of the Spirit is both experience and knowledge.[21] This way of knowing, rooted in individual and community, is not based on the reception and exercise of the more dramatic charisms. Rather, the Johannine writings reflect a quieter, more commonplace inner experience in individuals and community which brings the presence of the Spirit into conscious awareness, as the Spirit is experienced in Galatians 4:6 and Romans 8:14, the "Abba! Father!" passages.

Religious experience in biblical times was not an extraordinary event, but belonged to the normal, mature life of the Christian community. Experience of the Spirit was also a way of knowing. It crimps the force of the text in John 14:16-17 to exclude experience and knowledge: "I will ask the Father, and he will give you another Advocate, to be with you forever. This is the Spirit of truth, whom the world cannot receive, because it neither sees him nor knows him. You know him, because he abides with you, and he will

---

[20] Ibid. See the text of Philoxenus in "Memra de Philoxène de Mabboug sur l'inhabitation du Saint-Esprit," Antoine Tanghe, ed., *Muséon* 73 (1960) 51.

[21] Rudolf Schnackenburg, "Die johanneische Gemeinde und ihre Geisterfahrung," *Die Kirche des Anfangs*, Schnackenburg, Josef Ernst, and Joachim Wanke, eds. (Freiburg im Breisgau: Herder, 1978) 286.

be in you." This is even clearer in 1 John 2:27, where the author speaks of an anointing which abides in the believer, and in 3:9, concerning "God's seed" abiding. For John the possession of the Spirit is a way of knowing and an experienced reality, and does not refer to special manifestations of the Spirit in charisms (as in 1 Cor 12:7-11).[22]

In Paul also the Spirit is a way of knowing. Natural knowledge and understanding are not adequate to the truth the Spirit teaches (1 Cor 2:14f). In order to know a truth one must have a faculty proportionate to it. For us to know the mysteries of God, the Spirit must endow our knowing faculty with a power beyond human knowing. The Spirit is the proportionality which makes knowledge of God possible.[23] This is why pneumatology is in some sense epistemology, and to a degree determines the rules for speaking about the mystery. Within the proportionality that the Spirit gives, one can know Jesus, the image of the Father who sent him. With the same proportionality one can recognize the presence of God in history and the face of God's Son in the church.

In the fourth century Didymus the Blind indicated the magnitude of the hermeneutical problem: The Holy Spirit "will teach, not like those who have acquired an art or knowledge by study and industry, but as the very art, doctrine, and knowledge itself. . . . In this way all become doctors (of knowledge)."[24] This way of knowing in the Spirit cannot be verified by critical methods, and, therefore, cannot be a presupposition to a scientific method. The nonobjectivity and hiddenness of the Spirit are reason for the elusive quality of all knowing in the Spirit and all speech about the Spirit.

If one speaks of the work of creation and redemption in reference to the First and Second Persons, and refers sanctification to the Third Person, then the work of the Spirit falls less immediately under scrutiny than the other two. The Spirit is known by what is

[22] Eduard Schweizer, *Church Order in the New Testament* (London: SCM, 1961) 181–87, 209–10; "pneuma," *The Theological Dictionary of the New Testament* 6.423–24. James D. G. Dunn, *Jesus and the Spirit* (Philadelphia: Westminster, 1975) 297; Otto Kuss, *Der Römerbrief* (Regensburg: Pustet, 1963–78) 549–50.

[23] Richard Kugelman, "The First Letter to the Corinthians," *Jerome Biblical Commentary*, 258–59. See also Walter Kasper, *Gegenwart des Geistes: Aspekte der Pneumatologie* (Freiburg: Herder, 1979) 10.

[24] *On the Holy Spirit* 141; SC 386:275.

effected. But arguing back from effects does not leave a satisfying account of who the Spirit is. Persistent imprecision is one reason, in addition to the silence of scripture, why the early authors hesitate to make unambiguous statements about the person, origin, and divinity of the Spirit, and why it remains difficult to delineate what precisely knowledge in the Spirit is.

The elusive character of the Spirit pushed the early authors into uncomfortable positions about knowledge in the Spirit. Augustine scarcely spoke of the Holy Spirit except where he could not avoid it, such as when he found the Spirit in a citation he had invoked in order to support a thesis on which he had already decided. Augustine tends, as do his heirs both ancient and modern, to refer to grace in contexts where theologians of the East speak of the Spirit.[25] Hilary of Poitiers, attempting to give a pronounced and balanced trinitarian conclusion to his *On the Trinity,* devotes a section to the Father and the Son, and expresses frustration in lines devoted to the Holy Spirit: In his prayer peroration Hilary confesses that he holds fast the belief that the Spirit "is from you," but adds, "although I do not grasp it with my understanding." He recalls that there are other things he does not understand, including his own regeneration. Then, somewhat lamely, he concludes, "I shall assert nothing else about the Holy Spirit that is above the judgment of the human mind except that the Spirit is your Spirit. And I pledge myself to avoid a futile contest of words, but give myself to preserving the profession of unquestioning faith."[26]

Basil wrote his classic *On the Holy Spirit* in 374–375, but ten years earlier, when he is being pressed by the rationalist Eunomius, he confesses that he does not know very much about the Spirit. Basil defends himself: "Who then will be astonished if we confess, without blushing, our ignorance of the Holy Spirit, and if, nonetheless, we acquit ourselves with the doxology, which is an incontestable witness in its favor (of the Spirit not being a simple creature)?"[27] Basil devotes thirty-seven columns in Migne to the Father and forty to the Son, but is barely able to scrape together nine for the Spirit.

[25] Louis Bouyer, *Le Consolateur* (Paris: Cerf, 1980) 222.
[26] *On the Trinity* 12.56; CCSL 62.626.
[27] *Against Eunomius* 3.6; SC 305.168.

Even after centuries of reflection, writing on the Trinity manifests a certain impoverishment when it comes to the Third Person, as Karl Rahner has noted.[28] Very likely this will not change.

The displacement of pneumatology from its trinitarian context is a major cause of problems. Whatever helps are available for speaking meaningfully of knowing in the Spirit will come from the trinitarian context. As a discipline, pneumatology keeps slipping out of its frame, and in pneumatology Trinity is more than content—it is process, method, control, as of course also in christology. Basil said it all: "How can we be safe if we tear the Spirit from the Father and the Son?"[29]

ACQUIRING THE SPIRIT:
THE GOAL OF THE CHRISTIAN LIFE

Though "full life in the Spirit" was often equated in the tradition with the ascetic life in its celibate form, this is not the biblical view. Paul, speaking in a broader context, says that mature Christians "live by the Spirit" (Gal 5:16), are "led by the Spirit" (Gal 5:18), regulate their lives by "the law of the Spirit" (Rom 8:2), and therefore have "the mind of the Spirit" (Rom 8:6). The gift of the Spirit is the first gift in a total process that ends when the believer becomes a spiritual body, a mode of existence whose structure and dynamic are defined by the Spirit.[30]

As the Spirit makes Jesus the Son of God, so the Spirit makes believers share in the same life as the Father and the Son and become adopted sons and daughters in the Son. There is a strong tradition that God became what we are so we could become what God is—Irenaeus: "The Word of God, Jesus Christ our Lord, who, because of his superabundant love, made himself what we are in order to make of us what he is"; Athanasius: "God became human so humans could become God"; Gregory of Nazianzus: "God is made human; the human is rendered God"; Gregory of Nyssa: "Because our nature is mixed with the divine nature, our nature is made divine";

[28] William J. Hill, *The Three-Personed God: The Trinity as a Mystery of Salvation* (Washington, D.C.: Catholic University, 1982) 139, referencing Rahner.

[29] *On the Holy Spirit* 12.28; SC 17bis.346.

[30] Dunn, *Jesus and the Spirit*, 311.

Ephrem the Syrian: "He gave us divinity, we gave him humanity." Gregory of Nazianzus works backward from inner transformation to the divinity of the Spirit: "How could [the Spirit] not be God, the one through whom you become God?" Cyril of Jerusalem announces the principle that "whatever the Spirit touches becomes holy and transformed."[31]

Paul's admonition to "pray always" (1 Thess 5:17) makes sense only when situated in this already realized sharing in God: "For all who are led by the Spirit of God are children of God. . . . You have received a spirit of adoption. When we cry, 'Abba! Father!' it is that very Spirit bearing witness with our spirit that we are children of God" (Rom 8:14-16). The Spirit within, knowing with divine knowledge, is one with our knowing. A believer cries out to God not because participation is wanting, but because it is a present reality. In the Spirit one lives the life of God.

One can, of course, pray to the Spirit, but the burden of evidence is that the Spirit, as the very life of God, wants to pray in us and with us through Christ to the Father. One has the right to say "Abba! Father!" because one has received the Spirit and therefore has a real communion in the life proper to God, though it is a created participation. Further, what the Spirit leads us to beyond death is not so much the vision of God as the flowering of this communion along the spectrum of God's life, seeing from inside with the fully empowered eye of God. "It is through the Spirit that we are partakers of God."[32]

The present sharing has an unrealized ("already" but "not yet") dimension to it. The Spirit is the very newness we possess, as Thomas Aquinas says: "The new law consists chiefly in the grace of the Spirit." According to Ernst Käsemann, Paul taught that "Christianity is not a Jewish sect which believes in Jesus as the

---

[31] Irenaeus, *Against Heresies* 5.1.1; SC 153.14. Athanasius, *On the Incarnation of the Word* 54.3; SC 199.458. Gregory of Nazianzus, *Dogmatic Poem* 10.5; PG 37.465; *Oration* 39.17; SC 358.186. Gregory of Nyssa, *Catechetical Oration* 25, in *Opera*, Werner Jaeger, ed. (Leiden: Brill, 1952–) 3/4.64. Ephrem, *Hymns of Faith* 5.17; CSCO 155.17. Cyril, *Mystagogical Catecheses* 5.7; SC 126.154; Cyril is using this principle in a eucharistic context, but it has wider application.

[32] Hans Urs von Balthasar, *Creator Spirit* (San Francisco: Ignatius, 1993) 111. Athanasius, *Letters to Serapion* 1.24; SC 15.126.

Messiah. It is the breaking in of the new world of God characterized by the lordship of the Spirit." What Thomas and Käsemann point to as the newness has long been considered the goal of the Christian life, as by Athanasius: "The Word and the Son of the Father united to the flesh, made flesh a perfect man, so that we might be united to the Spirit, and might be made one Spirit. So the One (Son) is God bearing the Spirit, making us bearers of the Spirit."[33]

We have seen that Gregory of Nyssa identifies the whole kingdom with the Spirit when he adopts the variant reading of the Our Father: ". . . your Holy Spirit come upon us and cleanse us." Gregory also expresses the Holy Spirit's union with the Son in the anointing—the Son is the king, the Holy Spirit is the kingdom: "The Spirit is a living and substantial and distinctly subsisting kingdom, with which the only-begotten Christ is anointed and is king of all that is." Here again we have that essential reality: as the Spirit is the sole mediation of the sole Mediator, so the Spirit is the sole kingdom of the sole King. Symeon the New Theologian is in the same tradition: "The kingdom of heaven consists in the sharing in the Holy Spirit." Nicolas Cabasilas, a highly educated layman—not a monk—expounds a simple spiritual way in terms of the sacraments and life in Christ, accessible to all, whether married or monastic: "What in fact is the aim of Christ's sufferings, teachings and actions? Considered in relationship to us, it is none other than the descent of the Holy Spirit on the Church."[34]

In the twentieth century Karl Barth took over the language of goal: ". . . this sovereign goal and presupposition of all Christian teaching: *Credo in Spiritum Sanctum.*" Alexander Schmemann echoes the early Greek authors: "Cast in ecclesiological terms, the ultimate mystery of the church consists in knowing the Holy Spirit." John Meyendorff sums up the Orthodox sense: The Spirit "is the

[33] Thomas Aquinas, *Summa theologiae* I–II, q108, a1. Käsemann, *Commentary on Romans* (London: SCM, 1980) 191. Athanasius, *On the Incarnation and Against the Arians* 8; PG 26:996.

[34] Gregory, *On the Lord's Prayer* 3; *On the Holy Spirit Against the Macedonians* 16, in *Opera* 7/2.39; 3/1.102. See also Maximus the Confessor, *Explanation of the Lord's Prayer*; PG 90:884b. Symeon, *Catecheses* 6.110; SC 104.22. Nicolas Cabasilas, *Commentary on the Divine Liturgy* 37; SC 4bis.228.

very content of the kingdom."[35]

All of this is not theological rhetoric. According to Paul the purpose of the crucifixion is the imparting of the Spirit in faith (Gal 3:13-14).

Universal kingdom, universal horizon, the touch of God, ultimate goal—all these are reflections of the biblical teaching on the primacy of the Spirit as mediation, not only at the beginning but at every point along the redemptive process. God does not come to us except through the Son in the Spirit. And we do not go to God except in the Spirit through the Son. The Son and the Spirit do not stand "alongside" each other, or parallel to one another. Given the universality of the Spirit as the mediation of the Son, and given the equality of the mission of the Spirit with the mission of the Son, is this another reason to give the Spirit equal time? Equal time for equal missions? For instance, half of our time in proclamation should be given to the Son and half to the Spirit; or in our theology books there should be as many chapters on the Spirit as there are on the Son.

This would be a major misunderstanding of the trinitarian dynamic and of the role of the Spirit. No, we do as the apostles did after the transforming experience of Pentecost. They proclaimed Christ, and him crucified (Acts 2:22-36). But our proclamation is formed and informed with the Spirit in a way that makes the role of the Spirit evident. Implicit in that proclamation of Jesus Christ crucified and risen will be the conviction that the Christian life is a growth process in which the ascendancy of the Spirit is the goal. If the Spirit is the touch by which one has communion in the mystery of Christ, and if the Spirit is the only access to God, then the goal of the Christian life is the "acquisition" of the Spirit. The Spirit as goal is the kingdom Christ hands over to the Father.

WHAT IF?

The salvation of the whole created order is assured through the two missions from the Father, that of the Son and that of the Spirit. These two missions are present at the interior of each other, though

---

[35] Barth, *Church Dogmatics*, 4/1.650. Schmemann, *Of Water and the Spirit* (London: SPCK, 1974) 104. Meyendorff, *Byzantine Theology: Historical Trends and Doctrinal Themes*, 2nd ed. (New York: Fordham University, 1983) 169.

without confusion. They cannot exist divorced from each other. But in order to understand the unique character of each mission, it might be useful to look at this impossibility, that is, if the one mission of the Spirit did exist without the one mission of the Son, and *vice versa,* what would be the result?

The Spirit is communion *(koinonia),* sharing, participation, fellowship in trinitarian life (2 Cor 13:13; 1 John 1:1-10; 3:23-24). Without the mission of the Spirit there is neither communion with God, nor communion among believers. We remain separated from God, and scattered fragments among ourselves. Without the mission of the Spirit the mission of the Son cannot begin, has no goal, no terminus. Without the mission of the Spirit the history the Son constitutes by entering time at the Annunciation and at Bethlehem lacks the act of purposeful movement. Without the mission of the Spirit the son of Mary of Nazareth remains an unusual man without a substantive religious identity significant for life beyond the boundaries of his country. Without the mission of the Spirit the mysterious acts of Christ do not become real in us, but remain acts of an ancient wandering preacher who told memorable parables and lived a selfless life. Without the mission of the Spirit we cannot locate the Christ or his saving history, and the mission of the Son lacks the specific weight of God. Without the Spirit, the Son is the way, and the truth and the life, but without actualization. Without the mission of the Spirit the life in the vine and the branches is not one and the same. Without the mission of the Spirit we are not children carrying within a life which is already eternal. Without the mission of the Spirit we are not bearers of the seed which will spring forth in the resurrection. We will remain in our graves.

Without the mission of the Spirit the church remains in fixity, a splendid stasis, frozen in time, without movement, without an end. Without the mission of the Spirit what is left of faith and experience are the dried structural bones of religion. Liturgy is ceremony and ritual, prayer is formula, theology is the proposition of ideology that excites and changes no one; we remain without the knowledge of God, without touching or being touched by the reality of God. Without the mission of the Spirit no one can grasp the hem of the Son's garment, we never receive the eternal life extended to us, the sending of the Son is a dispatch into a void, a messenger who never arrives, a light illumining nothing, a road to nowhere, and the resurrection is a non-event. Without the personal mission of the Spirit we remain in our sin, and our graves are our permanent home. Without the mission of the Spirit the universal reach of the arms of the cross never become concrete reality in the church and the world. We are without hope of salvation.

Why is all of this true? Because the Spirit has exclusive possession of that road between God and humankind. Or rather the Holy Spirit is that road. Without the trinitarian highway that is the Spirit, God cannot reach us and we cannot reach God. We are closed up in our selves, and God is imprisoned in the splendor of divinity. These closed doors are flung open because the Spirit is the goal of the work of Christ, before he hands over the kingdom to the Father.

Without the mission of the Son the mission of the Spirit is devoid of the flesh and materiality that make salvation history possible. Without the mission of the Son, the mission of the Spirit floats above time, looking for flesh it can touch and transform. Without the mission of the Son the Spirit is a hand deprived of something to grasp, lacking a mystery to be present to, devoid of a mystery to make real in history and in our hearts, divested of a ministry to empower, bereft of children to transform into daughters and sons, wanting in offspring to gather into unity in the church and in human community. Without the mission of the Son the church is a mystical illusion, shadows upon the wall. Without the mission of the Son matter remains crass materiality, the universe never arrives at Easter, and sinks into decay. Without the mission of the Son the universality of the Spirit is emptied of its historic content.

Why is all of this true? Because without the Son the Spirit is a finger of God lacking a history to touch. Without the mission of the Son the Spirit is a ladder to nowhere, and history never arriving at the Father.

But the two missions are not separate. Cannot be divorced. Each is present at the interior of the other, a deep calling unto deep, light illumining light, witnessing to the love of the Father, bending over the world with troubled love, gathering humanity and the universe with the two divine arms, the Son and the Spirit, into the untroubled glory that is the ultimate consummation of all.

Bibliographies

MODERN SOURCES

À Lapide, Cornelius.
>   *Commentaria in Scripturam Sacram.* Paris: Vivès, 1866.
Adler, Ada, ed.
>   *Svidae Lexicon.* 5 vols. Stuttgart: Teubner, 1933.
Anastos, Milton.
>   "Basil's *Kata Eunomiou,* A Critical Analysis." In *Basil of Caesarea: Christian, Humanist, Ascetic.* Ed. Paul J. Fedwick, 67–136. Toronto: Pontifical Institute of Mediaeval Studies, 1981.
Aune, David E.
>   "The Significance of the Delay of the Parousia for Early Christianity." In *Current Issues in Biblical and Patristic Interpretation.* Ed. Gerald F. Hawthorne, 87–109. Grand Rapids: Eerdmans, 1975.

Badcock, F. J.
>   "Le credo primitif d'Afrique." *Revue Bénédictin* 45 (1933).
Balabanski, Vicky.
>   *Eschatology in the Making: Mark, Matthew and the Didache.* Cambridge: Cambridge University, 1997.
Bammel, Ernst.
>   "Schema und Vorlage von Didache 16." In *Studia Patristica* 4, part 2 (1961) (*Texte und Untersuchungen* 79).
Barnard, L. W.
>   "The Heresy of Tatian—Once Again." *Journal of Ecclesiastical History* 19 (1968) 10.

Barrett, C. K.

    The Gospel According to St. John. 2nd ed. London: SPCK, 1978.

    The Holy Spirit and the Gospel Tradition. London: SPCK, 1966.

    "The Place of Eschatology in the Fourth Gospel." *The Expository Times* 59 (1947–1948).

    "Why Do the Gospels Say So Little about the Spirit?" In *The Holy Spirit and the Gospel Tradition.* London: SPCK, 1966.

Barth, Karl.

    Church Dogmatics. Edinburgh: T. & T. Clark, 1936.

    The Epistle to the Romans. Oxford: University Press, 1933.

    Theologische Fragen und Antworten, Gesammelte Vorträge. Zollikon: Evangelischer Verlag, 1957.

Barth, Markus.

    Ephesians. 2 vols. Garden City: Doubleday, 1974.

Batiffol, Pierre.

    "Jérome de Jérusalem d'après un document inédit." *Revue des questions historiques* 39 (1886) 248–55.

Becker, Jürgen.

    Die Briefe an die Galater. Göttingen: Vandenhoeck & Ruprecht, 1976.

Bell, David N.

    The Image and Likeness: The Augustinian Spirituality of William of St. Thierry. Kalamazoo: Cistercian, 1984.

Berkhof, Henrikus.

    The Doctrine of the Holy Spirit. Atlanta: John Knox, 1964.

Bertrand, Frédéric.

    Mystique de Jésus chez Origène. Paris: Aubier, 1951.

Betz, Hans Dieter.

    "In Defense of the Spirit: Paul's Letter to the Galatians as a Document of Early Christian Apologetics." In *Aspects of Religious Propaganda in Judaism and Early Christianity.* Ed. Elisabeth Schüssler-Fiorenza, 99–114. Notre Dame: Notre Dame University, 1976.

    Galatians. Philadelphia: Fortress, 1979.

    "The Literary Composition and Function of Paul's Letter to the Galatians." *New Testament Studies* 21 (1974–1975) 353–79.

Bigg, Charles.

    The Christian Platonists of Alexandria. Oxford: Clarendon, 1886.

Blaser, Klauspeter.

    Verstoss zur Pneumatologie. Zurich: Theologisher Verlag, 1977.

Blenkinsopp, Joseph.

    Prophecy and Canon. Notre Dame: University of Notre Dame, 1977.

Bodard, Claude.
 "La bible, expression d'une expérience religieuse chez s. Bernard."
  In *Saint Bernard théologien: actes du Congrès de Dijon,
  15–19 septembre, 1953.* Rome: 1953.
Boff, Leonardo.
 Trinity and Society. Maryknoll: Orbis, 1988.
Bolli, Heinz, ed.
 Schleiermacher-Auswahl mit einem Nachwort von Karl Barth. Munich:
  Siebenstern-Taschenbuch, 1968.
Bonowitz, Bernard.
 "The Role of Experience in the Spiritual Life." *Analecta Cisterciensia*
  46 (1990).
Borchardt, C.F.A.
 Hilary of Poitiers' Role in the Arian Struggle. The Hague: Nijhoff, 1966.
Bouyer, Louis.
 Le Consolateur. Paris: Cerf, 1980.
Bovon, Francois.
 Luke the Theologian: Thirty-three Years of Research (1950– 1983).
  Allison Park, Pa.: Pickwick, 1987.
Brock, Sebastian.
 The Holy Spirit in the Syrian Baptismal Tradition. Kerala [India]:
  no publisher given, 1979.
Brooke, Odo.
 Studies in Monastic Theology. Kalamazoo: Cistercian, 1980.
Brown, David.
 The Divine Trinity. Lasalle, Ill.: Open Court, 1985.
Brown, Peter.
 Augustine of Hippo: A Biography. Berkeley: University of California,
  1967.
Brown, Raymond E.
 The Birth of the Messiah. Garden City: Doubleday, 1977.
 The Community of the Beloved Disciple. New York: Paulist, 1979.
 The Gospel According to John I–XII. Garden City: Doubleday, 1966.
 The Gospel According to John XIII–XXI. Garden City: Doubleday,
  1970.
Brox, Norbert.
 Der Hirt des Hermas. Göttingen: Vandenhoeck & Ruprecht, 1991.
Brunner, Emil.
 Vom Werk des Heiligen Geistes. Tübingen: Mohr [Siebeck], 1935.
Buber, Martin.
 I and Thou. Edinburgh: T. & T. Clark, 1937.

Büchsel, D. F.

    Der Geist Gottes im Neuen Testament. Gütersloh: Bertelsmann, 1926.

Buckley, Michael.

    At the Origins of Modern Atheism. New Haven: Yale University, 1987.

Bultmann, Rudolf.

    The Gospel of John. Philadelphia: Westminster, 1971.

    The History of the Synoptic Tradition. New York: Harper & Row, 1968.

    Theology of the New Testament. 2 vols. New York: Scribner, 1951.

Burge, Gary M.

    The Anointed Community: The Holy Spirit in the Johannine Tradition. Grand Rapids: Eerdmans, 1987.

Byrne, Brendan.

    Romans. Collegeville: The Liturgical Press, 1996.

Carmignac, Jean.

    "Les dangers de l'eschatologie." *New Testament Studies* 17 (1971) 365–90.

    Le mirage de l'eschatologie. Paris: Letouzey et Ane 1979.

Carroll, John T.

    "The Parousia of Jesus in the Synoptic Gospels and Acts." In *The Return of Jesus in Early Christianity.* Ed. John T. Carroll, 5–45. Peabody, Mass.: Hendrickson, 2000.

    Response to the End of History: Eschatology Situation in Luke–Acts. Decatur, Ga.: Scholars, 1988.

Catechism of the Catholic Church. Washington, D.C.: United States Catholic Conference, 1994.

Cavallera, Ferdinand.

    "La doctrine de saint Augustin sur l'Esprit Saint à propos du De trinitate." *Recherches de théologie ancienne et médiévale* 2 (1930) 365–87; 3 (1931) 5–19.

Cerfaux, Lucien.

    The Christian in the Theology of St. Paul. New York: Herder and Herder, 1967.

    "L'église et le règne de Dieu d'après saint Paul." *Ephemerides Theologicae Lovanienses* 2 (1925) 181–98.

Chadwick, Henry.

    The Church in Ancient Society: From Galilee to Gregory the Great. Oxford: Clarendon, 2001.

Chenu, Marie-Dominique.

    La théologie au douzième siècle. Paris: Vrin, 1966.

Chesnut, Roberta C.
  Three Monophysite Christologies. Oxford: University Press, 1976.
Clark, Mary.
  "Introduction." In *Marius Victorinus: Theological Treatises on the Trinity.* Washington, D.C.: Catholic University, 1981.
Coffey, David.
  Deus Trinitas: The Doctrine of the Triune God. New York: Oxford University Press, 1999.
  Grace: The Gift of the Holy Spirit. Manly, Australia: Catholic Institute of Sydney, 1979.
  "The Holy Spirit as the Mutual Love of the Father and the Son." *Theological Studies* 51 (1990) 193–229.
  "A Proper Mission of the Holy Spirit." *Theological Studies* 47 (1986) 227–50.
Colwell, E. C.
  "A Definite Rule for the Use of the Article in the Greek New Testament." *Journal of Biblical Literature* 52 (1933) 12–21.
Congar, Yves.
  I Believe in the Holy Spirit. New York: Seabury, 1983.
  Tradition and Traditions. New York: Macmillan, 1967.
Conzelmann, Hans.
  History of Primitive Christianity. Naperville, Ill.: Abingdon, 1973.
  An Outline of the Theology of the New Testament. London: SCM, 1969.
  The Theology of Luke. New York: Harper & Row, 1961.
Courth, Franz.
  Trinität in der Scholastik (Handbuch der Dogmengeschichte). Freiburg: Herder, 1985.
Courtonne, Yves, ed.
  Lettres. 3 vols. Paris: Société d'Édition "Les Belles Lettres," 1957–1966.
Cramer, Winfrid.
  Der Geist Gottes und des Menschen in frühsyrischer Theologie. Münster: Aschendorff, 1979.
Crouzel, Henri.
  Origen. San Francisco: Harper & Row, 1989.
Cullmann, Oscar.
  Early Christian Worship. London: SCM, 1953.

Daecke, Sigurd M.
  "Neue Konjunktur für den Geist." *Evangelische Kommentare* 9 (1975).

Daley, Brian.
    The Hope of the Early Church: A Handbook of Patristic Eschatology.
    New York: Cambridge University, 1991.

Daly, Robert J., ed.
    The Eucharist in the West. Collegeville: The Liturgical Press, 1998.

Daniélou, Jean.
    "Chrismation prébaptismale et divinité de l'Esprit chez Grégoire de
    Nysse." *Recherches de sciences religieuses* 56 (1968) 177–98.

Darlap, Adolf.
    "Der Begriff der Heilsgeschichte." In *Mysterium Salutis* 1. Ed.
    Johannes Feiner and Magnus Löhrer, 17–90. Einsiedeln:
    Benziger, 1965–1976.

De Halleux, André.
    "Towards an Ecumenical Agreement on the Procession of the Holy
    Spirit and the Addition of the *Filioque* to the Creed." In *Spirit
    of God, Spirit of Christ: Ecumenical Reflections on the Filioque
    Controversy.* Ed. Lukas Vischer, 69–84. London: SPCK, 1981.

De Lubac, Henri.
    The Christian Faith. San Francisco: Ignatius, 1986.

De Margerie, Bertrand.
    The Christian Trinity in History. Still River, Mass.: St. Bede's, 1982.

De Mendieta, Emmanuel A.
    *'Unwritten' and 'Secret' Apostolic Traditions in the Theological
    Thought of St. Basil of Caesarea (Scottish Journal of Theology
    Occasional Papers,* 13). Edinburgh: Oliver and Boyd, 1965.

Delling, Gerhard.
    Worship in the New Testament. Philadelphia: Westminster, 1962.

Dilschneider, Otto.
    "Geist und Kirche." In *Im Horizont des Geistes.* Ed. Claus Heitmann
    and Fidelis Schmelzer, 9–19. Paderborn: Schöningh, 1971.

Dodd, C. H.
    The Apostolic Preaching and its Developments. New York: Harper &
    Row, 1964.

Dörries, Hermann.
    *De Spiritu Sancto: Der Beitrag des Basilius zum Abschluss des
    trinitärischen Dogmas.* Göttingen: Vandenhoeck & Ruprecht,
    1956.

Driver, Tom F.
    Christ in a Changing World: Toward an Ethical Christology. New York:
    Crossroad, 1981.
    Patterns of Grace. San Francisco: Harper & Row, 1977.

Dunn, James D. G.

    Baptism in the Holy Spirit. Naperville, Ill.: Allenson, 1970.

    Christology in the Making: A New Testament Inquiry into the Origins of the Doctrine of the Incarnation. Philadelphia: Westminster, 1980.

    Jesus and the Spirit. Philadelphia: Westminster, 1975.

    Jesus and the Spirit: A Study of the Religious and Charismatic Experience of Jesus and the First Christians as Reflected in the New Testament. Grand Rapids: Eerdmans, 1997.

    "Spirit and Holy Spirit in the New Testament." In *The Christ and the Spirit: Collected Essays.* 2 vols. Grand Rapids: Eerdmans, 1991.

    Unity and Diversity in the New Testament. 2nd ed. Philadelphia: Trinity, 1990.

Durwell, F. X.

    "Pour une christologie selon l'Esprit." *Nouvelle Revue Théologique* 114 (1992) 651–77.

Eichrodt, Walter.

    Theology of the Old Testament. 2 vols. Philadelphia: Westminster, 1961.

Elliott-Binns, L. E.

    Galilean Christianity. Naperville, Ill.: Allenson, 1956.

Fassetta, Raffaele.

    "Le rôle de l'Esprit-Saint." *Analecta Cisterciencia* 46 (1990).

Fitzmyer, Joseph.

    The Gospel According to Luke I–IX. Garden City: Doubleday, 1981.

    The Gospel According to Luke X–XXIV. Garden City: Doubleday, 1985.

    "To Know Him and the Power of his Resurrection." In *To Advance the Gospel: New Testament Studies.* New York: Crossroad, 1981.

    Romans: A New Translation with Introduction and Commentary. New York: Doubleday, 1993.

Flannery, Austin, ed.

    Vatican Council II: The Conciliar and Post Conciliar Documents. Rev. ed. Northport, N.Y.: Costello, 1987.

Florensky, Pavel.

    "On the Holy Spirit." In *Ultimate Questions.* Ed. Alexander Schmemann, 137–72. New York: Holt, Rinehart and Winston, 1965.

Florovsky, George.

    "Eschatology in the Patristic Age: An Introduction." In *Studia Patristica* 2, part 2 (1955).

The Forgotten Trinity. The Report of the B.C.C. Study Commission on Trinitarian Doctrine Today. 3 vols. London: British Council of Churches, 1989.

Fortman, Edmund J.
    The Triune God: A Historical Study of the Doctrine of the Trinity. Grand Rapids: Baker, 1972.

Fransen, Peter.
    The New Life of Grace. London: Chapman, 1969.

Gallay, Paul, ed.
    Saint Grégoire de Nazianze: Lettres. 2 vols. Paris: Société d'Édition 'Les Belles Lettres,' 1964–1967.

Galtier, Paul.
    Le Saint Esprit en nous d'après les pères grecs. Rome: Gregorian University, 1946.

Giblet, Jean.
    "Pneumatologie et eschatologie." In *Credo in Spiritum Sanctum* 2. Ed. José Sariva Martins, 895–901. Vatican City: Libreria Editrice Vaticana, 1983.

Goertz, Hans-Jurgen.
    Geist und Wirklichkeit: Ein Studie zur Pneumatologie Erich Schaeders. Göttingen: Vandenhoeck & Ruprecht, 1980.

Gottwald, Norman K.
    The Hebrew Bible: A Socio-Literary Introduction. Philadelphia: Fortress, 1985.

Grant, Robert.
    Gods and the One God. London: SPCK, 1986.

Grässer, Erich.
    Das Problem der Parusievergöserung in den synoptischen Evangelien und in der Apostelgeschichte. 3rd ed. Berlin: Walter de Gruyter, 1977.

Graves, Charles Lee.
    "The Holy Spirit in the Theology of Sergius Bulgakov." Ph.D. diss.: University of Basel, 1970.

Gribomont, Jean.
    "Intransigence and Irenicism in Saint Basil's 'De Spiritu Sancto.'" *Word and Spirit* 1 (1979).

Gross, Jules.
    La divinisation du chrétien d'après les pères grecs. Paris: Gabalda, 1938.

Haenchen, Ernst.
    The Acts of the Apostles: A Commentary. Philadelphia: Westminster, 1971.

Hall, Jerome M.

    We Have the Mind of Christ: The Holy Spirit and Liturgical Memory in the Thought of Edward J. Kilmartin. Collegeville: The Liturgical Press, 2001.

Hamilton, Neill Quinn.

    The Holy Spirit and Eschatology in Paul. Edinburgh: Oliver and Boyd, 1957.

Hansen, Günther C., ed.

    Sokrates Kirchengeschicte. Berlin: Berlin-Brandenburgische Akademie, 1995.

Hanson, R.P.C.

    "The Achievement of Orthodoxy in the Fourth Century A.D." In *The Making of Orthodoxy,* Festschrift for Henry Chadwick. Ed. Rowan Williams, 142–56. New York: Cambridge University, 1989.

    The Search for the Christian Doctrine of God. Edinburgh: T. & T. Clark, 1988.

    Tradition in the Early Church. Philadelphia: Westminster, 1962.

    "The Transformation of Images in the Trinitarian Theology of the Fourth Century." In *Studia Patristica.* Oxford: Pergamon, 1982.

    "Witness from St. Patrick to the Creed of 381." *Analecta Bollandiana* 101 (1983).

Harrington, Daniel J.

    The Gospel of Matthew. Collegeville: The Liturgical Press, 1991.

Hauschild, Wolf-Dieter.

    Gottes Geist und der Mensch: Studien zur frühchristlichen Pneumatologie. Munich: Kaiser, 1972.

Hausherr, Irénée.

    "Les grands courants de la spiritualité orientale." *Orientalia Christiana Periodica* 1 (1935) 114–38.

Hausherr, Irénée, and Gabriel Horn, eds.

    Vie de Syméon le Nouveau Théologien. Rome: Pontifical Oriental Institute, 1928.

Havener, Ivan.

    "The Credal Formulae of the New Testament: A History of the Scholarly Research and a Contribution to the On-going Study." Ph.D. diss., University of Munich, 1976.

Hengel, Martin.

    The Charismatic Leader and His Followers. New York: Crossroad, 1981.

Hermann, Ingo.

    Kyrios und Pneuma. Munich: Kösel, 1961.

Hill, William J.
  The Three-Personed God: The Trinity as a Mystery of Salvation.
      Washington, D.C.: Catholic University, 1982.
Himes, Michael and Kenneth.
  Fullness of Faith: The Public Significance of Theology. New York:
      Paulist, 1993.
Holl, Karl.
  *Enthusiasmus und Bussgewalt beim griechischen Mönchtum: Eine
      Studie zu Symeon dem neuen Theologen.* Leipzig: Hinrisch,
      1898.
Holtz, Traugott.
  Der Erste Brief an die Thessalonicher. Einsiedeln: Benziger, 1986.
Hornus, J. M.
  "La divinité du Saint-Esprit comme condition du salut personnel
      selon Basile." *Verbum Caro* 23 (1969) 33–62.
Houssiau, Albert.
  "Le baptême selon Irénée de Lyon." *Ephemerides Theologicae
      Lovaniensis* 60 (1984) 45–59.
Hübner, Reinhard.
  "Gregor von Nyssa als Verfasser der sog. Ep. 38 des Basilius."
      In *Epektasis: mélanges patristiques offerts au cardinal Jean
      Daniélou.* Ed. Jacques Fontaine and Charles Kannengiesser,
      463–90. Paris: Beauchesne, 1972.

Isaye, Gaston.
  "L'unité de l'opération divine dans les écrits trinitaires de Saint
      Grégoire de Nysse." *Recherches de science religieuse* 27 (1937)
      422–39.

Jaschke, Hans-Jochen.
  Der Heilige Geist im Bekenntnis der Kirche. Münster: Aschendorff,
      1976.
Jeremias, Joachim.
  The Prayers of Jesus. Naperville, Ill.: Allenson, 1967.
Jevtich, Atanasije.
  "Between the 'Nicaeans' and the 'Easterners': The 'Catholic'
      Confession of Saint Basil." *St. Vladimir's Theological Quarterly*
      24 (1980) 235–52.
Johnson, Luke Timothy.
  The Acts of the Apostles. Collegeville: The Liturgical Press, 1992.

Jüngel, Eberhard.
"God's Being-As-Object." In *The Doctrine of the Trinity: God's Being Is in Becoming.* Grand Rapids: Eerdmans, 1976.
Jungmann, Josef.
The Place of Christ in Liturgical Prayer. Staten Island, N.Y.: Alba House, 1965.

Kannengiesser, Charles.
"Athanasius of Alexandria and the Holy Spirit between Nicaea I and Constantinople I." *Irish Theological Quarterly* 48 (1981).
Käsemann, Ernst.
"The Beginnings of Christian Theology." In *New Testament Questions of Today.* Philadelphia: Fortress, 1969.
Commentary on Romans. Grand Rapids: Eerdmans, 1980.
Romans. London: SCM, 1980.
Kasper, Walter.
Gegenwart des Geistes: Aspekte der Pneumatologie. Freiburg: Herder, 1979.
"Geschichtlichkeit der Dogmen?" *Stimmen der Zeit* 179 (1967) 401–16.
The God of Jesus Christ. New York: Crossroad, 1986.
Jesus the Christ. New York: Paulist, 1976.
Kilmartin, Edward.
"The Catholic Tradition of Eucharistic Theology: Towards the Third Millennium." *Theological Studies* 55 (1994) 405–57.
King, N. Q.
The Emperor Theodosius and the Establishment of Christianity. Philadelphia: Westminster, 1960.
Koch, Hal.
Pronoia und Paideusis: Studien über Origenes und sein Verhältnis zum Platonismus. Berlin: Walter de Gruyter, 1932.
Koch, Klaus.
The Prophets: The Assyrian Period. Philadelphia: Fortress, 1983.
The Prophets: The Babylonian and Persian Periods. Philadelphia: Fortress, 1982.
Köpf, Ulrich.
"Erfahrung als Voraussetzung bei Bernhard und seinen Hören." In *Religiöse Erfahrung in der Theologie Bernhards von Clairvaux.* Tübingen: Mohr [Siebeck], 1980.
"Die Rolle der Erfahrung im religiösen Leben nach dem Heiligen Bernhard." *Analecta Cisterciensia* 46 (1990).

Kremer, Jacob.
"Jesu Verheissung des Geistes." In *Die Kirche des Anfangs: Festschrift für Heinz Schürmann*. Ed. Rudolf Schnackenburg, Josef Ernst, and Joachim Wanke, 247–76. Freiburg im Briesgau: Herder, 1978.

Kretschmar, Georg.
"Le développement de la doctrine du Saint-Esprit du Nouveau Testament à Nicée." *Verbum Caro* 22 (1968) 5–55.
Studien zur frühchristlichen Trinitätstheologie. Tubingen: Mohr, 1956.

Krivocheine, Basil.
St. Symeon the New Theologian: Life-Spirituality-Doctrine. Crestwood, N.Y.: St. Vladimir's, 1986.

Kümmel, Werner Georg.
The New Testament: The History of the Investigation of Its Problems. 2nd ed. Nashville: Abingdon, 1969.

Kuss, Otto.
Der Römerbrief. Regensburg: Pustet, 1963–78.

LaCugna, Catherine Mowry.
God For Us: The Trinity and Christian Life. San Francisco: Harper, 1991.

Lagrange, Marie-Joseph.
Évangile selon saint Jean. 2nd ed. Paris: Lecoffre, 1925.

Lampe, G.W.H.
God as Spirit. New York: Oxford University Press, 1977.

Lebreton, Jules.
Histoire du dogme de la Trinité: des origines au concile de Nicée. 2 vols. Paris: Beauchesne, 1928.

Leclercq, Jean.
The Love of Learning and the Desire for God: A Study of Monastic Culture. 3rd ed. New York: Fordham University, 1982.
"The Schoolmen of the Twelfth Century." In *The Spirituality of the Middle Ages*. Ed. Jean Leclercq, François Vandenbroucke, Louis Bouyer, 223–42. New York: Desclée, 1968.

Léon-Dufour, Xavier.
"Bulletin d'exégèse du nouveau testament." *Recherches de science religieuse* 55 (1967) 566–86.

Lienhard, Joseph T.
"The 'Arian' Controversy: Some Categories Reconsidered." *Theological Studies* 48 (1987) 415–37.

Lohmeyer, Ernst.
Galiläa und Jerusalem. Göttingen: Vandenhoeck & Ruprecht, 1936.

Lonergan, Bernard.
  The Way to Nicaea: The Dialectical Development of Trinitarian Theology. Philadelphia: Westminster, 1976.
Lorenz, Rudolf.
  Arius judaizans? Untersuchungen zur dogmengeschichtlichen Einordnung des Arius. Göttingen: Vandenhoeck & Ruprecht, 1980.
Lossky, Vladimir.
  The Mystical Theology of the Eastern Church. Crestwood, N.Y.: St. Vladimir's, 1976.
Louth, Andrew.
  The Origins of the Mystical Tradition. Oxford: Clarendon, 1981.
Lührmann, Dieter.
  Der Brief an die Galater. Zurich: Theologischer Verlag, 1978.
Luislampe, Pia.
  Spiritus vivificans. Grundzüge einer Theologie des Heiligen Geistes nach Basilius von Caesarea. Münster: Aschendorff, 1981.
Lull, David J.
  The Spirit in Galatia: Paul's Interpretation of Pneuma as Divine Power. Chico, Calif.: Scholars Press, 1980.
Luneau, Auguste.
  L'histoire du salut chez les pères de l'église: la doctrine des ages du monde. Paris: Beauchesne, 1964.
Lyonnet, Stanislaus.
  "The Paraclete." In *The Christian Lives by the Spirit.* Ed. Ignace de la Potterie and Stanislaus Lyonnet. Staten Island: Alba, 1971.

Malet, André.
  Personne et amour dans la théologie trinitaire de saint Thomas d'Aquin. Paris: Vrin, 1956.
Maloney, George A.
  Russian Hesychasm: The Spirituality of Nil Sorskij. The Hague: Morton, 1973.
Marcel, Gabriel.
  The Mystery of Being. London: Harvill, 1950.
Marshall, Molly T.
  Joining the Dance: A Theology of the Spirit. Valley Forge, Pa.: Judson, 2003.
Martin, Francis.
  "Pauline Trinitarian Formulas and Church Unity." *Catholic Biblical Quarterly* 30 (1968) 199–219.

McBrien, Richard.
    Catholicism. 2 vols. Minneapolis: Winston, 1980.

McDonnell, Kilian.
    The Baptism of Jesus in the Jordan: The Trinitarian and Cosmic Order of Salvation. Collegeville: The Liturgical Press, 1996.
    "Does Origen Have a Trinitarian Doctrine of the Holy Spirit?" *Gregorianum* 75, 1 (1994) 5–35.
    "A Trinitarian Theology of the Holy Spirit?" *Theological Studies* 46 (1985) 191–93.

McGinn, Bernard.
    The Growth of Mysticism. New York: Crossroad, 1996.

McIntyre, John.
    "The Holy Spirit in Greek Patristic Thought." *Scottish Journal of Theology* 7 (1954) 353–75.

McNamee, John J.
    "The Role of the Spirit in Pentecostalism: A Comparative Study." Ph.D. diss.: University of Tübingen, 1974.

Meeks, M. Douglas.
    God the Economist. Minneapolis: Fortress, 1989.

Meier, John.
    A Marginal Jew: Rethinking the Historical Jesus. 2 vols. New York: Doubleday, 1991–1994.
    Matthew. Wilmington: Glazier, 1980.

Meijering, E. P.
    Orthodoxy and Platonism in Athanasius. Leiden: Brill, 1968.

Meredith, Anthony.
    The Cappadocians. Crestwood, N.Y.: St. Vladimir's, 1995.
    Gregory of Nyssa. New York: Routledge, 1999.

Meyendorff, John.
    Byzantine Theology: Historical Trends and Doctrinal Themes. 2nd ed. New York: Fordham University, 1983.
    St. Gregory Palamas and Orthodox Spirituality. Crestwood, N.Y.: St. Vladimir's, 1974.

Moingt, Joseph.
    Théologie trinitaire de Tertullien: Histoire, doctrine, methods. 4 vols. Paris: Aubier, 1966–1969.

Molnar, Paul D.
    "The Function of the Immanent Trinity in the Theology of Karl Barth: Implications for Today." *Scottish Journal of Theology* 42 (1989) 367–99.

Moloney, Francis J.
   The Gospel of John. Collegeville: The Liturgical Press, 1998.
Moltmann, Jürgen.
   History and the Triune God. New York: Seabury, 1992.
   Trinity and the Kingdom. New York: Harper & Row, 1981.
Montague, George.
   The Holy Spirit: Growth of a Biblical Tradition. New York: Paulist, 1976.
Mühlen, Heribert.
   "Das Christusereignis als Tat des Heiligen Geistes." In *Mysterium
      Salutis* 3, part 2. Ed. Johannes Feiner and Magnus Löhrer,
      513–44. Einsiedeln: Benziger, 1965–1976.
   *Der Heilige Geist als Person: Beitrag zur Frage nach der dem heiligen
      Geistes eigentumlichen Funktion in der Trinität, bei der
      Inkarnation und im Gnadenbund.* Münster: Aschendorff, 1963.
   *Una Mystica Persona. Die Kirche als das Mysterium der heilsgeschicht-
      lichen Identität des Heiligen Geistes in Christus und den Christen:
      Eine Person in vielen Personen.* 3rd ed. Munich: Schöningh,
      1968.
   "Soziale Geisterfahrung als Antwort auf eine einseitige Gotteslehre."
      In *Erfahrung und Theologie des Heiligen Geistes.* Ed. Claus
      Heitmann and Heribert Mühlen, 253–72. Munich: Kösel, 1974.
Murphy-O'Connor, Jerome.
   Paul: A Critical Life. Oxford: Clarendon, 1996.

Newman, John Henry.
   The Arians of the Fourth Century. 3rd ed. London: Pickering, 1876.
Nissiotis, Nikos.
   "Pneumatological Christology as a Presupposition of Ecclesiology."
      Oecumenica: Jahrbuch fur ökumenische Forschung 2 (1967)
      253–52.
Norris, Frederick W.
   *Faith Gives Fullness to Reasoning: The Five Theological Orations of
      Gregory Nazianzen.* Leiden: Brill, 1991.

O'Collins, Gerald.
   Christology. Oxford: University Press, 1995.
Orphanos, Markos A.
   "The Procession of the Holy Spirit According to Certain Later Greek
      Fathers." In *Spirit of God, Spirit of Christ: Ecumenical Reflec-
      tions on the Filioque Controversy.* Ed. Lukas Vischer, 21–45.
      London: SPCK, 1981.

Outler, Albert.
   "Veni Creator Spiritus: The Doctrine of the Holy Spirit."
      In *New Theology* 4. Ed. Martin E. Marty and Dean G. Peerman,
      195–209. London: Macmillan, 1967.

Pannenberg, Wolfhart.
   "Analogy and Doxology." In *Basic Questions in Theology*. London:
      SCM, 1970.
   The Apostle's Creed. Philadelphia: Westminster, 1972.
   Jesus: God and Man. Philadelphia: Westminster, 1968.
   "The Working of the Spirit in Creation and in the People of God."
      In *Spirit, Faith and Church*. Ed. Wolfhart Pannenberg, Avery
      Dulles, and Carl E. Braaten, 13–31. Philadelphia: Westminster,
      1969.
Parmentier, Martien.
   "The Doctrine of the Holy Spirit in the Works of Gregory of Nyssa."
      Ekklesiastikos Pharos 58 (1976) 387–444.
Pelikan, Jaroslav.
   The Emergence of the Catholic Tradition (100–600). Chicago: Univer-
      sity of Chicago, 1971.
   The Melody of Theology: A Philosophical Dictionary. Cambridge:
      Harvard, 1988.
   "The 'Spiritual Sense' of Scripture." In *Basil of Caesarea: Christian,
      Humanist, Ascetic*. Ed. Paul J. Fedwick, 337–60. Toronto:
      Pontifical Institute of Mediaeval Studies, 1981.
Porsch, Felix.
   *Pneuma und Wort: Ein exegetischer Beitrag zur Pneumatologie des
      Johannesevangeliums*. Frankfurt am Main: Knecht, 1974.

Quasten, Johannes.
   Patrology. 4 vols. Westminster, Md.: Christian Classics, 1986.

Rahner, Karl.
   "Der Dreifaltige Gott als Transzendenter Urgrund der
      Heilsgeschichte." In *Mysterium Salutis* 2. Ed. Johannes Feiner
      and Magnus Löhrer, 317–401. Einsiedeln: Benziger, 1965–1976.
   "Oneness and Threefoldness of God in Discussion with Islam."
      In *Theological Investigations*. 23 vols. New York: Crossroad,
      1966–1992.
   "Remarks on the Dogmatic Treatise 'De trinitate.'" In *Theological
      Investigations*. 23 vols. New York: Crossroad, 1966–1992.

"Some Implications of the Scholastic Concept of Uncreated Grace."
  In *Theological Investigations*. 23 vols. New York: Crossroad,
  1966–1992.
The Trinity. New York: Seabury, 1974.
Rahner, Karl, and Karl Lehmann.
  "Kerygma und Dogma." In *Mysterium Salutis* 1. Ed. Johannes Feiner
  and Magnus Löhrer, 622–707. Einsiedeln: Benziger,
  1965–1976.
Ratzinger, Joseph.
  Introduction to Christianity. New York: Herder and Herder, 1970.
Regli, Sigisbert.
  "Firmsakrament und christliche Erfahrung." In *Mysterium Salutis* 5.
  Ed. Johannes Feiner and Magnus Löhrer, 297–347. Einsiedeln:
  Benziger, 1965–1976.
Reumann, John.
  Righteousness in the New Testament. Philadelphia: Fortress, 1982.
Ritschl, Dietrich.
  "Historical Development and Implications of the Filioque Contro-
  versy." In *Spirit of God, Spirit of Christ: Ecumenical Reflections
  on the Filioque Controversy*. Ed. Lukas Vischer, 46–65. London:
  SPCK, 1981.
Ritter, Adolf-Martin.
  Das Konzil von Konstantinopel und sein Symbol. Göttingen:
  Vandenhoeck & Ruprecht, 1965.
Rosato, Philip.
  The Spirit as Lord: The Pneumatology of Karl Barth. Edinburgh:
  T. & T. Clark, 1981.
Rousseau, Philip.
  Basil of Caesarea. Berkeley: University of California, 1994.
Rüsch, Theodor.
  Die Entstehung der Lehre vom Heiligen Giest. Zurich: Zwingli, 1952.

Schaberg, Jane.
  The Father, Son, and the Holy Spirit: The Triadic Phrase in Matt 28:19b.
  Chico, Calif.: Scholars, 1982.
Schaeder, Erich.
  Das Geistproblem der Theologie. Leipzig: Deichert, 1924.
Scheeben, Matthias.
  Die Mysterien des Christentums. In *Gesammelte Schriften*. Ed. Josef
  Höfer. 8 vols. Freiburg im Briesgau: Herder, 1941.
The Mysteries of Christianity. St. Louis: Herder, 1947.

Scheffczyk, Leo.
"Die heilsökonomische Trinitätslehre des Rupert von Deutz und ihre dogmatische Bedeutung." In *Kirche und Überlieferung*. Ed. Johannes Betz and Heinrich Fries, 90–118. Freiburg: Herder, 1960.
"Lehramtliche Formulierungen und Dogmengeschichte der Trinität." In *Mysterium Salutis* 2. Ed. Johannes Feiner and Magnus Löhrer, 146–220. Einsiedeln: Benziger, 1965–1976.
"Uneingelöste Traditionen der Trinitätslehre." In *Trinität: Aktuelle Perspektiven der Theologie*. Ed. Eugen Drewermann, et al., 47–72. Freiburg: Herder, 1984.
Schierse, Franz J.
"Die neutestamentliche Trinitätsoffenbarung." In *Mysterium Salutis* 2. Ed. Johannes Feiner and Magnus Löhrer, 85–131. Einsiedeln: Benziger, 1965–1976.
Schlink, Edmund.
The Coming Christ and the Coming Church. Philadelphia: Fortress, 1967.
Schmaus, Michael.
Die psychologische Trinitätslehre des heilgen Augustinus. Münster: Aschendorff, 1927.
"Die Trinitätslehre des Simon von Tournai." *Recherches de théologie ancienne et médiévale* 3 (1931) 371–96.
Schmemann, Alexander.
Of Water and the Spirit. London: SPCK, 1974.
Schmithals, Walter.
"Geisterfahrung als Christuserfahrung." In *Erfahrung und Theologie des Heiligen Geistes*. Ed. Claus Heitmann and Heribert Mühlen, 101–17. Munich: Kösel, 1974.
Paul and James. Naperville, Ill.: Allenson, 1965.
Schnackenburg, Rudolf.
Brief an die Epheser. Zürich: Benziger, 1982.
The Gospel According to St. John. New York: Herder & Herder, 1968.
The Gospel According to St. John. 3 vols. New York: Crossroad, 1982.
"Die johanneische Gemeinde und ihre Geisterfahrung." In *Die Kirche des Anfangs: Festschrift für Heinz Schürmann*. Ed. Rudolf Schnackenburg, Josef Ernst, and Joachim Wanke. Freiburg im Briesgau: Herder, 1978.
Schoedel, W. R.
Ignatius of Antioch. Philadelphia: Fortress, 1985.
Schoonenberg, Piet.
"Trinity–the Consummated Covenant. Theses on the Doctrine of the Trinitarian God." *Studies in Religion/Sciences Religieuses* 5 (1975–1976) 111–16.

Schuck, Johannes.
  *Das Hohe Lied des Hl. Bernhard von Clairvaux: Dokumente zur
    mittelalterlichen Christus- und Brautmystik.* Paderborn:
    Schöningh, 1926.
Schütz, Christian.
  Einführung in die Pneumatologie. Darmstadt: Wissenschaftliche
    Buchgesellschaft, 1985.
Schweizer, Eduard.
  Church Order in the New Testament. London: SCM, 1961.
  The Spirit of God. Philadelphia: Fortress, 1980.
  "The Spirit of Power." *Interpretation* 6 (1952) 259–78.
Sekki, Arthur E.
  The Meaning of Ruach at Qumran. Atlanta: Scholars, 1989.
Sesboüé, Bernard.
  "Bulletin de théologie dogmatique: Pneumatologie." *Recherches des
    sciences religieuses* 76 (1988) 115–28.
Shapland, C.R.B.
  The Letters of Saint Athanasius concerning the Holy Spirit. New York:
    Philosophical Library, 1951.
Sieben, Hermann Josef.
  Die Konzilsidee der alten Kirche. Paderborn: Schöningh, 1979.
Siman, Emmanuel Pataq.
  *L'expérience de l'Esprit par l'église d'après la tradition syrienne
    d'Antioche.* Paris: Beauchesne, 1971.
Simonetti, Manlio.
  La crisi ariana nel IV secolo. Rome: Augustinianum, 1975.
Sirks, G. J.
  "The Cinderella of Theology: The Doctrine of the Holy Spirit."
    Harvard Theological Review 50 (1957) 77–99.
Staats, Reinhart.
  "The Nicene-Constantinople Creed as a Foundation for Church
    Unity: Protestant Thoughts on Its Centenary, 1981."
    Irish Theological Quarterly 48 (1981).
Stead, Christopher.
  Divine Substance. Oxford: Clarendon, 1977.
Stock, Brian.
  *The Implications of Literacy: Written Language and Models of
    Interpretation in the Eleventh and Twelfth Centuries.*
    Princeton: Princeton University, 1983.
Studer, Basil.
  Trinity and Incarnation. Collegeville: The Liturgical Press,
    1993.

Swete, H. B.
> *On the Early History of the Doctrine of the Holy Spirit.* Cambridge:
> Deighton and Bell, 1873.

Tabbernee, William.
> "Revelation 21 and the Montanist 'New Jerusalem.'" *Australian
> Biblical Review* 37 (1989) 52–60.

Tanner, Norman.
> *Decrees of the Ecumenical Councils.* 2 vols. Georgetown: Georgetown
> University, 1990.

Terrien, Samuel.
> *The Elusive Presence.* New York: Harper & Row, 1978.

Thielicke, Helmut.
> *The Evangelical Faith.* 3 vols. Grand Rapids: Eerdmans, 1974.

Thomas, Robert.
> "William of St. Thierry: Our Life in the Trinity." *Monastic Studies*
> 3 (1965) 139–63.

Thompson, John.
> *Modern Trinitarian Perspectives.* New York: Oxford University Press,
> 1994.

Thomson, Robert W., ed.
> *The Teaching of Saint Gregory: An Early Armenian Catechism.*
> Cambridge: Harvard, 1970.

Thüsing, Wilhelm.
> *Per Christum in Deum: Studien zum Verhältnis von Christozentrik
> und Theozentrik in den paulinischen Hauptbriefen.* 2nd ed.
> Munster: Aschendorff, 1968.

Überweg, Friedrich, and Bernhard Geyer.
> *Die patristische und die scholastische Philosophie.* 13th ed. Basel:
> B. Schwabe, 1956.

Vandenbussche, E.
> "La Part de la dialectique dans la théologie d'Eunomius 'le techno-
> logue.'" *Revue d'histoire ecclésiastique* 40 (1944) 47–72.

Vagaggini, Cyprian.
> *Theological Dimensions of the Liturgy.* Collegeville: The Liturgical
> Press, 1976.

Vaggione, Richard P., ed.
> *Eunomius: The Extant Works.* Oxford: Clarendon, 1987.

Verdeyen, Paul.
> *La théologie mystique de Guillaume de Saint-Thierry.* Paris: FAC, 1990.

Von Balthasar, Hans Urs.
  Creator Spirit. San Francisco: Ignatius, 1993.
  Origen: Spirit and Fire. Washington, D.C.: Catholic University, 1984.
  Richard von Sankt-Victor: Die Dreieinigkeit. Einsiedeln: Benziger,
    1980.
  Theo-Drama. San Francisco: Ignatius, 1992.
Von Campenhausen, Hans.
  The Fathers of the Greek Church. New York: Pantheon, 1959.
Von Rad, Gerhard.
  Old Testament Theology. 2 vols. New York: Harper & Row, 1962.

Wainwright, Arthur W.
  The Trinity in the New Testament. London: SPCK, 1962.
Wainwright, Geoffrey.
  Doxology. London: Epworth, 1980.
Ware, Kallistos.
  "The Eastern Tradition from the Tenth to the Twentieth Century."
    In *The Study of Spirituality*. Ed. Cheslyn Jones, et al, 235–58.
    New York: Oxford University Press, 1986.
Welker, Michael.
  God as Spirit. Minneapolis: Fortress, 1994.
Wendland, Hans Dietrich.
  Die Briefe an die Korinther. Göttingen: Vandenhoeck & Ruprecht,
    1968.
Wiles, Maurice.
  Archetypal Heresy: Arianism through the Centuries. Oxford: Clarendon,
    1996.
  "Eunomius: Hair-splitting Dialectician or Defender of the
    Accessibility of Salvation?" In *The Making of Orthodoxy*,
    Festschrift for Henry Chadwick. Ed. Rowan Williams, 157–72.
    New York: Cambridge University, 1989.
  "The Holy Spirit in Christian Theology." In *Explorations in Theology* 4.
    London: SCM, 1979.
Williams, R. R.
  "Logic versus Experience in the Order of Credal Formulae."
    New Testament Studies 1 (1954) 42–44.
Williams, Rowan.
  Arius: Heresy and Tradition. Grand Rapids: Eerdmans, 2002.
Wilson, Christian.
  *Toward a Reassessment of the Shepherd of Hermas: Its Date and Its
    Pneumatology*. Lewiston, Me.: Mellen Biblical Press, 1993.

Windisch, Hans.

    The Spirit-Paraclete in the Fourth Gospel. Philadelphia: Fortress, 1968.

Winkler, Gabriele.

    "Ein bedeutsamer Zusammenhang zwischen der Erkenntnis und
        Ruhe in Matt 11, 27–29 und dem Ruhen des Geistes auf Jesus
        am Jordan. Eine Analyse zur Geist-Christologie in syrischen
        und armenischen Quellen." *Muséon* 96 (1983) 267–326.

Winslow.

    The Dynamics of Salvation: A Study in Gregory of Nazianzus.
        Cambridge, Mass.: Philadelphia Patristic Foundation, 1979.

Wipfler, Heinz.

    *Die Trinitätsspekulation des Petrus von Poitiers und die
        Trinitätsspekulation des Richard von St. Viktor. Ein Vergleich.*
        Münster: Aschendorff, 1965.

Wolfson, Harry A.

    The Philosophy of the Church Fathers. 2nd ed. Cambridge: Harvard, 1964.

Wrede, William.

    The Messianic Secret. Cambridge: Clarke, 1971.

Young, Frances.

    From Nicaea to Chalcedon. Philadelphia: Fortress, 1983.

Zehnle, Richard F.

    Peter's Pentecost Discourse. Nashville: Abingdon, 1971.

Zizioulas, John.

    Being as Communion: Studies in Personhood and the Church. Crest-
        wood: St. Vladimir's, 1985.

    "Implications ecclésiologiques de deux types de pneumatologie."
        In *Communio Sanctorum: Mélanges offerts à Jean Jacques von
        Allmen.* 141–54. Geneva: Labor et Fides, 1982.

    "The Teaching of the 2nd Ecumenical Council on the Holy Spirit in
        Historical and Ecumenical Perspective." In *Credo in Spiritum
        Sanctum* 1. Ed. José Sariva Martins, 29–54. Vatican City:
        Libreria Editrice Vaticana, 1983.

ANCIENT AND MEDIEVAL SOURCES

Amphilochius

    Synodal Letter, PG 39

Aphrahat

    Demonstrations, SC 349

Aquinas, Thomas
  Summa theologiae
Athanasius
  Commentary on the Psalms, PG 27
  Festal Letter, CSCO 151
  History of the Arians, PG 25
  On the Incarnation of the Word, SC 199
  To John and Antiochus, PG 26
  Letter to the African Bishops, PG 26
  Letter to the Emperor Jovian, PG 26
  Letter on the Synods of Arminum and Seleucia, PG 26
  Letters to Serapion, SC 15, 17
  On the Synods of Ariminum and Seleucia, PG 26
  To Marcellinus on the Interpretation of the Psalms, PG 27
  To Palladius, PG 26
  Tome to the People of Antioch, PG 26
Augustine
  Confessions, CCSL 27
  On Faith and the Creed, in *Augustine: De Fide et Symbolo*. Ed. E. P.
    Meijering. Amsterdam: Gieben, 1987.
  Questions on the Heptateuch, CSEL 28/2
Basil
  Against Eunomius, SC 305
  Apology, SC 305
  On the Holy Spirit, SC 17
Bernard of Clairvaux
  On the Ascension, in *S. Bernardi Opera*. Ed. Jean Leclercq, C. H. Talbot,
    H. M. Rochais. Rome: Editiones Cisterciensis, 1957–1977.
  On Consideration, in *S. Bernardi Opera*
  On the Dedication of a Church, in *S. Bernardi Opera*
  On Grace and Free Will, in *S. Bernardi Opera*
  On Quadragesima, in *S. Bernardi Opera*
  On the Vigil of Christmas, in *S. Bernardi Opera*
  Praise of the New Knighthood, in *S. Bernardi Opera*
  Sermons on Diverse Topics, in *S. Bernardi Opera*
  Song of Songs, in *S. Bernardi Opera*
Cabasilas, Nicolas
  Commentary on the Divine Liturgy, SC 4
Clement of Alexandria
  Miscellaneous Studies (Stromata), SC 30
Clement of Rome
  To the Corinthians, SC 167

Cyril of Alexandria
> *Commentary on John,* in *Sancti Patris Nostri Cyrilli Archiepiscopi Alexandrini Opera.* Ed. Philip E. Pusey. 7 vols. Brussels: Culture et Civilisation, 1965.

Cyril of Jerusalem
> *Catechetical Lectures,* in *Cyrilli Hierosolymarum Archiepiscopi Opera Quae Supersunt Omnia.* 2 vols. Ed. W. C. Reischl and J. Rupp. Munich: Keck, 1848/1850.
> *Mystagogical Catecheses,* SC 126

Cyrus of Edessa
> *Explanation of the Passion,* CSCO 356

Didymus the Blind
> *On the Trinity,* PG 39
> *Treatise on the Holy Spirit,* SC 386

Ephrem the Syrian
> *Commentary on the Concordant Gospel or Diatessaron,* SC 121
> *Hymns on Faith,* CSCO 155

Epiphanius
> *Panarion,* PG 41

Gregory of Nazianzus
> *De Vita Sua.* Ed. Christoph Jungck. Heildelberg: Winter, 1994.
> *Discourse,* SC 250
> *Discourse in Honor of Athanasius, Bishop of Alexandria,* SC 270
> *Fifth Theological Oration,* SC 250
> *Oration,* SC 250

Gregory of Nyssa
> *Against Eunomius,* PG 45
> *Against the Macedonians,* PG 45
> *In That "When"* (Homily), PG 44
> *Life of Moses,* SC 1
> *On the Lord's Prayer,* PG 44
> *Oration* ("When all things are subjected to him"), in *Opera.* Ed. Werner Jaeger. Leiden: Brill, 1952– .
> *To Ablabius That There are not Three Gods,* PG 45

Hilary of Poitiers
> *Against Constantius,* PL 10
> *Commentary on the Psalms,* CSEL 22, SC 347
> *From an Historical Work,* PL 10
> *On Matthew,* SC 254
> *On the Trinity,* CCSL 62, CCh 62

Hugh of St. Victor
> *Didascalicon,* PL 176

Hippolytus
    Refutation of All Heresies, in *Refutatio Omnium Haeresium.* Ed.
        Miroslav Marcovich. New York: De Gruyter, 1986.
Ignatius of Antioch
    Ephesians, SC 10
Irenaeus
    Against Heresies, SC 100, 153, 211
    Demonstration of the Apostolic Preaching, SC 406
    To the Ephesians, SC 10
    To the Romans, SC 10
Jerome the Greek
    Comment Useful to Some Christian, PG 40
Justin Martyr
    First Apology, in *Saint Justin: Apologies.* Ed. André Wartelle. Paris:
        Études Augustiniennes, 1987.
Maximus the Confessor
    Explanation of the Lord's Prayer, PG 90
    On the Divine Names, PG 4
Niceta of Remesiana
    The Power of the Holy Spirit, PL 52
Origen
    Commentary on John, SC 120, 385
    Commentary on Romans, PG 14
    Homilies on Exodus, SC 16
    Homilies on Genesis, SC 7
    Homilies on Jeremiah, SC 238
    Homilies on the Song of Songs, SC 37
    On First Principles, SC 252, 268
    On John, SC 157
Pseudo-Dionysius
    Letter, PG 3
Richard of St. Victor
    On the Grace of Contemplation or *Benjamin major,* PL 196
    On the Preparation of the Soul for Contemplation or *Benjamin Minor,*
        PL 196
    On the Trinity PL 196
Rupert of Deutz
    On the Apocalypse, PG 169
Second Letter of Clement, in *Die apostolischen Väter.* Ed. Karl Bihlmeyer.
    Tübingen: Mohr [Siebeck], 1956.
Shepherd of Hermas, SC 53

Symeon the New Theologian
> *Catecheses,* SC 104
> *Ethics,* SC 122, 129
> *Hymn,* SC 174
> *Theological Chapters Gnostic and Practical,* SC 51

Tatian
> *Oration to the Greeks,* in Tatiani, Oratio ad Graecos. Ed. Miroslav Marcovich. Berlin: Walter de Gruyter. 1995.

Tertullian
> *On Modesty,* SC 394, CCh 2
> *On Penitence,* SC 316
> *On the Resurrection,* CCh 2
> *On the Spectacles,* SC 332

Theodoret of Cyrrhus
> *Résumé of Heretical Fables,* PG 83

William of St. Thierry
> *Meditations,* SC 324
> *The Mirror of the Faith,* SC 301
> *On Contemplating God,* SC 61
> *On the Nature and Dignity of Love,* PL 184
> *On the Nature of Body and Soul,* PL 180
> *The Prayer of Dom William,* SC 61
> *On Romans,* CCCM 86
> *On the Song of Songs,* SC 82

Victorinus, Marius
> *Against Arius,* CSEL 83/1
> *Hymn,* CSEL 83/1
> *On Ephesians,* CSEL 83/2

Index of Subjects

Ad gentes divinitus (Decree on the Missionary Activity of the Church), 198, 199
Alexandrian synods, 76–77
Angels, 13–14, 73
Apocalyptic, 33, 39–40, 51
Apollinarianism, 156
Arianism, 24, 72, 73–75, 76, 121, 123n, 131, 155
Ascension, 57

Baptism, 21–22, 25, 50, 93, 95, 136, 146, 169, 170–71, 173, 203–04, 215–16
of Jesus, 67–68, 84, 93, 96, 146, 168–69, 192
Binitarianism (Father and Son), 8, 12, 16–17, 116, 216

Christology, 4–5, 12–13, 69–70, 88–90, 96–97, 109–10, 123–25, 165, 193–94, 199, 203–05
Contemplation, 27, 31, 174, 177, 181
Correlative principle, 75, 128, 129
Council of Constantinople, 149–59
Council of Nicaea, 17, 71, 74, 123–25, 154–55
Crucifixion, 166–67, 205

Divinization, 73, 75, 126, 134–35, 146–47, 180, 224–25
Doxology, 24–25, 28–31, 132–33, 139

Eastern theology, 85–86, 87, 89, 114
Ecclesiology, 42, 53, 59, 8, 109, 110, 184, 197, 204
Epistemology, 214, 222
Eschatology, 33–34, 39–48, 50–53, 204
in the Old Testament 34–36, 52
Exorcisms of Jesus, 39, 40

Faith, 186–87
Filioque, 85

Galilee, 57–58
Gnosticism, 49
Grace, 86, 223

Hermeneutics, 218–19, 222
Homoousios (the same substance), 16, 17, 18, 72, 74, 121, 123–24, 132, 135, 136n, 138, 157
of the Spirit, 18, 74, 106, 127, 137, 154, 159
Homotimos (the same honor), 18–19, 25, 137–38

procession of, 82–83, 85, 87,
102–03, 156
and prophecy, 194
in public life, 210–11
as reality, 91
as source of communal life, 107,
162–64
in the Trinity, 3–4, 17, 22–23,
24–26, 49, 61, 68–70, 73,
75, 76–78, 83, 86–87, 91–97,
100–01, 102–04, 106–07,
112, 114–17, 119–20, 128,
132–38, 145–47, 155–57,
177–78, 180, 184, 199–200,
208–09, 218

universality of, 112, 117–18,
195–96, 206–07, 211, 213,
227

Trinity
dynamic of, 3–4, 22–26, 92,
100–01, 201, 209–10
models of, 7–8
mystery of, 23–24, 26, 27, 118
in New Testament, 4–7, 67–70
Tropici (*see also* Macedonians,
Pneumatomachoi), 76, 127

Wisdom, 12

Index of Ancient and Medieval Authors

Index of Modern Authors

Old Testament

Index of Scripture References

Index of Scripture References